THE SOCIAL IMPERATIVE

THE SOCIAL IMPERATIVE

RACE, CLOSE READING, AND
CONTEMPORARY LITERARY CRITICISM

PAULA M. L. MOYA

Stanford University Press
Stanford, California

Stanford University Press
Stanford, California

Chapter 1 has previously appeared as Moya, Paula M. L. "Racism Is Not Intellectual: Interracial Friendship, Multicultural Literature, and Decolonizing Epistemologies." *Decolonizing Epistemologies*. Ed. Ada Isasi-Díaz and Eduardo Mendieta. New York: Fordham University Press, 2012. Print. Reprinted with permission.

Parts of Chapter 3 have previously appeared in Moya, Paula M. L. "Another Way to Be: Women of Color, Literature, and Myth." *Doing Race: 21 Essays for the 21st Century*. Ed. Hazel Rose Markus and Paula M. L. Moya. New York: Norton, 2010. 483–508; 18. Print. Reprinted with permission.

Parts of Chapter 3 have previously appeared in Moya, Paula M. L. "Dancing with the Devil— When the Devil Is Gay." *Gay Latino Studies*. Ed. Michael R. Hames-García and Ernesto J. Martínez. Durham: Duke University Press, 2011. Print. Reprinted with permission.

Printed in the United States of America on acid-free, archival-quality paper

Library of Congress Cataloging-in-Publication Data

Moya, Paula M. L., author.
  The social imperative : race, close reading, and contemporary literary criticism / Paula M.L. Moya.
    pages cm
  Includes bibliographical references and index.
  ISBN 978-0-8047-9570-8 (cloth : alk. paper) — ISBN 978-0-8047-9702-3 (pbk. : alk. paper)
  1. American fiction—History and criticism. 2. American fiction—Social aspects. 3. Race in literature. I. Title.
  PS374.R32M69 2015
  813.009'355—dc23

                                        2015021847

ISBN 978-0-8047-9703-0 (electronic)

Typeset by Bruce Lundquist in 10/14 Minion Pro

Debe haber otro modo que no se llame Safo
ni Mesalina ni María Egipciaca
ni Magdalena ni Clemencia Isaura.

Otro modo de ser humano y libre.

Otro modo de ser.

Rosario Castellanos, "Meditación en el umbral"

CONTENTS

ACKNOWLEDGMENTS

I have many people to thank for helping me to write this book. First and foremost are the scholars who have been involved in the Future of Minority Studies Research Project (FMS) and Stanford University's Center for Comparative Studies in Race and Ethnicity (CCSRE), in whose company I have been working out the ideas in this book for more than a dozen years. At FMS, they include Johnnella Butler, Joseph Jordan, Amie Macdonald, Satya Mohanty, Chandra Talpade Mohanty, Susan Sánchez-Casal, Beverly Guy Sheftall, Tobin Siebers, John Su, Sean Teuton, Alan Wald, and Kay Yandell. Linda Martín Alcoff is for me an inspiration and a primary interlocutor; I am grateful for her advice and the kind words of encouragement she gave me at a crucial juncture. Both Michael Hames-García and Ernesto Martínez are models of the kind of scholar I want to be; I am ever grateful for their work and for their friendship. The valuable feedback and support I received from each of them at different points during the writing of this book is something I strive always to reciprocate. At CCSRE, there are almost too many colleagues to mention. In addition to all the contributors to my co-edited volume *Doing Race: 21 Essays for the 21st Century*, I am indebted to my many faculty colleagues who generously lectured over the years in the "Introduction to Comparative Studies in Race and Ethnicity" class that I regularly team-teach with Hazel Markus. José David Saldívar and James Campbell gave me much appreciated feedback on different chapters of the manuscript, and Samy Alim, Jennifer Brody, Al Camarillo, Prudence Carter, Jennifer Eberhardt, MarYam Hamedani, Monica McDermott, Gary Segura, Matthew Snipp, David Palumbo-Liu, Claude Steele, Dorothy Steele, Jeanne Tsai, and Chris Queen have been generous over the years with their ideas, scholarship, friendship, and support. Also, the symposium organized by José David Saldívar on Junot Díaz at Stanford University was key to the development of my chapter on Díaz's fiction.

I thank my faculty colleagues in the English Department at Stanford University for their conviviality. The Literary Lab, as run by Franco Moretti, Matthew Jockers, and Mark Algee-Hewitt, has significantly influenced the framing of this book. Gavin Jones provided helpful comments on the entire manuscript, while being a model of what a department chair should be. As always, I am grateful to Alex Woloch for his scholarship and his friendship. Sianne Ngai, Vaughn Rasberry, and Shelley Fisher Fishkin have been exemplary Americanist colleagues. Mark McGurl's leadership at the Center for the Study of the Novel and in the Post45 collective has had the effect of expanding my scholarly circle, even as his scholarship has provoked my thinking. Other colleagues across Stanford have been similarly instrumental in providing space and intellectual support for my work. They include Shelley Correll of the Clayman Institute; Debra Satz of the Center for Ethics and Society; Roland Greene of the website Arcade: Literature, Humanities, and the World; Patti Gumport of the Office of the Vice Provost for Graduate Studies; and Helen Longino in the Department of Philosophy. I count myself very lucky to work alongside staff professionals such as Nicole Bridges, Alyce Boster, Judy Candell, Katie Dooling, Dagmar Logie, Laura Ma, Rachel Meisels, and Nelia Peralta. Monica Moore deserves special acknowledgment; my work as Director of the Program in Modern Thought and Literature has been a joy, for which she deserves much of the credit.

Like most teachers, I learn as much or more from my students as they learn from me. I appreciate the undergraduate students who took my classes "Narrative and Narrative Theory" and "Introduction to Comparative Studies in Race and Ethnicity." I am also grateful to the graduate students who enrolled in "Concepts of Modernity: Philosophical Foundations"; "Concepts of Modernity: Culture and Society in the Age of Globalization"; "Theories of Race and Ethnicity"; and "Feminist Theory: Thinking Through/With/About the Gendered Body." Current and former students whose scholarship pushed forward my own thinking, or else who gave me feedback on pieces of this manuscript, include Cameron Awkward-Rich, Guadalupe Carrillo, Karli Cerankowski, Maria de Lourdes Medrano, Julie Minich, J. D. Porter, Elda María Román, Carmen Sanjuan-Pastor, Amir Tevel, and Jennifer Harford Vargas—and also Teresa Jimenez, who, in addition, provided research support for the chapter on A Mercy. Also for research support I thank Laura Austin and Gina Arnold. I am grateful to Corey Masao Johnson for his co-coordination with me of the Interdisciplinary Working Group in Critical Theory, a workshop sponsored by the Program in Modern Thought and Literature and the Stanford Humanities Center. That forum provided a rich environment within which to work out the details of my theoretical framework.

As central as Stanford University has been to the writing of this book, I would be remiss if I did not acknowledge how important it was to be able to workshop parts of it in front of audiences around the country and in Switzerland and Germany. I begin by thanking Barbara Buchenau, who invited me to keynote a conference at the Georg-August-Universität Göttingen, and subsequently asked me to participate in research colloquia at the Universität Bern and the Universität Duisburg-Essen. Peter Schneck allowed me to share some ideas in a keynote at the German Association of American Studies in Jena, and Laura Bieger and Irwin Collier invited me to present at the John-F.-Kennedy-Institut für Nordamerikastudien at the Freie Universität Berlin. Sally Haslanger's invitation to participate in the National Humanities Center's blog *On the Human* allowed me to finally articulate the link I intuited between the disciplines of literary studies and social psychology. Ada Maria Isasi-Díaz included me as a keynote speaker in an important gathering of Latina/o philosophers and thinkers at Drew University, as did José Medina and Andrea Pitts for a meeting of Latina feminist philosophers at Vanderbilt University. Michael Hames-García and Ernesto Martínez have both hosted me numerous times at the University of Oregon in interdisciplinary forums where I had the opportunity to present material from this book. Maureen Harkin generously arranged for me to speak to the English Department and to American Studies faculty and students at Reed College, while Mary Pat Brady and Helena María Viramontes organized a talk for me at Cornell University that was sponsored by the English Department, the Latino Studies Program, and the Minority, Indigenous, and Third World Studies scholars. Asma Barles invited me to present to the Center for the Study of Culture, Race, and Ethnicity at Ithaca College, and Frederick Aldama arranged for me to speak at The Ohio State University to faculty and students affiliated with Women, Gender, and Sexuality Studies and the Latino and Latin American Space for Enrichment and Research. Donald Pease twice invited me as a speaker for his tremendously intellectually exciting Futures of American Studies summer seminars, and Shelley Correll and José David Saldívar asked me to give a talk at a public event on intersectional feminism in Los Angeles, co-sponsored by Ina Coleman and The Feminist Majority Foundation. Finally, Joshua Glasgow provided me with a terrific audience at a talk sponsored by the Center for Ethics, Law, and Society at Sonoma

State University. I am grateful for the feedback I received from these audiences, and also from those at presentations I gave at the Critical Ethnic Studies Association conference, Modern Language Association conferences, the "Haciendo Caminos" conference at John Jay College, and the Center for the Study of the Novel at Stanford University. I want also to thank Helena María Viramontes and Junot Díaz for their fiction and their friendship; in addition, I am grateful to Helena for her example and to Junot for doing an interview with me for the *Boston Review*.

I am happy to be publishing this book with Stanford University Press. I appreciate the model of professionalism that Editor-in-Chief Kate Wahl has shown throughout our work on the Stanford Studies in Comparative Race and Ethnicity book series, and for Senior Editor Emily-Jane Cohen's expert and sensitive shepherding of this book through the acquisitions process. I am grateful to her for substantive feedback on the framing of the book, as I am for the insightful comments on the manuscript from former Post•45 series editor Michael Szalay and two other anonymous readers for the press. Thanks are due also to Friederike Sundaram, Gigi Mark, and Elspeth MacHattie for seeing the book through the process of production.

Hazel Rose Markus deserves her own paragraph, a fact that she might find odd in light of her fundamentally interdependent orientation toward the social world. Hazel is by now so deeply interwoven into the many strands of my personal and professional lives—not to mention the personal and professional lives of countless others of the institutions and individuals I have acknowledged above—that she almost never appears by herself, either in print or in person. But just this once I will set her apart to acknowledge the profound influence that she, her work, and the work of her colleagues and students have had on me. Quite simply, I could not have written *this* book without her, and for that I am deeply grateful.

I would like to thank my father, R. F. Moya, for his advice, his support, and our weekly conversations; my mother, Patricia Black Esterly, for her beauty, her unselfishness, and what she has taught me about making the most of what one has been given; my sister Linda for giving me someone to look up to and for explaining the methods and reasoning used in cognitive neuroscience; my sister Caryn for always having the courage of her convictions; and my brother Eric for philosophical conversations and for explaining concretely the mind-body connection. I am grateful to my daughters, Halina Victoria Martínez and Eva María Lourdes Martínez, for growing themselves up into beautiful, intelligent, kind, and motivated young women; I marvel that I have the great good luck to be their mother.

Finally, I dedicate this book to my beloved husband, Ramón Saldívar, who patiently, generously, and lovingly saw me through the writing of this book. I am as grateful for his scholarly example as I am for the encouragement he provides whenever I feel discouraged. I cannot ask for a more perfect interlocutor—sometimes challenging, often teaching, but acting always with abundant gentleness and care. My love and appreciation are boundless.

THE SOCIAL IMPERATIVE

INTRODUCTION
Schemas and Racial Literacy

The Search for Method

Since beginning my career in 1996, I have worked extensively in three interdisciplinary programs at Stanford University: Comparative Studies in Race and Ethnicity; Feminist, Gender, and Sexuality Studies; and Modern Thought and Literature.[1] Because of this, I have been expected by students in these programs to explain how my work on race, ethnicity, gender, and sexuality can be distinguished from that of a sociologist, a historian, or a social psychologist. I have also been challenged by faculty colleagues working in the social and natural sciences to demonstrate how literary criticism might contribute to an understanding of these world-making social fictions. Some of my non-humanist colleagues have gone so far as to signal doubt, through both word and deed, about the value of literary criticism for the production of knowledge generally.

The challenges to literary studies coming from students and scholars outside the discipline have been heightened by a rising sense of crisis among scholars within it. When I began graduate school at Cornell University, literary critics felt an excitement about our profession and especially about literary and cultural "theory." There was a shared belief among a sizeable portion of the profession regarding the political efficacy of cultural critique. Throughout the late 1980s and into the '90s, this excitement was manifested in the rock star status within literary criticism of a few academics, of whom Jacques Derrida, Judith Butler, Edward Said, and Fredric Jameson were the most prominent. This was accompanied by the slightly lesser renown of others similarly associated with poststructuralist, psychoanalytic, postcolonial, or Marxist literary and cultural theories and methods. Over time, the shine of these academic luminaries has faded, and literary critics have searched in vain for their successors. By the late 1990s, the time of theory and its attendant methods seemed to have come to a definitive end. As the new millennium opened, conferences and books with titles like *Post-Theory: New Directions in Criticism* (McQuillan), *After Theory* (Eagleton), and *Theory after "Theory"* (Elliott and Attridge) appeared to proliferate. They signaled, with confidence, the end of an era in which literary critics—whether they were "for" or "against" it—at least knew what "it" was. What no one in the profession has been nearly as confident about ever since is what "it" is now, or even if—perhaps especially if—there is an "it" now.

One difficulty has been the intransigence of culture in the face of our critiques. But literary studies as a discipline has also been troubled by falling enrollments and a lack of support from governmental funding sources and university administrations in the face of an uncertain economy and the increasing corporatization of the university. Over the past decade, departments in the humanities have experienced shutdowns, consolidations, cancelled searches, and shrinking tenure-line faculties. Such pressures have affected the way literary critics view their professional practice, spawning a variety of approaches that constitute nothing less than a field-wide search for method. Critics like Hillary Chute, Frederick Aldama, and Katherine Hayles have turned to new narrative forms, expanding the purview of literary studies to include video games or graphic novels or electronic media.[2] Others like Lawrence Buell, Ursula Heise, and Timothy Morton have extended the traditional concerns of cultural criticism by examining the damage that humans are doing to animals and the environment.[3] Other approaches have taken the form of interdisciplinary engagements that look to the methods and scholarship of non-literary, sometimes even non-humanities, disciplines. Some engagements, like philosophy and literature or law and literature, have been around for a while.[4] But others stretch the definition of what it means to be a humanities scholar. Scholars such as Brian Boyd, Lisa Zunshine, Frederick Aldama, and Blakey Vermeule have mined scholarship in the field of cognitive neuroscience to explore the links between fiction, cognition, and perception in what was called by the *New York Times* the "Next Big Thing in English" (Cohen).[5] Meanwhile, other critics such as Franco Moretti, Matthew Jockers, Mark Algee-Hewitt, and Ted Underwood have pioneered quantitative literary analysis, a kind of literary studies that applies machine learning algorithms to large digital collections.[6] I, too, am participating in this general trend, although my own interdisciplinary engagements have been with social and cultural psychology. In part, this has been inspired by my experience as a co-teacher and co-author with the social and cultural psychologist Hazel Rose Markus—with whom I share an interest in the workings of race and ethnicity, and with whom I have published a volume of collected essays on the subject called *Doing Race: 21 Essays for the 21st Century* (2010). But my turn to social and cultural psychology has also been powerfully motivated by my growing understanding of literature as a mode, as well as an object, of inquiry. As will become clearer over the course of this book, I draw on the scholarship and insights of social and cultural psychology for empirical support, and some of their concepts have deeply influenced the way I approach literary analysis.[7]

Not all literary critics have responded to the sense of crisis by looking beyond the traditional objects or boundaries of our discipline. Some have retrenched, turning their gaze inward, in order to advocate a kind of a "doing what we do, but doing it better." For example, in a 2007 essay on the "New Formalism" in "The Changing Profession" section of *PMLA*, Marjorie Levinson documents an increased attention to the practice of close reading and a renewed commitment to the individual literary text by critics across the ideological spectrum. Levinson cautiously divides New Formalists into two groups: "normative" formalists and "activist" formalists.[8] According to Levinson, normative formalists work with an Aristotelian model of the artwork and assert the necessity of returning to a more traditional kind of aesthetic appreciation of the literary work as something distinct from its sociohistorical or political import. Activist formalists, by comparison, work with a dialectical model of the artwork and presume that an attention to form can be continuous with a concern for sociohistorical analysis (558–59). Although the differences between the normative and activist formalists are significant, what they share is important for indicating the general direction of the movement Levinson highlights. Both groups assign to the category of literature "a special kind or concept of [literary] form," and both agree that a methodological response to the "transformation of literary studies into sociohistorical study over the past several decades" is overdue. Both assert the "critical (and self-critical) agency of which artworks are capable," and both "seek to reinstate close reading at the curricular center of the discipline" (560). At the heart of both types of New Formalism, Levinson explains, is a "kind of aesthetic or formal commitment" that, more than anything else, seeks to "generate community around the idea of form" (562, 561). To the question of whether the individual literary work should remain a significant object of study for literary critics, Levinson answers with a resounding "yes." According to Levinson, the literary work gives us "unique access to the dynamic historical formation that inhabits the still form of form itself" (566).

Another interesting example of the turn inward that has garnered a fair amount of attention over the past few years is found in Stephen Best's and Sharon Marcus's co-authored introductory essay to the 2009 special issue of *Representations* devoted to "the way we read now." Intended as a rejection of the "symptomatic reading" they see as exemplified by Fredric Jameson's *The Political Unconscious: Narrative as a Socially Symbolic Act* (1981), Best and Marcus propose "surface reading" as "the best way to move past the impasses created by what has become an excessive emphasis on ideological demystification" (18). Arguing for a set of reading practices that would be "free from having a political agenda that determines in advance how we interpret texts," Best and Marcus point to a future free of the "paranoia and suspicion" characteristic of the "heroic" criticism practiced by "revolutionary critics, and those pursuing various forms of identity politics (feminism, queer studies, critical race studies)" (16). Without answering the question of whether it is possible for literary scholars to "set aside our [unconscious and unknowable] responses" to "the state of things," they nevertheless insist that we "strive to produce undistorted, complete descriptions of them" (18). Gesturing toward a method in which literary critics adopt "some of the methods of science," embrace the "act of bearing witness to the given," valorize the "neutrality of description," and refuse to "celebrate or condemn their objects of study," they urge us to produce work that "seeks to occupy a paradoxical space of minimal critical agency" (17–18).[9]

Apart from introducing the special issue, Best and Marcus aim in their piece to "perform a self-assessment, to survey the present" of contemporary practices in literary criticism (2). Best and Marcus's formulations betray a sense of urgency and a profound disillusionment with the unmet promises of hitherto dominant methods in literary criticism. Their observation, for instance, that the "disasters and triumphs of the last decade have shown that literary criticism alone is not sufficient to effect [political] change" indicates that they might have once believed that it was (2). The fact that they are now "skeptical about the very possibility of radical freedom and dubious that literature or its criticism can explain our oppression or provide the keys to our liberation," suggests that they might have been, in the past, true believers (2). Their willingness to raise the question of "why literary criticism matters if it is not political activism by another name" underscores their own possible prior motivations for participating in the business of literary criticism (2). And finally, their mention of the chance that surface reading "might easily be dismissed as politically quietist" highlights an assumption running throughout the piece that literature and literary criticism do, still, serve crucial ideological functions in society (16).[10]

If literary critics have been laboring under the illusion that our writings alone are sufficient to effect political change, or that radical freedom is ever possible, or that literature or its criticism can provide the keys to our liberation, then Best and Marcus do us a service by alerting us to the reality of our situation. But there is an important disjuncture between saying, as Jameson does, that a reader can never assume that "the text means just what it says" (*Political* 60), and saying, as Best and Marcus imply Jameson means, that "domination can only do its work when veiled" (2). Similarly, there is a great deal of analytical space between believing that literary criticism has the ultimate power to interpret and change the world, and believing that it has none at all.[11] It is within this analytical space, and in response to the various kinds of pressures I describe above, that my present inquiry is situated.

This book, then, is an attempt to answer four theoretical questions with methodological implications that have preoccupied me over the past decade. They are: What is the power of a work of literature to affect a reader's perception of his or her world? How might a nuanced and insightful interpretation of a given text affect our perception of that text—and by extension, of the worlds it represents? What is the status of "close reading" within a literary critical landscape that includes quantitative formalism and cognitive approaches to literature? And, how important is it that literary critics maintain a focus on the individual literary text? (Versions of these questions that signal the anxiety of the moment are displayed in Figure 1.)

These questions are not new, but their answers have changed and taken on increased urgency in the context of a changing American society in which literacy about race and ethnicity will be more needed than ever.[12] They have emerged from my encounters with some of the most compelling trends in contemporary literary studies, and against the background of my intellectual re-formation as an interdisciplinary scholar of race and ethnicity who works across the humanities and the social sciences. Knowing that I am not unique— that I share disciplinary questions, confusions, assumptions, and methods with many of my colleagues who work across a range of literary archives—provides

1. Does literature still matter?

2. Do literary critics still matter?

3. Does my training still matter?

4. Does the literary "text" still matter, or should we all become literary historians or sociologists of literature?

FIGURE 1. Questions: anxious versions.

an important motivation for this book. The project itself is the culmination of my decade-long effort to understand how I interpret particular works of literature, and to articulate to myself and to others, both within and outside the discipline, why literary close reading remains an important critical endeavor. When it comes to understanding how significant social categories like race, ethnicity, gender, and sexuality structure individual experience and identity, as well as why it is necessary to appreciate and engage "worlds of sense" that are anchored in experiences and identities other than one's own, there may be no more efficient and effective approach than the close reading of individual works of literature.[13]

I begin by defining the key term—literature—before explaining how I understand the practice of close reading. After surveying the problem of literary criticism's relationship to science and the scientific method, I argue for the necessity of reconceiving that relationship. Next, I introduce the social psychological concept of *schema* before elaborating its significance for the way literature works. After turning to a consideration of the relationship between literary evaluation and objectivity, I suggest how literature can help to build racial literacy. In the process, I give provisional answers to the questions that have motivated this book. The success of those answers, of course, can only be demonstrated by the close readings I provide in the book's remaining chapters.

What Is Literature? What Is Close Reading?

When I use the term *literature*, I am referring to a trans-historical and trans-individual social institution—one that influences, and is influenced by, the ideas, practices, and behaviors of all the actors within its sphere. The institutional nature of literature accounts for why sociological approaches to literature, like the one so brilliantly modeled by Pierre Bourdieu in *The Field of Cultural Production*, can be so revealing.[14] It is also why quantitative approaches to literature, which study units of analysis at scales other than the singular literary text, are beginning to yield such intriguing results. Indeed, it is because literature exists as an institution within what social psychologists describe as the "culture cycle" that professionalized literary critics can take literature as an object of study in the first place (see Figure 2). If literature were not fundamentally ideological—if it were not so revealing of the complex ways in which our diverse cultural ideas inform and motivate our equally diverse practices and behaviors—there would be little reason to retain literature as a field of study in the academy.

Given that I understand literature as an institution, why do I maintain a commitment to close reading—and to its correlative object, the individual literary text? The answer to this question is related to the kind of social institution literature is. Literature is most usefully understood as a system (made up of even smaller systems) of formalized activities enabling social communication via culturally-specific forms of aesthetic expression. These activities (writing, reading, publishing, reviewing, advertising, and discussing) operate within a field of interaction involving a variety of sentient and non-sentient "actors" commonly associated with the literary field (Latour, *Modern*; Latour, *Reassembling*; Bourdieu). Some of these actors are the humans to whom people give the names of writer, reader, reviewer, publisher, or advertiser; others are

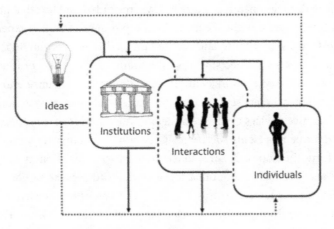

FIGURE 2. The culture cycle.
SOURCE: Adapted from Markus and Conner.

the culturally-specific forms of aesthetic expression (novels, magazines, essays, newspapers) through which and with which those writers and readers interact.

Literature, in other words, is a dynamic system of communication through which the manifold ideologies that shape and motivate humans' diverse cultural practices are circulated. Some of those ideologies include the ones in which I am particularly interested—race, ethnicity, gender, and sexuality. Importantly, the singular literary text (or group of texts, as in a multivolume series) is the primary means through which the author and reader encounter and interact with that system as a whole. I appreciate why literary critics, particularly those working in literary history, quantitative formalism, or narratology, might study genre or syntax at a scale other than the literary work; by so doing, they reveal aspects of the literary system that come into view at a larger or smaller scale. For a literary critic interested in producing knowledge about the institution of literature as it operates across time and place, working at scales larger and smaller than the literary text is a disciplinary imperative. Even so, analyzing the singular literary text remains a crucial project for our discipline. Consider this: writers do not write, nor do readers read, literary genres per se.[15] Cervantes did not write "the novel"; rather, he wrote *Don Quixote*, which has since become the prototype of the novel. Similarly, while it is true that writers write, and readers read, clauses, sentences, and paragraphs—they generally do so as constituent parts of the literary work as a whole. It is at the scale of the individual literary text, or group of closely-interwoven texts, that authors most meaningfully communicate with their readers, and around which readers frequently communicate with each other. It is, moreover, via the individual text that literature is a sensitive indicator of the ideological underpinnings of human experience.

Importantly, works of literature are not only vehicles of communicative expression. As aesthetic objects, works of literature are also acts of interpretation. In order to create a work, authors must choose and organize into a more or less coherent whole a set of images, metaphors, character-types, and other formal narrative devices available to them in their worlds of sense. A work of literature never represents society as it really is, but rather filters through a literary form the hopes, dreams, illusions, and (sometimes faulty or partial) knowledge of the author about that social world. And because authors are cultural beings, their hopes, dreams, illusions, and bodies of knowledge are not unique to themselves (Markus and Conner; Markus, Kitayama, and Heiman). Instead, those hopes and dreams engage—sometimes positively, sometimes negatively—the pervasive sociocultural ideas of the society within which an author lives. A work of literature is thus a creative linguistic engagement, in the form of an oral or written artifact, with the historically-situated cultural and political tensions expressed at the level of individual experience. Like other aesthetic artifacts, such as a film, a painting, a piece of music, or a drama, a work of literature is a formal representation that mediates authors' (and subsequently readers') apprehension of the societies within which they live. This means that a close reading of a work of literature is not merely an encounter with the self; depending on how careful the reading is, and how willing readers are to have their received ideas challenged, it can also be an encounter with an other—even a radical other. A close reading of a work of literature can thus serve as an excavation of, and a meditation on, the pervasive sociocultural ideas—such as race, ethnicity, gender, and sexuality—of the social worlds, as well as the worlds of sense, within which both authors and readers live.

By *close reading*, I mean the kind of intensive reading and re-reading that calls for a heightened attention to literary language and form, considering both as semantic structures that mediate authors' and readers' perceptions of the social world. As a historical matter, close reading has been a fundamental aspect of literary critical practice since at least the mid-twentieth century, when the New Criticism developed it as an interpretive technique. But as John Guillory points out in his recent essay "Close Reading," its foundations were laid in the 1920s in the "psychology of reading approach" pioneered by I. A. Richards in *Principles of Literary Criticism* and *Practical Criticism*. Richards, according to Guillory, wanted to activate in his undergraduate students "an underlying cognitive potentiality" in order to train them in "literary judgment" (12). This potentiality involved the "focusing of attention in reading," and Richards believed that it would put literary criticism on the "surer, scientific footing" it needed to be legitimized as a discipline (12). As I argue throughout this book, close reading ought to remain central to our disciplinary practice, and we ought to return to the concerns with attention, training, and judgment that motivated Richards's investigations in the first place. Apart from being the most powerful discipline-specific tool we have at our disposal, close reading is also something that we literary critics do exceptionally well. But close reading, as I understand and practice it, is not antagonistic to what Franco Moretti calls "distant reading." Nor does it preclude or gainsay sociological or historicist approaches, quantitative formalism, or even psychoanalytic, Marxist, or other so-called "symptomatic" ways of reading a text.[16] Close reading can be stifling when it neglects consideration of the social, historical, economic, political, and cultural contexts from which a text emerges. And it can be dangerously mystifying if it actively obscures the ideological investments that motivate any creative or interpretive endeavor. But when it involves a heightened attention to literary language and form in a way that acknowledges the shaping force of culture and society on a text's development and expression, then close reading is an indispensable tool for excavating the ideological investments promoted by any given text. My approach is thus *socioformal*, and it is deeply informed by the methods and scholarship of social and cultural psychology.[17] I attend to the social dimension of literary form by describing how the thematic and formal features of a text mediate the historically-situated cultural and political tensions expressed in a work of literature.

As a scholar interested in the workings of race, ethnicity, gender, and sexuality, my close reading practice involves a respectful engagement with the thought and feeling of some profound thinkers and cultural critics who are working through significant social problems in a literary form. Writers like Junot Díaz, Toni Morrison, Helena María Viramontes, and Manuel Muñoz communicate with me (and with others) through works of literature rather than philosophical tracts, films, or other forms of visual art. Thinking through literature is one of the best ways to confront social issues such as race, ethnicity, gender, and sexuality because literature allows writer and reader alike to explore them in all their particularity and embeddedness in the social world—which is, after all, the only way that they enter the world as issues in the first place.

The Problem of Science for Literary Method

The questions of what literature (and literary criticism) can do, as well as what literature actually does, to readers are perennial ones for literary criticism.[18] Such queries have long been tied to the question of our discipline's relationship to the scientific method. Literature, many have argued, is about feeling, emotion, and the development of subjectivity. What do science, objectivity, and rationality have to do with that? Jane P. Tompkins touches on these issues in her trenchant précis of literary criticism's shifting concern with the power of language to affect human cognition and behavior. In her contributions to the edited collection *Reader-Response Criticism: From Formalism to Post-Structuralism*, Tompkins defines "reader-response criticism" as work that is associated with critics who use the words "*reader, the reading process*, and *response* to mark out an area of investigation."[19] Reader-response criticism, she avers, is "not a conceptually-unified critical position," but is defined by practitioners that represent a variety of theoretical orientations: New Criticism, structuralism, phenomenology, psychoanalysis, and deconstruction (ix). What unites reader-response critics, according to Tompkins, is a belief that the "effects" of a poem, "psychological and otherwise, are essential to any accurate description of its meaning, since that meaning has no effective existence outside of its realization in the mind of a reader" (ix).

In the course of tracing first a departure from and then a return to literary criticism's concern with the power of literature to affect a reader, Tompkins argues that reader-response criticism brought literary criticism back (or at least very close) to the place where the Greek rhetoricians began (xxv, 226). After making a quick run through the ages, Tompkins suggests why New Criticism was so dismissive of what Wimsatt and Beardsley termed in 1949 the "Affective Fallacy" (Tompkins ix, 223). If formalism developed as a response to the challenge posed by the increasing status and influence of science at the beginning of the twentieth century, then New Criticism went one step further by "attempting, in effect, to beat science at its own game" (222). New Critics wanted to "prove that their discipline was as rigorous as any science by mounting a discourse that was tough-minded, logical, detached, and above all, objective" (224). The solution they came to was to declare poetic language "ontologically distinct from scientific language, and the objects of its investigation ontologically separate from (and by implication superior to) the objects of scientific research" (222). In this way, New Criticism sought to justify the sort of specialized reading practice that only trained, disciplined, and rigorously "objective" literary critics could provide. By Tompkins's account, New Criticism took criticism as far in the direction of scientific rigor and positivist objectivity as it could possibly go while still retaining a rigorously distinct disciplinary identity. The only problem was that, in focusing so narrowly on the formal aspects of the text, New Critics had to ignore or actively dismiss anything having to do with how actual readers responded to literary texts.

According to Tompkins, the American and German versions of response-centered critical theory were united by one central trend that distinguished them from New Criticism—namely, the turn away from the objectivity of the text and toward the subjectivity of the reader. "The objectivity of the text is the concept that these essays, whether they intended it or not, eventually destroy" (Tompkins x).[20] She documents how, over the course of about thirty years, literary critics shifted the way they wrote about literary meaning. From 1950 to

1980, literary meaning migrated from being located in the objective features of the text, to being found in the interaction between the text and its reader, to being a function of the mind of the reader, and finally to being a result of the interpretive strategies that constitute meaning itself. For later proponents of response-centered critical theory like Stanley Fish, the text itself finally disappears, such that the focus of literary critical attention becomes the interpretive capacities of the reader rather than the contents of the work (xxiii; see also Fish 183). While generally approving this trend, Tompkins finally disapproves of reader-response criticism's continuing commitment to the activity of analyzing individual texts. She writes:

> It seems, then, that there is no escape from interpretation, not because the text
> is undecidable, as the deconstructionists would have it, but because the institu-
> tional context within which the critic works—a context created by the doctrines
> of literary formalism—dictates that interpretation is the only activity that will be
> recognized as doing what criticism is supposed to do. (225)

Holding out hope that literary criticism will yet reinvent itself in a way that will prove its relevance for the production of knowledge, Tompkins closes her introductory essay by invoking Walter Benn Michaels's Peircean conception of the self: "'the self, like the work, is a text'" (xxiv). It is perhaps instructive that Tompkins misquotes Michaels slightly—transposing "world" to "work"— thereby making the reader and the literary text indistinguishable; Michaels's actual words are "[t]he self, like the *world*, is a text" (Michaels 199, emphasis added). After all, Tompkins's larger argument is that reader-response criticism develops to the point where the activities with which we associate readers and texts are similarly indistinguishable: "Reading and writing join hands, change places, and finally become distinguishable only as two names for the same activity" (x). For Tompkins, the propitious result of literary criticism's turn toward the reader can be found not in reader-response criticism per se, but rather in the theoretical insights espoused by its later proponents such as Michaels, Fish, and Jonathan Culler. Writing at the dawn of the 1980s, Tompkins looks forward to realizing within literary critical practice the theoretical insights of those who, having perceived that "language [is] constitutive of reality," "shift away from the analysis of individual texts and toward an investigation of what it is that makes texts visible in the first place" (226, 225). With a nod to Foucault, Tompkins suggests that, from the moment of her writing forward, the "questions that propose themselves within this critical framework therefore concern, broadly, the relations of discourse and power" (226). Heralding a final break with formalism, Tompkins confidently declares that it is the "perception of language as a form of power" that promises the most for literary criticism's future (226).

Writing now from the perspective of the second decade of the twenty-first century, I propose that we have followed Tompkins's poststructuralist-influenced path about as far as it will go. Because investigations into the relations between discourse and power have not provided the answers, solved the contradictions, or filled the void that set the process in motion in the first place, it is time to enact a Hegelian *Aufhebung* (Hegel). Literary critics need to step back, rethink the terms we have been using to conduct our investigations, and start over again from a different and slightly more self-conscious vantage point informed by the methods that have come before. But in invoking Hegel, I do not mean to suggest that literary criticism has attained (or even ever will attain) a state of perfect self-actualization. Rather, I mean to suggest that the time is favorable for sublating the best methods and insights from both formalist and reader-response criticism, even as we go back to the problem that set us on that path in the first place. Literary critics need, in other words, to re-conceptualize literary criticism's relationship to science and the scientific method. Instead of trying either to outdo scientists on the terrain of objectivity or to undermine the foundations of science by declaring scientific objectivity to be founded on the lie of language, instead of either claiming privileged status for literary language or denying the existence of any pre-discursive reality to which literary works refer, we would do well to develop more nuanced understandings of subjects (readers) and objects (texts), taking the time and the trouble to tease out the complicated and fascinating relationship between them. But the answers to the kinds of questions literary critics have been asking—questions about how humans make meaning from their interactions with other humans and other objects (including literary texts) that they encounter in their social worlds—cannot be answered from within literary criticism alone. And while science cannot by itself provide the answers we seek either, it can be a valuable partner in our efforts to find them.

Consider in this vein the work of social psychologist David Kidd, who in collaboration with his doctoral advisor, Emanuele Castano, ran a series of experiments designed to show that reading literary fiction challenges readers cognitively in a way that might have potentially beneficial effects.[21] In a presentation he gave at Stanford in March 2014, Kidd noted that reading literary fiction—as opposed to reading non-fiction, popular genre fiction, or nothing at all—improves a test subject's ability to perform well on social psychological tests of both cognitive and affective theory of mind (ToM). ToM is a social psychological theory that posits an ability to attribute mental states to others as well as oneself, such that one understands that others might have beliefs, desires, and intentions that are different from one's own.[22] In explaining his findings, Kidd pointed to several features of literary fiction that might account for his results. He noted that literary fictions typically highlight human subjectivity and the existence of multiple perspectives while also requiring readers to integrate several streams of information at once. They frequently plunge readers into unfamiliar situations, requiring them to pay attention to types of people they might normally never encounter, or to interactions they might usually sail through without real engagement (as when they interact with a cashier at the grocery store). Such features of literary fiction, Kidd suggested, might have the effect of interrupting readers' taken-for-granted social scripts and of disrupting readers' customary egocentrism. They might, as a result, have oriented his test subjects outward to other people, in effect priming them to do better on the tests they had to complete immediately after finishing their reading assignments. The implication is that reading literary fiction might enhance a person's ability to accurately discern other people's feelings and intentions in the real world outside literature—a skill that is central to the successful navigation of complex social relationships in a multifaceted multicultural world like our own.

There is much to say about how literary critics might engage the sort of work David Kidd is doing. For example, while it is comforting to assume that a person's ability to do well on laboratory tests is functionally equivalent to that person's ability to understand and empathize with the intentions of other people in real-life settings, the studies Kidd has done to date demonstrate only the first, and not the second.[23] Additionally, Kidd's preliminary conclusions remain at a fairly abstract level; his hypotheses and conclusions reference literary fiction as a category, rather than particular works of literature; and about a general ability to impute intentions to others, rather than about specific aesthetic responses to particular texts. Moreover, Kidd's findings are relatively preliminary, insofar as he cannot be sure that the specific features of literary fiction he cites are what produced his results. To know that, similar results to his would have to be obtained using other measures, and additional studies would have to be done to isolate the precise literary mechanisms at work.[24] This is where the kind of expertise that literary critics have and can bring to the table becomes crucial for further studies. Still, the work Kidd is doing is exciting, and full of potential for helping literary critics understand why our disciplinary objects of study remain so compelling to so many people in our techno-mediated and digital age.

Schemas

One tool that literary critics need in our efforts to better understand how literature works—that is, how specific texts affect specific readers—is the social psychological concept of *schema*. While a novel or short story might move one reader to great depths of emotion, it can leave another untouched. This is an obvious point, but not a trivial one. It is, however, a point that has been too often overlooked—as much in some forms of reader-response criticism that generalize the literary critic's interpretation as "the" reader's response as in some so-called "symptomatic" approaches that purport to tell us what the text "really" means. Key to the impact a text will have on a reader is the manner and extent to which *that* text activates for *that* reader a set of cognitive-affective structures social psychologists refer to as schemas. Because schema is such a core concept for me but remains unfamiliar to most literary critics, I need first to elaborate it before returning to its significance for interpreting literary works. An understanding of schemas allows for a fuller appreciation of the social—that is, the trans-individual and trans-historical—significance of the subjective while also acknowledging the particularity of individual responses to any given text.

In social psychology, and as I mean to use the term, schema refers to the active organization of past experiences (physical and emotional) and past reactions (sensory-motor and cognitive-affective) through which a person apprehends and interacts with incoming stimuli. As structures that have been built up through a person's past behavior and experiences in specific domains, schemas serve "as patterns for one's current and future behavior" in those and perceptually-related domains (Markus and Kitayama 229–30). Schemas are central to cognition insofar as they allow a person to "go beyond the information given," to fill in the gaps, and to extrapolate from what is known or from what is given to what might be apparent or might not yet have appeared (Bruner). Schemas thus have a temporal dimension characterized by evolution across time—they are anticipatory as well as retrospective, even as they orient a person's behavior in the present.

A substantial body of experimental psychological work supports the existence and functioning of schemas. The term was first applied to psychological phenomena in 1920 by the English neurologist Henry Head; subsequently, the English psychologist Frederic Bartlett used it in reference to the cognitive processes and the overt actions involved in the organization of past experiences for the purposes of understanding and recall.[25] The concept was also central to the work of developmental psychologist Jean Piaget, who used it to help explain the way children develop their cognitive skills (Markus and Zajonc 144). Over the past century, numerous psychologists have elaborated the concept by demonstrating that the activation of schemas derived from past experience is fundamental to people's ability to organize information coherently enough to perceive and remember.

In the service of showing how schemas work to direct attention, condition perception, and shape interpretation, I offer here as an example a psychological study from a paper published in 1972 by the psychologists John Bransford and Marcia Johnson. The study involved giving the following auditory set of instructions to study participants. I ask you, reader, to engage now in this thought experiment with me. Read the passage shown below, and note for yourself as you read what you think it is about.

> The procedure is actually quite simple. First you arrange things into different groups. Of course, one pile may be sufficient depending on how much there is to do. If you have to go somewhere else due to lack of facilities that is the next step, otherwise you are pretty well set. It is important not to overdo things. That is, it is better to do too few things at once than too many. In the short run this may not seem important, but complications can easily arise. A mistake can be expensive as well. At first the whole procedure will seem complicated. Soon, however, it will become just another facet of life. It is difficult to foresee any end to the necessity for this task in the immediate future, but then one never can tell. After the procedure is completed one arranges the materials into different groups again. Then they can be put into their appropriate places. Eventually they will be used once more and the whole cycle will have to be repeated. However, that is part of life.

Did you understand what this passage was about? Stop here before reading further and consider your answer.

Now let me pose a different question. Have you ever had any experience with washing clothes? Yes? And if you had known beforehand that the passage offered instructions for sorting and washing clothes, would it have been easier for you to comprehend the passage?

In setting up the portion of the study pertaining to this passage, Bransford and Johnson created three experimental conditions. In the first condition, the study participants were given the instructions, as I've done here, without preamble; this was the No Topic condition. In the second, Topic After, condition, the participants were told *after* reading the passage that the instructions pertained to washing clothes. In the third, Topic Before, condition, study participants were informed *before* they read the passage that they would be given instructions related to washing clothes. All the participants were subsequently tested on their recall of the passage. What Bransford and Johnson found was that those participants who were given the topic of "washing clothes" prior to reading the passage were significantly better at remembering the details of the passage afterward. They concluded that an "activated semantic context" had to be present during the "ongoing process of comprehension" in order for test subjects to comprehend the meaning of the paragraph well enough to remember it (724). In other words, simply having prior knowledge about the procedures involved in washing clothes was not enough to ensure comprehension of the passage. Test subjects had to know about those procedures and then also to know that their knowledge about the procedures involved in washing clothes would be relevant to the passage they were about to read. Only when test subjects' schema for washing clothes was *activated* did the passage make enough sense for them to be able to understand it well enough to remember it.[26]

The Bransford and Johnson study is important not only because it showed the role that schemas play in comprehension and recall, but also because it suggested a "useful strategy" by which experimental social psychologists could manipulate the experimental context to investigate "the interaction of prior knowledge and present input events" (725). This useful strategy, of course, is what is now familiarly known as the "prime." The action of directing someone's attention to a particular feature of the environment is what social scientists refer to as "priming." It involves activating, in an experimental setting, test subjects' schemas—most often those related to a structurally significant feature of society such as race, class, gender, ethnicity, age, religion, or social status. Social psychologists have used priming to great effect over the past several decades to test the existence and import of various schemas, as well as to demonstrate that people behave differently depending on the schemas that are activated for them in a given context. Still other psychologists have used priming to show that people often fail to perceive something that is right in front of them when their attention is directed toward something else.

In a famous experiment conducted by psychologists Christopher Chabris and Daniel Simons in 1999, and recounted in a book titled *The Invisible Gorilla: And Other Ways Our Intuitions Deceive Us* (2010), test subjects were tasked with watching a short video in which a group of young people, some wearing black and some wearing white, move slowly around in a circle while passing two balls among themselves. After being told that they are participating in a "test of selective attention," test subjects are instructed to count the number of times the people wearing white pass the ball. After the ball passing starts, a figure wearing a black gorilla suit enters the frame of the video from the right, walks into the middle of the circle, and beats its chest before exiting to the left.[27] What is so interesting about this experiment is that about half the people viewing the video for the first time fail to see the gorilla. Of course, the gorilla is completely obvious to all the subjects after they have been shown that it is there; once someone has participated in this experiment, she can never again *not* see the gorilla. But as the updated version of the experiment created in 2010 demonstrates, even those who have seen the experiment before—who know that the gorilla will be coming through, and who are therefore hyper-attentive to details in the video—even they will miss other fairly obvious elements of the situation, such as the fact that the background curtain changes color and that one of the players wearing black exits the game. The point is simply that there will always be more stimuli in the environment than one can possibly apprehend. For this reason, perception is not a matter of looking out on the world and seeing what is there. Rather, perception is about filtering the barrage of incoming stimuli so that some small part of it can be observed. What Chabris and Simons demonstrate is that schemas operate as perceptual filters. Schemas direct the viewer's attention, thereby conditioning her perception, and so shaping the resulting interpretation.

Before I go further, I want to emphasize two important points. First, schemas are self-relevant. Second, they are learned. Because "the fundamental units of the self-system, the core conceptions . . . [are] predicated on significant interpersonal relationships," a person's set of schemas develops and evolves over the course of her life in conjunction with her identity as a Being in a world full of other Beings (Markus and Kitayama 227). Not only does a person possess many different schemas, but also her schemas are built up over time in domains that she considers important or in which she has had significant experiences. Many, if not most, of an individual's schemas will be shared with others who are similarly situated within a particular society—so, for instance, racial, gender, religious, and class schemas are often shared across a demographic group. Other schemas will be particular to the person, and will be shaped by her idiosyncratic likes and dislikes (a love of fashion) or by her past experiences (the fact that she is newly pregnant, or was beaten as a child). Schemas are necessarily shaped by those facets of a person's Being that hold sociocultural experiential significance for her or for others in the social and historical contexts in which she lives.[28]

As illustrated by the invisible gorilla experiments, not all of a person's schemas will be operative at any given moment. A particular schema will be activated when something in the immediate environment cues its usefulness for guiding a person's understanding and behavior in that situation. Consider the way freshmen who enter my classes at Stanford University all have a schema for "attending a university lecture." They expect to enter a large classroom at an assigned hour and sit down in one of a number of chairs, all of which will be facing toward the side of the room in which is located a lectern and possibly a blackboard, whiteboard, or projection screen. They expect to remain quiet for a predetermined amount of time while I stand up at the front and talk to them. They understand that I want them to note down some of what I say using either a pen and paper or the word-processing function of their computers. They understand that I do not want them to browse the web while I am talking, although they also know that I will not be able to prevent that behavior from where I am standing. Finally, they know that they may be expected to respond to what I have said near the end of the assigned hour, and that they should not get up and leave in the middle of my talking or before the assigned hour has come to a close. Where did they get this schema for attending a university lecture? Why do I not have to tell them how to behave the first time we meet? The answer, of course, is that they have built this schema up over years of primary and secondary schooling, and also by observing the role modeling of their university peers. Schemas are cognitive-affective structures that help us to deal more effectively with new situations; they help us to act appropriately in new situations by allowing us to build on our knowledge of past situations that are similar in relevant ways.

As the schema for attending university lectures example indicates, people share common schemas with those with whom they share contexts. But a person's particular set of schemas will also be shaped by her idiosyncratic experiences, and her likes and dislikes as they change over time. For example, before I bought a Honda automobile in 1998, I had a very poorly elaborated schema for cars. I might have been able to tell you what color a given car was, but I could not have told you whether it was a sedan or a coupe, a Toyota or a Chevrolet, a four-cylinder or an eight-cylinder car. I had never needed a schema for cars; the men in my life had guided my previous car purchases. Until I was faced with the prospect of having to buy a car on my own, I had not thought much about a car's shape, its horsepower, or its cultural capital. If anything, I had a slight aversion to caring about those things because of my past experience with men and what seemed to me to be their excessive caring about cars, and especially about cars' cultural capital. I did not realize that I had a poorly elaborated schema for cars; I knew that cars existed, and I assumed I understood them as well as the next person—or at least as much as anybody needed to understand them. The only time I became aware that others might have a much fuller and richer framework for perceiving cars was when someone would point out what seemed to be a really arcane difference between one four-wheeled vehicle with an engine and another. Years pass, people change, and I now have a moderately good schema for cars—at least for how they look, if not their inner workings. I recognize Hondas of a particular era (because I ended up buying one), Priuses (because I later purchased one), and BMWs (because my husband has one, and because he and I visited the BMW Museum in Munich together). At this stage in my life my head turns when I see a Porsche Boxster or a Tesla, and I *will* notice if a car looks different from one that I have seen before.

What all this means is that the number, content, and complexity of the schemas available to a person at any given time will have significant implications for that person's cognition, emotion, and motivation. As Hazel Markus and Shinobu Kitayama note in their foundational essay on the mutual constitution of culture and the self, "the greater the familiarity with the stimulus materials, the more elaborate the schemata for framing the problem, and the better the problem solving" (231). A person's ability to develop schemas is thus an essential aspect of survival and adaptability to changing circumstances. I am reminded of Michael Dorris's memoir of raising a child who suffered from fetal alcohol syndrome. The key difficulty the young boy faced was his apparent inability to learn from experience in a way that would allow him to understand the future consequences of his actions. We can conceptualize this by noting that his brain damage interfered with his capacity to build the numerous and elaborated schemas necessary for survival in a dangerous and complex world.

Schemas in Literature

As a literary critic, what interests me is how the concept of schema aids in analyzing the way that literature works—as a system of social communication through which information, ideas, and norms are transmitted from author to reader, and among different communities of readers. There are several ways to approach this question. One is by attending to the different schemas readers bring with them to the scene of reading; I address this issue below and throughout the remaining chapters of this book. Another is by paying attention to the way schemas are embedded into a work of literature through the use of various narrative features. Consider by way of illustration an incident in the life of the character Thomas Cromwell in Hilary Mantel's Booker Prize–winning novel *Wolf Hall*. With this example, I show how Mantel employs specific narrative strategies to help her readers build a schema that allows them to understand and empathize with her protagonist. The scene also illustrates how Mantel depicts Cromwell using an idiosyncratic learned schema to interpret a situation in a way that another character might not.

The first time the reader meets Thomas he is "felled, dazed, silent." He has fallen down, having been "knocked full length on the cobbles of the yard" by his abusive father, Walter Cromwell (3). The reader comes to find out that Walter has a nasty habit of sneaking up behind his wife and children and knocking them down with whatever blunt object is to hand. This time, Walter nearly kills Thomas, and as soon as his sister patches him up so that he can walk, this scrawny beat-up boy, whose only resources are a quick intelligence and a willingness to work until he drops, runs away to foreign lands to make his way in the world. Unsurprisingly, given his childhood experiences, Thomas begins his life as a fighter; part of making his way involves dark alleys, violent encounters, and soldiering. At some point in his maturation, unspecified in the novel, Thomas moves from soldiering to provisioning, from physical fights to diplomatic encounters, and from working for scraps to managing other men's business affairs. Accordingly, when the novel joins up with him again twenty-seven years later, our hero is managing the business affairs of Cardinal Thomas Wolsey, who at the time is the chief advisor to King Henry VIII. Late one evening, Cromwell is sitting with Cardinal Wolsey in the Cardinal's house in a firelit room, teasing the Cardinal about a rumor that he is pretending to withhold. This is where the scene opens:

> Laughing, the cardinal pushes back his chair, and his shadow rises with him. Firelit, it leaps. His arm darts out, his reach is long, his hand is like the hand of God.
>
> But when God closes his hand, his subject is across the room, back to the wall.
>
> The cardinal gives ground. His shadow wavers. It wavers and comes to rest. He is still. The wall records the movement of his breath. His head inclines. In a halo of light he seems to pause, to examine his handful of nothing. He splays his fingers, his giant firelit hand. He places it flat on his desk. It vanishes, melted into the cloth of damask. He sits down again. His head is bowed; his face, half-dark.
>
> He Thomas, also Tomos, Tommaso and Thomaes Cromwell, withdraws his past selves into his present body and edges back to where he was before. His single shadow slides against the wall, a visitor not sure of his welcome. Which of these Thomases saw the blow coming? There are moments when a memory moves right through you. You shy, you duck, you run; or else the past takes your fist and actuates it, without the intervention of will. Suppose you have a knife in your fist? That's how murder happens. (58–59)

We can see here that, as a result of his past experiences, Thomas has developed a schema for unexpected and quick movements in dark spaces. This idiosyncratic schema in turn affects Thomas's interpretation of Cardinal Wolsey's actions and intentions. It motivates his behavior, and it does so well below the level of conscious deliberation: "the past takes your fist and actuates it, without the intervention of will." The spatio-temporal dimensions of the schema are evident; we note that Thomas brings his experiences with past similar spaces into the present space. Furthermore, Thomas's reaction to the Cardinal's sudden movement is relevant to his sense of self in relation to his environment and other Beings. In other words, Thomas responds to his immediate context, but that response derives from his past experiences with other Beings within the various sociocultural contexts to which he has been exposed. This last fact is nicely suggested by reference in the text to the different names the character has answered to over the course of his foreign travels: "He Thomas, also Tomos, Tommaso and Thomaes Cromwell, withdraws his past selves into his present body." Of course, because Thomas's cognitive-affective and sensory-motor processing of the Cardinal's sudden movement does take place below the level of his conscious deliberation, even he cannot say for sure exactly what prompted his response: "Which of these Thomases saw the blow coming?" It bears notice, finally, that our hero "saw" a blow that was not going to come. Thomas's perception of the Cardinal's intention was flawed; it was overdetermined by his past in a way that causes him to misapprehend his present. After some awkwardness between them, the cardinal finally says to Thomas: "I really would like the London gossip. But I wasn't planning to beat it out of you" (59). Schemas, then, are more than just mental states that people use to perceive the world around them. They *are* mental states—they are conceptual frameworks that predispose us to select, organize, integrate, and remember some subset of the barrage of incoming stimuli to which we are constantly subjected. But schemas also involve us completely as embodied Beings. The schemas a person builds for dealing with particular emotions, circumstances, and situations derive as much from her past sensory-motor experiences as from what she has cognized in the process of observing herself and others.

In analyzing how schemas are embedded into literature, it is important to note the large amount of contextual information Mantel provides in the lead-up to this scene, together with the explicit interpretive commentary she includes in the passage itself. Because *Wolf Hall* is, in part, a sympathetic character study of a fictional person based on the historical figure of Thomas Cromwell, Mantel includes the two fictional incidents I have flagged (his beating at the hands of his father, and his dramatic flinch at the Cardinal's sudden movement) to help her reader build a sympathetic schema for interpreting Cromwell's personality and subsequent behavior. Mantel is a skilled novelist who presumably wants her readers to understand and appreciate why her protagonist acts the way he does over the course of the events in *Wolf Hall* and its Booker prize–winning sequel, *Bring Up the Bodies*. Because Mantel understands that she cannot reliably depend on her reader's ability to read Cromwell's mind on the basis of his external actions alone, she wisely scaffolds our understanding by depicting him in situations of vulnerability, and by providing us access, through the use of free indirect discourse, to Thomas's subjective experience of his vulnerability. It is in this way that a writer can craft a novel so as to teach a reader how best to read it.

The second way I approach the question of how schemas help us in analyzing literature is by attending to how readers' schemas affect their encounters with particular texts. At the most basic level, different readers bring to the scene of reading widely divergent sets of schemas. The set of schemas any person possesses will be constituted by her bodies of knowledge, her collection of ignorances, her sociocultural biases, and her dispositional attitudes toward learning about new and different situations. For this reason, not all texts will mean the same thing to all readers. Some readers will bring to the reading of a novel like Jane Austen's *Pride and Prejudice* an extensive knowledge of literary history, a heightened attention to rhetorical language, and an understanding of narrative form that has been developed over the course of reading many examples of various kinds of novels. Others might bring a general knowledge of the historical era or the geographical area in which the novel is set, but lack the more specialized reading practices of a trained literary critic. Yet another reader might know little about the historical era or the cultural context, but harbor a personal concern about the difficulty of finding an appropriate romantic partner. Each of these readers would necessarily experience the novel very differently; in a non-trivial sense, it would be a different novel for each of them. This is what compels me to elaborate the multiple contexts (sociocultural and historical) from which a text emerges and into which it becomes actualized as a work of literature. Because I am interested in what the "text itself is saying," I can neither confine myself to examining the text's surface nor proceed as if the text says the same thing to every reader. Instead, I excavate the schemas embedded in the text by attending to the work's formal narrative features in a way that acknowledges the shaping force of culture and society on its development and expression. This requires me to attend to the text's surface, but only as the most immediately perceptible part of a network of significations that reaches out toward the social world and into the mind of the socioculturally-situated reader.

Knowing how schemas work allows us to think more complexly about the concept of literary value. As my own experience with cars illustrates, a person who lacks or has a poorly elaborated schema for a given set of stimuli may not even realize it. She may fail to pick up on relevant cues in the environment (or in the literary text), perceiving them as so much noise, as useless and inchoate information. Or she may fail to perceive them at all—she may be distracted by other aspects of the environment or text or by other stimuli in the reading environment. Moreover, because schemas form the basis of a person's self-esteem, they tend to resist information that the person deems threatening or that is inconsistent with her own view of herself as a good person (Markus and Zajonc; Tavris and Aronson). This is why, when a person is reading a work of literature that is structured according to schemas with which she is unfamiliar or to which, because of her past experiences, she has a conscious or unconscious aversion, she may initially judge it negatively as being poorly organized or excessively sentimental or simply not good. She may then locate the fault not in herself or in her inability to fully appreciate the text's schematics but in the text itself—as if meaning were static and somehow contained within the boundaries of a material object. But as critics of reception aesthetics such as Wolfgang Iser and Winfried Fluck have pointed out, meaning is never static, and it does not exist outside the actualization of a text by a reader (Fluck "Why," 367; Fluck "Search"). Insofar as literature is a system of formalized mechanisms enabling social communication via culturally-specific forms of aesthetic expression, the meaning of any given work of literature is only fully realized in the particular interaction(s) between a text and its readers.

Value, in any case, is a relative term. As Karl Marx illustrated so effectively in *Capital*, something (a coat) only has value relative to something or someone else (twenty yards of linen or a person who needs a coat), and for a particular purpose (exchange or use) (126–77).[29] Works of literature have value because they are culturally consecrated textual objects through which authors, publishers, merchants, reviewers, and readers communicate with each other. Particular works hold up various kinds of mirrors—sometimes highly distorted ones—to their author and their readers. When we read them, works of literature amuse us, fill our time, and, when their structures or their themes reflect our basic values and commitments, make us feel that we are good and worthy Beings in the world. Particular works may be valuable to literary historians or narratologists because they are paradigmatic examples of a particular narrative genre or epoch or else because they are the exception that proves the rule. Other works may be valuable to critics who work in specific historical eras because they were written or produced during that time or because they effectively mediate the tensions that are a defining aspect of that particular locale and epoch. Yet other works are valuable to readers because they help those readers grow and learn by exposing them to new situations and information. Whenever a person reads a literary work of substantial complexity, the possibility exists for her to engage in a kind of "'world'-traveling" whereby she enters into another, and (depending on who she is and what the book is about) possibly alien, world (Lugones 77–100). The social world or worlds depicted in the book might be set in the future or in the past, they might be completely imaginary, or they may depict societies that are geographically and culturally distant from the reader. A reader who takes up a story or book about a social world that is far from her own will be exposed to situations, feelings, attitudes, and characters (implied people) that she does not encounter in her everyday life. Moreover, because of their transportability through space and time, some stories and books allow readers who live in a racially segregated and economically stratified society like ours to be exposed to a variety of alternative perspectives (or worlds of sense) they might otherwise never encounter. Although some people do have friends from a wide variety of racial, cultural, and economic backgrounds, many more people associate only with those who are very similar to them. In the case of some works of literature written by racial, ethnic, or gendered "others," the effect can be (although it is not always the case) that readers are pulled in and given a kind of access to social worlds (and to worlds of sense) to which they might not otherwise be exposed, even if they live and work side by side with people of other races. The activity of reading good literature can expand the reader's horizon of possibility for encountering, living with, and loving characters (e.g., implied people) different from themselves.

In arguing for the relativity of literary value, I have a friendly and unlikely precursor in the literary critic Wayne C. Booth. In *The Company We Keep: An Ethics of Fiction*, Booth argues against the search for universal standards of literary evaluation.[30] He suggests that a search for a universal standard is misguided for several reasons—not least because it implies that value judgments are arrived at by deduction. After working through the logical errors of that faulty premise, he proposes a model of literary evaluation that more nearly approximates how people actually judge. In proposing the neologism "coduction"—from *co* ("together") and *ducere* ("to lead, draw out, bring, bring out")—Booth explains that, "we arrive at our sense of value in narratives in precisely the way we arrive at our sense of value in persons: by *experiencing* them in an immeasurably rich context of others that are both like and unlike them." "Every appraisal of a narrative," Booth insists, "is implicitly a comparison between the always complex experience we have had in its presence and what we have known before" (70–71). "Judgment," he reminds us "always requires a community" (72). Coduction occurs "whenever we say to the world (or prepare ourselves to say): 'Of the works of this general kind that I have experienced, comparing my experience with other more or less qualified observers, this one seems to me among the better (or weaker) ones, or the best (or worst). Here are my reasons'" (72–73). Booth further recognizes that the judgment about a work's literary value does not end with a statement of fact, but rather is open to ongoing negotiation with judgments of others who have read the same text.

He writes: "Every such statement [of value] implicitly calls for continuing conversation: 'How does my coduction compare with yours?'" (73). In his neologism, Booth effectively captures the contextual, comparative, perspectival, and conversational nature of all literary evaluation. And while Booth's understanding of perspectivalism is perhaps less robust than a schema-influenced understanding, his discussions in *The Company We Keep* of what he has learned over time from feminist critics suggest that he is aware of the importance of always considering the place from which any particular judgment derives.

This is not to say that literary critics cannot identify some works of literature that we might collectively want to designate as "great." But such judgments cannot be a priori, and they cannot be tied to one absolute and abstract criterion such as "complexity." Instead, judgments of literary "greatness" that hold true across time and space will most likely satisfy at least these two conditions: first, that the work will have embedded within itself (in its form and its language) a wide variety of schemas, at least some of which speak eloquently to a large number of people; and second, that a large number of people have developed a set of schemas—through exposure or education or both—that make the work accessible and enjoyable for them to read. The works of Shakespeare provide an excellent example of this, particularly for native speakers of English who will have grown up with many of his metaphors as foundational elements of their conceptual universe. But judgments of value, even about the works of Shakespeare, will always be situated in time and space, although the time might be long and the space expansive. Such judgments can never be universal or absolute because, to invoke Marx yet again, value refers to social relations (which are contingent and variable) and not to the essential properties of things. Just as not every work of literature moves everyone in the same way, so not every work of literature is equally valuable to all people. Literary critics need a conceptual vocabulary capable of registering this basic and all too easily ignored fact, even as we need a way to track the linkages between institutional structures of power and literary "value."

Schemas and the Problem of Objectivity

In arguing for the relativity of literary value, I am not committing myself to epistemological relativism. Insofar as I take the scientific method seriously, I am obliged to work with a conception of *objectivity*. But my understanding of objectivity is different from that of many of my colleagues who work in the humanities. Instead of equating objectivity with detachment, impartiality, and absolute certainty about a fixed and unchanging "Truth," I work with a fallibilistic conception of objectivity that accounts for the role of perceptual bias in the practice of interpretation. Under this conception, any claim to truth is subject to testing and revision in light of changing circumstances and more compelling evidence. Objectivity thus represents an ideal as well as a temporary achievement; it is something to be aimed for in the quest for good, verifiable, evidence-based knowledge.

A fallibilistic conception of objectivity is consistent with the post-positivist realist theoretical framework elaborated in *Reclaiming Identity* (Moya and Hames-García 2000) and *Learning from Experience* (Moya 2002). I and other scholars with whom I co-founded the Future of Minority Studies Research Project developed that framework over the course of the 1990s and 2000s. We did so to account for the epistemic significance and social salience of minority identities.[31] In opposition to then-dominant views of identity in the humanities, which tended to see racial and gender identities as fictitious and ideologically dangerous mystifications, we argued that identities are better understood as socially significant and context-specific ideological constructs that refer in mediated but non-arbitrary ways to verifiable aspects of the social world.[32] Insofar as identities track social relations, they are contextual and subject to change in response to the transformation of social relations; identities come into being through the kinds of experiences people have, and they inform the way people interpret the social worlds they live in. Under this conception, identities are not reducible to social categories (i.e., woman, Black, Chicana, gay, etc.), nor do they refer exclusively to people's subjective (raceless, genderless, bodiless) senses of self. Rather, *identity* refers to the complex and mediated way a multiply-situated and embodied human being looks out onto and interprets the social world she lives in. At stake in our realist defense of the epistemic significance of identities was an attempt to understand and explain why women and people of color so frequently draw upon their identities as both ground and framework for understanding their situations of subordination. It was also a way of limning the complex and mediated, but persistent and analyzable, referential relationship between racial and gender representations (in literature and elsewhere) and racial and gender dynamics in the societies in which we, as human beings negatively affected by these dynamics, must live.

As a realist, I hold that there are aspects of "the real" that exceed humans' mental or discursive constructions of it. While our human understandings may provide our only access to reality, humans' mental or discursive constructions of our shared social world do not constitute the totality of what makes it real. Instead, that which literary critic Stacy Alaimo calls the "more-than-human world" shapes and constrains the range of our human imaginings and behaviors, and provides an important reference point in any sort of interpretive debate about the meaning of a text, picture, social identity, or natural phenomenon (238). The part of "reality" that exceeds humans' mental and discursive constructions of it is also what occasions some "truths" to carry over across particular historical and cultural contexts. For that reason, and unless one is delusional, that which a person encounters in the process of being in the world is simultaneously outside the self and in the mind. A perceiver neither constructs the totality of the person, object, or phenomenon she perceives nor can she ever perceive it "in itself," free of the schemas that allow her to assimilate it to some structure of her understanding. The key principle to keep in mind is that there is a relationship—a relationship that can be traced and communicated—between the perceptible features of the phenomenon under consideration and an interpreter's schematic understanding of it. For this reason, the range of phenomena about which I am willing to make a claim for objectivity is necessarily bounded. I am not willing, for example, to argue that someone does not feel what she claims to feel or does not perceive what she claims to perceive. Feelings and perceptions are very subjective—even if they are shaped by ideas, institutions, and interactions that transcend individuals. I am, however, willing to argue that what an individual perceives may be less than accurate or else badly distorted by ideology. A person's perception of a given phenomenon, in other words, might have a weaker or more ideologically-mediated relationship to reality than some other competing perception to which one might compare it.

The post-positivist realism I sketched out above has important resonances with the agential realism that has been articulated by feminist physicist and philosopher Karen Barad over approximately the same period of time.[33] Throughout her work and in her article "Posthumanist Performativity," Barad builds on the work of the Nobel Prize–winning physicist Niels Bohr to rethink the relationship between nature and culture. According to Barad, there are no essential and unchanging boundaries between human and non-human, culture and nature, subject and object, knower and known, and word and world (137). Rather, every distinction we humans draw in the course of conceptualizing our world is a specific agential practice/intra-action/performance through which we enact specific exclusionary boundaries for the purpose of making sense of it (134). Barad's "posthumanist performativity" is resolutely anti-ideal-ist and decidedly materialist. In the course of reminding her readers that "we are part of the nature that we seek to understand" (146), she argues against what she calls the "inscription model of [social] constructivism" whereby—through the language of production, as in gender *produces* sex—"culture is figured as an external force acting on passive nature" (142–43). For Barad, "nature is neither a passive surface awaiting the mark of culture nor the end product of cultural performances." It is, rather, "an active factor in processes of materialization" (145). She writes: "Reality is not composed of things-in-themselves or things-behind-phenomena, but of 'things'-in-phenomena" (135). Having refused the hard and fast distinction between subject and object, or knower and known, Barad pushes us to reconsider the separation of episte-mology and ontology. Such a distinction, she suggests, is a reverberation of a metaphysics that assumes an inherent difference between human and non-human, subject and object, mind and body, matter and discourse. Making the point that practices of knowing and being are not isolatable but rather mutually implicated, and that, moreover, "[w]e do not obtain knowledge by standing outside of the world; we know because 'we' are of the world," Barad calls for an "*onto-epistem-ology*," in which scholars are engaged in the "study of practices of knowing in being" (147). Because, like Barad, I understand myself as being engaged in the "study of practices of knowing in being," I recognize that knowledge can be evaluated only in relation to particular historical, cul-tural, and material contexts. This is why I consider both from where a given knowledge-claim is derived, as well as whose interests it will serve, in any eval-uation of its significance and truth-value.

Building Racial Literacy

Over my career, I have studied the ideological, institutional, and interpersonal mechanisms by which particular populations of people (especially women and people of color within the United States) are placed into and become en-tangled in positions of relative powerlessness. I have also investigated the way those same populations incorporate, as well as actively resist, the downwardly socially constituting and exclusionary ideas and practices to which they are subjected (Thomas). These preoccupations are what drive my interdisciplinary engagements—real-world problems involving complex and evolving world-systems like race and gender demand solutions that are not located within any one discipline. Through sustained conversations over many years with colleagues outside my discipline, I have learned what different disciplines regard as evidence, and which methods are best for answering different kinds of research questions. I have noted that, with notable exceptions, when literary critics visit other disciplinary terrains, they do not always do justice to the research methods developed there. The reverse is also true; I have been dismayed to see how often historians and philosophers—even well-known and respected ones—read a work of literature as if it were a straightforward or ahistorical piece of evidence for their argument. What I have realized is that while I, as a literary critic, have much to learn from other disciplines, I also have a great deal to offer to them. For one thing, literary critics are sophisticated explicators of the ideology of aesthetic form and the polysemous referentiality of literary language. As a literary critic, I turn to works of literature rather than to surveys, lab experiments, or primary source archives to garner my evidence and present my findings about the ways in which race, ethnicity, gender, and sexuality matter to people's lives. One of my goals in writing this book has thus been to illustrate the value of literacy criticism for the interdisciplinary study of race and ethnicity. I do so by highlighting the effectiveness of close reading—a method perfected within literary criticism—for helping to build racial literacy.

The concept of racial literacy has been elaborated to great effect, albeit in somewhat different ways, by the legal scholar Lani Guinier and the sociologist France Winddance Twine. In a 2004 article published in the *Journal of American History*, Guinier contrasts "racial literacy" to the more common "racial liberalism." Noting that many of the social, political, and economic problems that many legal scholars assumed would be ameliorated by the *Brown v. Board of Education* ruling still exist, Guinier points to the racial liberalism upon which the case rested. In her review of *Brown*, Guinier argues that its focus on the psychological damage done by racism to black children in a school setting, without a concurrent discussion about how racial segregation affects whites' self-conceptions more broadly, had the effect of positing racism as a problem of individual bad actors operating with bad intentions. Moreover, the Warren Court's preoccupation with de jure educational segregation figured Jim Crow as the primary evil in need of remedy rather than as a visible symptom of a larger economic and political system designed to create racialized hierarchies for the purpose of justifying inequitable resource distribution (Guinier 98–99).[34] Guinier's point is that the larger and arguably more important conversation about the unequal distribution of facilities, staff members, and budgets across school districts was neglected, and as a result, racial equality was redefined as the absence of formal, legal barriers that separated the races, rather than as a fair and just redistribution of resources across racial groups (Guinier 95).

Despite being anti-racist in character, racial liberalism suffers from the limitations of liberalism generally—most notably in the way it conceives of the individual as the source (and end) of all thought, feeling, and action (Moya and Markus 33). Because it figures racism primarily as a psychological and interpersonal challenge for individuals, racial liberalism obscures the systemic, trans-individual, and ever-mutating nature of race. But, as Guinier knows, race is not primarily a problem of individuals—even if our experience of it sometimes makes it feel that way. Rather, race is foundational (having been inscribed in the U.S. constitution), systemic (having been structured into our social, political, and economic institutions), and flexible (constantly adapting to both support, and mask, financial and power relations). Guinier's call, then, for a "new racial literacy" is a way of redirecting attention to the systemic and institutional nature of race. If racial liberalism obscures the social, political, and economic interests and institutions that support our nation's white supremacist racial hierarchy, then racial literacy is designed to make those systems legible—so that we might "treat the disease and not just the symptoms" (Guinier 100).

Guinier defines racial literacy as "the capacity to decipher the durable racial grammar that structures racialized hierarchies and frames the narrative of our republic" (100). She offers a kind of "thought experiment" regarding what the practice of racial literacy might entail (115). Race, she says, is "an instrument of social, geographic, and economic control." It works as a "decoy" helping to "cloak the maldistribution of material resources" in favor of the rich and powerful, while also offering a "psychological bribe" to working-class and poor whites (114). Accordingly, becoming racially literate requires one to understand that the answers to how race is working in any given situation are contextual rather than universal. For the racially literate, race is neither the problem nor the answer to the analysis being undertaken. Rather, "racial literacy is an interactive process in which race functions as a tool of diagnosis, feedback, and assessment" (115). Moreover, becoming racially literate involves examining the relationship between race and power, attending always to the structural, as well as the individual and interpersonal, nature of race. And finally, racial literacy requires that the analyst interrogate the dynamic relationship between race (as a system of social distinction and economic control) and other crosscutting and intermeshing vectors of power and oppression. Guinier mentions class, geography, and gender; I would add to her list disability, sexuality, and religion. For Guinier, then, racial literacy involves moving beyond a single-issue justice paradigm based on formal racial equality to a contemplation of what it will take to create "a moral consensus" about the role of government and the place of the public in ameliorating the most negative effects of inequality more broadly (115).

In her 2010 book, *A White Side of Black Britain*, France Winddance Twine develops a concept of racial literacy that is distinct from but shares important resonances with the concept as articulated by Guinier. Over a period of about ten years, from April 1995 to June 2005, Twine used a variety of ethnographic methods to conduct research about white mothers of African-descent children in Leicester and London, England. In the course of interviewing, interacting with, and observing her research subjects, Twine noticed that some subset of the mothers, especially those who had been involved in anti-racist education or activism, developed a "sociological imagination" that allowed them become racially literate (109). For Twine, racial literacy describes "an analytical orientation and a set of practices that reflect shifts in perceptions of race, racism and whiteness. It is a way of perceiving and responding to racism that generates a repertoire of discursive and material practices" (92). Twine elaborates the concept in relation to numerous stories about the way these white mothers navigated their changed relationship to the racial dynamics of British society as a consequence of having given birth to children of African descent (109). She provides specific examples to show that these women were able to locate themselves and their problems in a broader historical and national context, identify the unquestioned assumptions structuring racial relationships in their communities, and analyze the racial logics and ideologies used by their families and neighbors in an attempt to regulate their gendered behavior. Because her conception of racial literacy was developed over years in conjunction with her research among actual people living in the world, Twine's account of what racial literacy includes is helpfully specific. She explains:

> The components of racial literacy include the following: (1) the definition of racism as a contemporary problem rather than a historical legacy; (2) an understanding of the ways that experiences of racism and racialization are mediated by class, gender inequality, and heterosexuality; (3) a recognition of the cultural and symbolic value of whiteness; (4) an understanding that racial identities are learned and an outcome of social practices; (5) the possession of a racial grammar and vocabulary to discuss race, racism, and antiracism; and (6) the ability to interpret racial codes and racialized practices. (92)

Of particular importance to Twine throughout her book is how these women are able to transmit their understandings of race and racism, along with strategies for dealing with everyday racism, to their African-descent children.

Together, Guinier's and Twine's conceptions contain the core elements of the notion of racial literacy with which I am working in this book. As Hazel Markus and I argue in the introduction to *Doing Race*, race is a historically derived and institutionalized system of ideas and practices that emerged gradually over the course of several hundred years in connection with European colonialism and the rise of the capitalist world-system. It involves creating groups based on perceived physical and behavioral characteristics; associating differential capacities, power, and privilege with these characteristics; and then justifying the resulting inequalities (Moya and Markus). As a flexible instrument of social distinction and economic control that works in geographically- and culturally-specific ways, race operates reliably to justify and obscure the inequitable distribution of social and natural resources. People who have developed racial literacy therefore refuse to reify the individual as the source (and end) of all thought, feeling, and action. Instead, they engage their sociological imaginations to perceive individuals as Beings who, in belonging to particular historical moments and geographical locales, are shaped by and also shape the larger social worlds of which they are part.

It is the centrality of perception to what Markus and I call "doing race" that motivates my focus on schemas in an analysis of the way literature can help to build racial literacy. For reasons related to the kind of aesthetic objects that works of literature are, literature is an especially valuable medium for exploring the way race, ethnicity, gender, and sexuality are materialized in human lives. Apart from allowing readers to "world"-travel, literature can also facilitate a kind of "time"-travel. All narratives, by definition, have a sequence of events that unfold successively through time (story time as well the real time of the reader) even when the narration of the story is not linear. A narrative might begin generations in the past and then carry the reader up through the present and into the future. The significance of this feature for the study of race, ethnicity, gender, and sexuality reveals itself when one considers the effects of time on the development of a self, or the effects of past historical events on the shape of present-day political and cultural institutions. Such effects are difficult for most people who are living in the present to perceive or understand. They can only be revealed over time—whether that time is measured by the span of a person's lifetime or by centuries of record keeping. The time-traveling features of some works of literature can thus enable a reader to imaginatively comprehend how a character's "now" self might have been shaped by a "past" self, as well as how that character will evolve into a "future" self. And because the operations of race, ethnicity, gender, and sexuality are dynamic and extend through time, the time-traveling features of literature make it a particularly effective way of exploring and representing the complex manner through which these social processes affect people's experiences and shape their identities. As in the example of Octavia Butler's novel *Kindred*—which tells the story of a black woman from the twentieth century who is pulled back into time into chattel slavery and then returns to the present only to find that she has lost an arm—literature can show how past oppressive structures do damage to possible future selves.[35]

Furthermore, literature can powerfully engage readers' emotions in ways that have the potential to alter readerly schemas. In its actualized form, literature does not just take up space on our bedside table; rather, it drags us down or lifts us up, altering our moods, pulling on our attention, and exciting our feelings. Sometimes it carries readers forward, as when they finish the first novel in a trilogy and immediately download the second and third so that they can keep reading. When readers read a novel, they are subject to its own peculiar type of acceleration. As the narrative discourse speeds up and slows down, as the plot moves forward and backward in fictional time, readers' experience of time goes careening around, backward into the past, forward into the future, sometimes slowing to the kind of crawl that they might rarely experience in their non-literary lives. Literature does not just have the power to capture a reader's attention, it actually displaces it, moving it from here to there. In so doing, it orients readers in new directions and enriches their schemas for interpreting both the fictional social worlds they enter temporarily and the real everyday social worlds in which they live. Occasionally, the work of literature "changes our lives," motivating readers to the kinds of concrete actions that bring profound changes in their life possibilities. Unless literary critics attend to the way works of literature can both figuratively and literally "move" us, they miss something essential about the thing itself. And finally, most literary narratives take as their customary focus the lives-over-time of a range of characters in a way that can provide material for readers' meditations on the complexities of social dynamics. By representing the interconnected lives of different characters that are all negotiating multiple and overlapping structures of power and privilege, a good work of literature can suggest to its readers how race, ethnicity, gender, and sexuality constrain and enable characters' bodies, behaviors, and ideologies. In this way, some works of literature allow a reader to perceive (or a literary critic to analyze) the way race, ethnicity, gender, and sexuality actually *matter*—both in the sense of being important and meaningful and in the sense of becoming materialized in individual lives.

In the chapters that follow, I explore through socioformal close readings of poems, essays, short stories, and novels by authors such as Lorna Dee Cervantes, Helena María Viramontes, Toni Morrison, Junot Díaz, Audre Lorde, and Manuel Muñoz the ideological, institutional, and interpersonal mechanisms by which race is done. My explorations are undertaken in the company of one or more literary works and, at a mediated remove, of the authors of those works. In each case, I have chosen my text for the quality of engagement that it brings to an exploration of the complicated relationship between the activity of reading and the dynamics that create and maintain racialized gender. So, for example, I am absorbed by the way Junot Díaz confronts his own internalized racism, and works through it toward decolonial self-love. I am compelled by the way Toni Morrison explores the ethical relationship of selves to others as it is played out in the friendship of two black women in mid-twentieth century Ohio. I am interested in how a vestigial schema from a centuries-old and moribund cosmological religion survives in the work of Helena María Viramontes, and is then put to work in the service of finding another, more just, way of being in the world. I am intrigued by Toni Morrison's exploration of race as an enactment of perception that works in the service of establishing social and economic hierarchy. These authors are doing a kind of work; through their fiction they are seeking answers to the kinds of questions that I and others are asking about our own lives. Accordingly, my close readings are designed to illuminate something about the work of literature (and by extension about the human self) that some readers perhaps did not understand before. But they are also intended as sustained explorations of the workings of race and ethnicity. In the process, I model a form of close reading that interprets a literary work's themes, structure, plot, and symbolism in terms of the ideas and practices that reflect, promote, and contest the pervasive sociocultural ideals of the world(s) with which the work engages.

As artifacts of the imagination, literary works are by their very nature engaged in imagining ways of being in the world. Sometimes they do it by depicting social worlds that look very similar to our own, with characters that are similar to people we know; sometimes they do it by depicting worlds and characters that are wholly alien to us. Whether a work of literature is realistic or fantastical, despairing or hopeful, it is almost always an ethical engagement with some past, future, familiar, or foreign social world. However convoluted and mediated the referential relationships among authors, texts, worlds, and readers may be, a good close reading of a literary work can help us understand something important about the way we humans make meaning about ourselves and the worlds in which we live. Describing our relationship to these worlds through the process of making meaning, as I have, underscores nothing less than the workings of the social imperative.

1

RACISM IS NOT INTELLECTUAL
The Dialogic Potential of Multicultural Literature

Racism is not intellectual.
I can not reason these scars away.
Lorna Dee Cervantes

There is no Frigate like a Book
To take us Lands away
Emily Dickinson

In a searingly powerful poem that serves as the fulcrum of her award-winning first book of poetry, *Emplumada,* the Chicana poet Lorna Dee Cervantes responds to a young, white male acquaintance who has charged her with being altogether too concerned with the existence of racial discord. Over the course of "Poem for the Young White Man Who Asked Me How I, an Intelligent, Well-Read Person Could Believe in the War Between Races," Cervantes attempts to explain to her interlocutor why she has been unable to transcend the emotional predispositions and what Raymond Williams has called "structures of feeling" that have mediated her race-conscious perspective on their shared social world (*Marxism* 129–34). Hers is a perspective, she contends, that has its roots in the emotionally toxic fallout of her everyday experiences of racism: the schoolyard experiences that have left her with an "'excuse me' tongue, and [the] / nagging preoccupation with the feeling of not being good enough"; the "slaps on the face" that her daily experiences of racism bring to her; the powerful enmity she feels from the "real enemy" outside her door who "hates [her]." In response to the young man's implied argument that any perspective that participates in the logic of race-consciousness is the result of error-prone beliefs which can and should be eradicated through education, Cervantes insists that the accusation he has leveled at her cannot be adequately answered within the terms he has set forth: "Racism," she tells him, "is not intellectual. / I can not reason these scars away" (36).

If racism is not intellectual—if a committed anti-racist cannot fight it with facts, then how can we fight it? How might we go about the process of changing people's emotional horizons?—which is clearly a part of what needs to happen if the problem of racism is to be ameliorated. In this chapter, I explore two possible avenues: interracial friendships and multicultural literature.[1] Insofar as emotions are key to the doing of race, a sustained examination of how emotions about race figure into human motivation must be central to any attempt to move beyond the ideologies and socioeconomic arrangements that sustain racial inequality. Moreover, as a medium of communication that involves the active use of imagination—on the part of the reader as well as the author—literature is one of the key sites in which the social order can be imaginatively examined and reshaped. Both friendships and works of literature have the potential to move people emotionally by activating structures of identification and empathy toward others not like themselves. Books, novels, stories, and poems are important venues within which authors and readers alike can imagine alternative ways of being in this world—or even alternative social worlds.

Racism Is Not Intellectual

Cervantes's assertion that racism is both imbued with emotion and resistant to pure reason has found resonance over the past decades in the work of philosophers and psychologists alike. For example, in a paper he gave at the 2001 "Passions of the Color Line" conference, Michael Stocker argues against the philosophical view that emotions involve or arise from beliefs alone. Such an account, he explains, "undergirds the hopeful view that racism or at least the emotions of racism could be eliminated by changing the beliefs giving rise to those emotions."[2] Stocker makes his argument by drawing on the work of Sartre to trace out the intractability of feelings of loathing and contempt among anti-Semites who are confronted with evidence that logically contradicts the rationalizations they construct to justify their feelings. He then demonstrates the futility of trying to change beliefs without attending to the emotions they are inextricably bound up with:

> It would not be enough that anti-Semites come to see that a particular act by a particular Jew is an everyday, ordinary act, or is even a fine act. That thought

must be integrated into, and seen to conflict with, their anti-Semitism. And further, *this conflict must matter to them*. It cannot be seen just as a puzzling anomaly, of the sort that besets many, if not most, theories and generalizations. Nor can it be defended against in ways that stop it from mattering to them or moving them. They must be—and this means that almost certainly they must make themselves be—emotionally available and open to that thought and (what I see as) its obvious implications. ("Some Issues" 13–14, emphasis added)

Stocker's point bears repeating: if the anti-Semite is not, at a profound level, emotionally moved or bothered by the contradiction between what she observes and what she "knows," she need not make adjustments to her way of thinking. Even if she acknowledges that the act she has observed is a "fine act," she can interpret it as an anomaly—as the proverbial exception to the general rule. In this way she can incorporate the act into her consciousness without having her anti-Semitic beliefs challenged in the least. Her emotional involvement is thus a prerequisite to overcoming her logically unfounded views about Jews.

The philosophers Eduardo Mendieta and William Wilkerson also reject the rigid distinction between thought and emotion. In his contribution to the "Passions of the Color Line" conference, Mendieta prefaces his analysis of exoticization as a technology of the racist self with an argument against the view that sees a bifurcation between mind and body. He observes that "the parceling between emotions and ideas, or between emotive responses and cognition, is but a manifestation of a [by now discredited] technology of the self, which dictates that we have to attribute to our biological natures an element of unpredictability and animalistic connotation, and to our cognitive and mental capacities a calculative, predictive nature."[3] Such a technology of the self, Mendieta reminds us, has arisen as a result of a historically contingent (specifically Cartesian) regime of subjection that fails to account for the way in which emotions are both cognitive and evaluative. Contra this view, Mendieta sees emotions as epistemically valuable. Emotions, he explains, "place us in particular relationships to the world, which is made up of things as well as other selves." Insofar as emotions help us to make sense of others and ourselves, they serve as crucial hermeneutic devices—they "interpret the world for us."

Similarly, in a compelling essay about the experience of coming out as gay or lesbian, William Wilkerson presents some phenomenological considerations about experience that suggest thought and emotion are necessarily bound up with one another (256–67). Drawing on the work of philosophers in both the analytic and continental traditions, Wilkerson argues that emotions are more than simply decorations or distractions to our thoughts:

> [O]ur moods and emotional states are not merely an extra feeling laid over our ordinary thoughts and behaviors; they are part of a horizon that actually changes and molds our thoughts and behaviors, even as our behaviors and experience reinforce our emotions. If I am angry, my anger is not just a reaction to frustrating happenings or disappointed expectations. Rather, my anger has both a reactive and an anticipatory element. . . . When I am writing while angry and my pencil breaks, I may lash out in frustration, even though in a different mood I may simply get up and sharpen it and begin again. The experience is altered by the antecedent context of being angry, and being angry is not just an inner feeling but also a whole style of being in the world. (259–60)

Although Wilkerson chooses anger as the illustrative emotion in his example, his argument holds for all sorts of emotional states. Indeed, Wilkerson suggests that emotional states—as much as "taken-for-granted cultural meanings" and sedimented "habits of action and thought"—inevitably guide the initial direction that any interpretation may take by directing the interpreter's attention to some elements of the hermeneutic situation while obscuring others (260).

One of Wilkerson's aims in his essay is to defend the realist contention that attending to one's own and others' emotions is necessary for unlocking the epistemic potential of cultural identities. Elsewhere, I have argued that while emotions are always experienced subjectively, the meanings they embody transcend the individuals who are doing the experiencing (see Moya, "Symphony"; Moya, "Introduction"; Moya, *Learning*, esp. 49–57).[4] Insofar as people learn from others around them what are considered to be appropriate emotional reactions to specific social situations, emotions are at least partially conditioned by the particular social and historical contexts into which they emerge. In other words, emotions are mediated by the shared ideologies through which individuals construct their social identities. As such, emotions necessarily refer outward—beyond individuals—to historically- and culturally-specific sorts of social relations and economic arrangements.

Under the view I am articulating here, emotions are not merely subjective; they are not circumscribed within one body, nor do they have their origin in an individual psyche. Rather, they literally "embody" larger social meanings and entrenched social arrangements. Recent work in the field of social psychology now provides empirical evidence for this view. Social psychologist Jeanne Tsai

and her colleagues have run a number of studies over the past decade showing the cultural causes and behavioral consequences of what is considered to
be an "ideal affect," and the importance of cultural and situational factors for
understanding the links between self and emotion (see, e.g., Tsai; Wong and
Tsai; Chentsova-Dutton and Tsai). Thus, through attending to the meanings
and origins of our often inchoate feelings, we humans can begin to discern the
outlines of the social arrangements that sometimes constrain, and sometimes
enable, our relational lives (Fanon). It is in this way that emotions have crucial
epistemic value.

I have spent the past few pages arguing for the inextricable link between
thought, emotion, and motivation primarily because claims about race and racism that are made by people of color are often dismissed by others as based in
emotion—and as therefore irrational and epistemically unjustified. In present-
ing a case for the necessary interconnectedness between what goes on in our
hearts and in our minds, I hope to forestall an easy dismissal of the idea that
interracial friendships and multicultural literature can contribute to the project
of decolonizing epistemologies. Rather than suggesting that the race-conscious
perspectives and claims of people of color are not based in emotion, I acknowledge that they often are—even as I insist that such perspectives and claims can
be both rational and epistemically justified. Moreover, rather than "clouding
the issue" or "derailing the conversation," emotions surrounding race and racism must be seen as precisely that which the committed anti-racist seeks to
understand.

As I use it in this chapter, *racism* describes a complex of ideas, emotions,
and practices having to do with the denigration, hatred, dispossession, and/
or exploitation of people who are visually, and often culturally, different from
oneself in a way that is understood to be innate, indelible, and unchangeable.[5]
Racism is expressed in multiple registers, including through folk beliefs, laws,
court decisions, institutional structures, and everyday interactions. In the subjective realm, those who are exposed to the racism of others experience it as
emotional pain, anger, and self-doubt. In the economic realm, victims of racism experience it as a lack of opportunity or the physical dispossession of personal or communal property. In both cases, the harms caused by racism are
long lasting and can be handed down over many generations. Children who
grow up in racist environments imbibe social attitudes about race along with
their mothers' milk, and children whose parents have been emotionally scarred
by their own experiences of social denigration often inherit lifelong preoccupa-

tions with, as Cervantes suggests, the "feeling of not being good enough" (36). On a psychological level, it can be difficult for the racist and her victim alike to transcend the attitudes and interactions learned in childhood. In addition, the significant economic advantages gained by the ancestors of many white Americans at a time when the forebears of most racial minorities could be (and often were) legally dispossessed of their lands and labor have not dissipated. Although some people of color have succeeded in substantially improving their economic status, the majority of them confront a systemic economic disadvantage relative to white Americans—a situation that has been, and continues to be, perpetuated across generations both through differential access to educational and employment opportunities and the ongoing effects of institutional and interpersonal racism (Markus and Moya; Desmond and Emirbayer; Omi and Winant). Moreover, racial minorities have had to cope with this disadvantage in a society that measures people's worth largely in terms of what kind of home they live in, what kind of car they drive, and what sort of school they attend; and that assumes that what people have is what they—in some sort of moral sense—deserve. Given all this, it should not be surprising that the statements about race and racism made by people who are the victims of racism are often thoroughly imbued with expressions of strong emotion—pain, regret, outrage, resentment. Conversely, because many people who participate in racist practices do so unwittingly and unintentionally simply as a result of being part of a society that is organized according to race, it should not be surprising that their reactions to the emotionally-charged claims of their accusers frequently cover the spectrum from denial and defensiveness, through shame, to a self-righteous claiming of racial privilege (Markus and Moya). To the extent that the anti-racist person is interested in understanding the intransigence of something as apparently "irrational" as race, the emotions surrounding race and racism must be seen as precisely that which she seeks to understand. A necessary part of any anti-racist project will thus be a consideration of the strong and varied emotions that are the warp and the woof of the fabric of racial relations in this country.

The Transformative Potential of Interracial Friendship

In her book *What Are Friends For?*, feminist philosopher Marilyn Friedman makes a cogent and compelling argument for understanding the institution of friendship as providing important opportunities for moral growth. Building on the work of Carol Gilligan, as well as on the work of Gilligan's critics, Friedman explores the sort of profound moral growth that can result from a deep and sustained attention to the best interests of a person other than oneself. She takes as her paradigmatic case the relation of friendship, and identifies several features of friendship that make it conducive to fostering moral growth. By friendship, Friedman means "a relationship that is based on approximate equality (in at least some respects) and a mutuality of affection, interest, and benevolence. Friendship in this sense can occur between or among lovers or familial relations as well as between or among people not otherwise affiliated with one another" (189). Although my own interests are directed less toward the potential friendships hold for moral growth than toward the potential that interracial friendships hold for expanding and changing people's emotional horizons, I find Friedman's account useful for her insightful explication of the dynamics of a certain type of friendship. Rather than including in my discussion every sort of relationship across cultures to which some people may give the name of "friendship," I focus on the sorts of relationships that are predicated on a strong degree of voluntarism, mutuality, sharing, and trust—that is, the type of friendship described and identified by Aristotle in his *Nicomachean Ethics* as a "complete" or "perfect" friendship.[6] In what follows, I both build on and depart from Friedman's account to examine the way that interracial friendships can contribute in significant ways to the changing of people's racial schemas. I start by enumerating several features that are common to complete friendships before returning to a consideration of specifically interracial friendships. I propose that the sharing of experiences about race and racism within interracial friendships that are predicated on a strong degree of voluntarism, mutuality, sharing, and trust can lead not only to emotional growth regarding the illogic and evils of racism, but also to an increase in the two friends' shared understanding about the way race functions in our society to maintain current relations of power.

There are several features of complete friendship that make it particularly conducive to epistemic and emotional transformation. The first and perhaps most important characteristic is that it is a voluntary association. When a person says that she is friends with someone, she usually means at least these two things: (1) that she has *chosen* her friend because she feels affection for her, and (2) that her friendship with the friend exists independently of biological or attributed kinship ties. This is not to say that one cannot be friends with a member of one's family—friendships among family members are both possible and frequent. Nevertheless, when one develops a friendship with a biological child or a sister-in-law, describing that relation as a "friend" implies that there is a crucial sense in which the relationship transcends the kinship tie. Moreover, the voluntary nature of complete friendship ensures that it is inherently self-regulating in the way that other sorts of relationships often are not. In general, economic, familial, and social considerations weigh much more heavily on marital, sibling, and parental relations than they do on friendship. As noted by the feminist philosopher Marilyn Frye, it "is one mark of a voluntary association that the one person can survive displeasing the other, defying the other, dissociating from the other" (73). Indeed, because friendships exist with comparatively less institutional support than marriages and other familial structures, the relationship will survive only as long as both friends attend to it—at least intermittently. Once one person ceases absolutely to participate in the complex negotiations required to keep each attentive to the other, or begins to demand more from the relationship than the other is willing to provide, the friendship will founder or cease to exist. Indeed, the always-present threat of the friendship's dissolution discourages both coercion and the possibility of taking one's friend for granted.

A natural consequence of the egalitarian nature of voluntary friendships is that friends who wish to maintain their relationship will be disposed to take an interest in and show respect for each other's perspectives—even when those perspectives differ from one's own. Accordingly, friends often come to understand each other as *particular others* who are related to, but not coincident with, the self. In other words, persons engaged in a complete friendship are more likely than those engaged in other sorts of relationships (i.e., marital or parent-child relationships) to see each other with what Frye calls a *Loving Eye*. According to Frye, seeing with a loving eye is a way of looking at an other that requires a certain kind of self-knowledge—that is, the "knowledge of the scope and boundary of the self." In particular, Frye explains, "it is a matter of being able to tell one's own interests from those of others and of knowing where one's self leaves off and another begins" (75). Because the loving eye does not confuse the other with the self, it "is one that pays a certain sort of attention." It is "the eye of one who knows that to know the seen, one must consult something other than one's own will and interests and fears and imagination. One must look at the thing. One must look and listen and check and question" (75). The loving eye thus exists on one end of a continuum at the other end of which is the *Arrogant Eye*. In contrast to the loving eye, Frye explains, the arrogant eye organizes everything—including the interests, desires, and needs of the other—with reference to himself and his own interests (66–67).

The kind of emotional openness encapsulated by Frye in her concept of the loving eye is a necessary prerequisite to a third important aspect of friendship—the sharing of experiences and stories. Close friends frequently share stories about things that have happened to them and that bear for them some moral or epistemic significance. This activity of sharing stories is important not only because it provides an occasion for amusement and social bonding, but also because it provides an opportunity for friends to learn from each other. As one friend recounts an experience to the other, she necessarily interprets the meaning of the event she is relating. In the process, she draws upon the wide range of schemas—cultural myths, social meanings, and bodies of knowledge—that she has access to. She thus gives her friend access to an experience and an interpretive framework that may be unfamiliar (or even objectionable) to the friend. Friedman explains, "In friendship, our commitments to our friends, as such, afford us access to whole ranges of experience beyond our own. . . . Friendship enables us to come to know the experiences and perspectives of our friends *from their own points of view*" (197–98, emphasis added).[7] Moreover, because we care about the people with whom we form friendships, we are inclined "to *take our friends seriously* and to take seriously what our friends care about" (Friedman 192–93). Taking a friend seriously may mean that a person reconsiders her own experiences, values, and interpretations in light of the experiences, values, and interpretations of that friend. Alternatively, it may mean that the person feels compelled to engage her friend in conversation—or even argue with or rebuke her—when she touches upon a subject, like race, about which they each have strong feelings. In both cases, a person's response will be conditioned by the intensity and nature of her emotional investment—in the friend *and* in the issue under consideration.

This brings me to one of the most crucial aspects of a voluntary friendship—the fact that friends are likely to trust each other. As Friedman notes, the parties to a friendship are likely to have confidence that their friend will bear "reliable 'moral witness'" (189). Indeed, it is when friends trust each other's epistemic capacity (and moral goodness) that the sharing of stories can help both parties expand their epistemic and emotional horizons. This is because a person who trusts her friend's judgment is less likely to dismiss, outright, an interpretation of a story provided by the friend that radically differs from one she herself might have come up with. The listener may be doubtful, and may initially treat the story or the interpretation with suspicion. However, because she risks losing an important relationship if she persists in being dismissive or contemptuous, she will be compelled to consider seriously, even for the purpose of arguing against, the interpretation that her friend has advanced. Just as "friends don't let friends drive drunk," the person who cares deeply about her friend's character and well-being is unlikely to simply ignore those viewpoints her friend holds that she finds deeply problematic.

The interactive process that occurs when friends share stories is enhanced when one friend, in the act of helping, is called upon to participate in the process of interpreting the meaning of the other's experience. It is a common practice for a person who is having some sort of trouble—in her marriage, at her job, with her children, with the law—to seek advice from a friend she trusts. Sometimes she needs material help, but often she needs help with comprehending and analyzing the dilemma she is facing. In such a situation, she shares with her friend the details of her quandary, advances a tentative interpretation, and then seeks amendments to her reading of the situation. When the circumstances are especially troubling—as in those cases where the worldviews or abstract moral values of either friend are challenged—the process of analysis will be protracted, interactive, and even conflictive. This interactive (and occasionally conflictive) process can amount to a "testing" of the viewpoints and abstract moral guidelines both hold. It should be noted that the emotional component of this process is absolutely key to its success. Unless both friends feel an emotional stake in the outcome of the discussion, one or both might well retreat into a position of epistemic or moral relativism. The problem with a relativist position is that it discourages genuine involvement in the dispute and prevents the person who holds it from evaluating the different interpretations as better and worse, as more and less truthful. Only when both friends care about and respect each other enough to take the other seriously, and have sufficient confidence in the other's affection to risk pushing the other past her comfort zone, does this interactive process contribute to their collective epistemic and emotional growth.

I turn now to a consideration of the significance of specifically *interracial* friendships. In her account of the opportunities presented by friendships for promoting moral growth, Friedman acknowledges that the kind of deep-level moral growth she esteems is a potential that is not always realized. She notes that "[t]he more alike friends are, the less likely they are to afford each other radically divergent moral perspectives in which to participate vicariously"

(202–03). Friedman does not elaborate extensively on this insight, nor does she extend her investigation into the realm of race. However, to the extent that a person is interested in the way friendships across difference might challenge her schemas to the point where she begins to change her understanding of the ideas, institutions, and interactions that create the difference between her and her friend, it makes sense to do so.

To begin with, I acknowledge that people rarely become close friends with others who are radically different in every way (in terms of race, class, gender, sexuality, age, political commitment, religious affiliation, etc.) from themselves. This is partly because people make friends with others with whom they come into sustained contact; people find their friends at work, at play, in school, at church, or in their neighborhoods. Consequently, when a person makes friends with others who have been racialized differently from herself, usually they are like her in at least a few other salient ways. For example, when two people who work together become friends, it is generally because they are comparably situated in the hierarchy of their organization. They are likely to be comparably compensated and have a similar standard of living. The two friends may share a commitment to their profession or company and value similar kinds of activities and material goods. The most salient difference between them, in such a case, might well be how they are situated in the racial hierarchy of the United States.

Because race matters considerably for people's life experiences and opportunities in American society, friends who are differentially situated in the U.S. racial hierarchy are more likely to have had different experiences in (and to possess different schemas about) their shared world than those who are substantially similarly situated within the racial hierarchy. In the case of two friends associated with different races, the strong potential exists that one friend will eventually share with the other her interpretation of an event that her friend might either perceive quite differently or never have had the opportunity to experience personally. Depending on how they are each identified in terms of gender, class, and sexuality, their differing views regarding what is at stake or what is to be done in response to the event might be widely divergent. It is in the process of talking through their contrary perspectives, and in discovering what it is about their own *particular* lives that might have caused them to think and feel so differently, that they might begin to realize how differently they perceive the situation. Thus, it is often against this backdrop of sameness of other parts of their lives that two friends of different races have the opportunity to

compare the difficulties and opportunities that come their way. Through such
a process of comparison, they can learn about the differential effects of race
on people located differently within the racial order, and begin the process of
building a shared racial schema.

The opportunities for building richer and more accurate racial schemas, I
contend, are especially rich in the case of two non-white friends who are of different racial or cultural backgrounds. As people who have been victimized by
racism—as people who have been forced to respond in some way to numerous
unfair and inaccurate assumptions about their mental and moral capacities—
people of color are more likely than white people to be attuned to the multifarious dynamics of the way race is done. Not only have they had to grapple with
the prejudice they encounter in their own lives, but—by virtue of their close
proximity to family members, friends, and neighbors who share their racial
group associations—they are likely to have been witness to a wide range of racist experiences particular to their own group. Furthermore, they are familiar
with the incredible variety of strategies (humor, denial, self-segregation, racism directed toward members of other racial groups, armed resistance, self-
affirmation, reverse racism, etc.) that people in their communities employ to
counteract racism's painful and debilitating effects. As a result of their socially-
located experiences, non-white people have access to a virtual storehouse of
emotionally-charged pieces of information about race and racism—even if
they never figure out how best to organize, interpret, synthesize, or process that
information. Furthermore, many people of color have developed what W.E.B.
Du Bois termed a "double-consciousness"; they understand that there is more
than one way of interpreting a racially-charged situation (5).[8] Insofar as people
of color are accustomed to the disjuncture between their own interpretations
of racial incidents and hegemonic or "commonsense" interpretations of those
same events (think here of the initial media coverage of the 1992 Los Angeles uprising versus the subsequent interpretations provided by the people who
were directly affected by it), they may in fact be more open than most white
people are to the possibility that there are alternative valid perspectives about
the issue of race. People of color are thus likely to make better interlocutors for
each other when the subject is race and racism. And finally, because two non-
white friends from different racial groups are differentially situated within the
system of white supremacy, their mutual exposure to each other's situations can
help them to better understand *together* the overall dynamics of what is an incredibly complex system. To be sure, while blacks, Latina/os, Asians, American

Indians, and Arabs are all disadvantaged within the system of white supremacy, the system itself is sufficiently variegated that it affects each of these groups (and significant subgroups within them) differently (Alcoff, "Anti-Latino"). For all these reasons, when a person of color shares her observations and feelings about race with a non-white friend associated with a different racial group, both friends are admirably positioned to begin the difficult process of analyzing together the complexity and perniciousness of racial formations in the U.S. in a way that leads to the development of a racial schema that more adequately accounts for the dynamics of race.[9]

Friendship between two people who are differently situated within the racial order thus enables an emotionally- and epistemically-productive kind of particularizing of consciousness. When a friend you love and trust has a radically different reaction to a particular issue or event than you do, you are presented with the opportunity to realize that the view you hold on that issue is not the only—and perhaps not even the best—view to have. Indeed, friends who take each other's differences seriously are less inclined than those people whose values have never been profoundly challenged *by people they care about* to understand their way of thinking or being in the world as the "normal" or "right" way be. A healthy particularizing of consciousness—which I contend is a significant effect of interracial friendships that endure over time—is a key step in moving away from a positivist conception of objectivity. As such, it is the first step toward a fallible and non-dogmatic conception of how a community of people can (collectively) develop a better way of interacting with each other. In the case of interracial friendships, a friend who understands that her way of interpreting a racial situation is only one way (and maybe not the best way) is well on her way toward understanding the way race is done in the United States. Thus, a friendship between two people associated with different racial groups always holds at least the potential for expanding each friend's emotional horizons and improving her racial schemas.

The Dialogic Potential of Multicultural Literature

Engagement with a literary work written by a racial other replicates some of the dynamics of an interracial friendship, but has the advantage of being more flexible in space and time. My purpose in making this point is not to suggest that reading multicultural literature is necessarily more effective or more important for improving our racial schemas than is fostering a friendship with someone associated with a different race. Rather, I want to suggest that reading and teaching novels by socially subordinated people can provide a particularly rich context for learning about the interactions, institutions, and ideas that create and maintain different forms of inequality.

My interest in what and how readers can learn from literature was initially piqued by an anecdote that Marilyn Friedman includes in her book. At a 1987 American Philosophical Association conference where she presented a version of her argument, David Solomon asked Friedman whether works of literature could inspire the same sort of moral transformation that she attributed to friendship. Her response was not to deny the possibility but to downplay it.[10] She explains:

> The literary work may be more articulate than my friend, but I can talk to my friend and she can answer me in her own terms, directly responsive to what I say and what I ask her. By contrast, I may have to extract "responses" from the fixed number of sentences in a literary work and I am limited to interpreting those responses in my own, possibly uncomprehending, terms. (201)

Curiously, Friedman's account in this particular description of how communication between friends works simplifies her own very interesting and complex account of the potential that friendship holds for moral growth. On one hand it implies an unconstrained and unending responsiveness on the part of the friend who is being questioned, and on the other it ignores the possibility that the questioner will be unable to hear her friend's responses (should they be forthcoming) in her friend's "own terms." Thus, Friedman inadvertently paints here a picture of intersubjective communication that is too transparent, too immediate. In fact, communication between friends—particularly among those who are talking about something on which they hold differing views—can be very oblique or be conducted in fits and starts. If the matter at hand is an especially difficult one, if it seriously challenges one or the other of the pair, then it is quite likely that the listener will initially, and perhaps even repeatedly, hear her friend's responses in *her* own (as opposed to her *friend's* own) terms. Moreover, the listening friend's ability to "get it" may come years later, after the fact, in a moment of private contemplation and reinterpretation of what her friend was telling her so many years before.

I am not sure why Friedman felt the need to downplay literature as a source for moral transformation. Perhaps she felt unprepared to deal adequately with Solomon's question, or perhaps she interpreted it (unnecessarily, I believe) as a challenge to her argument. Whatever her rationale, Friedman's defensive response causes her to paint a static and ultimately inadequate picture of the experience of writing and reading fiction. She writes:

> Moreover, my friend's life continues to unfold in new directions that may surprise even her; while she lives, her life is still an open book whose chapters she does not wholly author as a mere self-confirmation of her own preexisting moral commitments. Thus, the lived experiences of friends have the potential for a kind of authenticity and spontaneity not available in novels, leaving only biography and autobiography as relevant analogues. (201–02)

With this explanation, Friedman inadvertently disparages the literariness of autobiographies and biographies, such as the way they are plotted by an author who selects and arranges certain biographical facts (but not others) of the life under consideration. More crucially, Friedman underestimates the complexity and semantic open-endedness of literary texts. Most importantly, she misunderstands how readers engage with works of literature that move them in profound ways. In fact, the activity of reading literature is rich in the potential for world-shaping and world-altering dialogic encounters for at least the following three reasons: (1) reading is a practice involving a person's intellectual and emotional engagement with a text; (2) reading expands a reader's horizon of possibility for experiential encounters; and (3) works of literature are heteroglossic textual mediations of complex social relations.

To begin with, a reader of a long, narrative work such as a novel will engage with it both intellectually and emotionally. In the process of reading, a reader is called upon to participate in an act of interpretation, to actively make sense of the narrative and of the characters that inhabit it. This interactive process is far more dialogic and open-ended than Friedman's description of the reader who must "extract 'responses' from the fixed number of sentences in a literary work" would imply. After all, if a reader is not sufficiently engaged by a novel, she will put it down and stop reading; she will decline the offer of friendship (or profit or amusement) that the narrative proposes to her and go her separate way.[11] If, however, she finds herself drawn into the novelistic world presented to her, her involvement will be both cognitive and emotive. The two processes necessarily go together—it is virtually impossible to follow a story line or remember the details of a novelistic setting without caring in some sort of positive or negative way about the characters whose adventures and dilemmas power the story line and provide fodder for the reader's ruminations about her own life.

Second, reading a novel can expand a reader's horizon of possibility for experiential encounters even further than the realm of friendship can. When a person reads a complex literary work of substantial length, the potential exists for her to engage in what the feminist philosopher María Lugones calls "'world'-traveling," whereby she enters into another, and (depending on who she is and what the book is about) possibly quite alien, world (77–100). A reader who takes up a book about a world that is far from her own will be exposed to situations, feelings, attitudes, and characters (implied people) that she does not encounter in her everyday life. In this way, literature has at least one significant advantage over a friendship: a book can enter, and imaginatively transport the reader, to spaces, times, and places that she herself cannot physically encounter; as my chapter epigraph by Emily Dickinson suggests, a book can "take us Lands away." Moreover, because it offers transportability through space and time, the book as a particular kind of object can allow a reader who lives in a racially segregated and economically stratified society like our own to be exposed to a variety of alternative perspectives that she might not otherwise be exposed to. Although some people do have friends from a wide variety of racial, cultural, and economic backgrounds, many more people associate only with those who are very similar to themselves. As Friedman admits, "Our choices of friends are indeed constrained, both by the limited range of our acquaintances and by the responses of others to us as we extend gestures of friendship toward them. Thus, friendship is voluntary only within the limits imposed by certain external constraints" (209). So, in the case of literature written by racial and cultural others, the effect can be that the reader is pulled in and given a kind of access to a way of conceptualizing the world that she might otherwise never be exposed to, even if she lives and works side by side with people of other races.

Third, in the case of a long, complex narrative like a novel, the engagement a reader has with a text can be profound. It is true that a reader's engagement with a novel can be an encounter of the type that leaves her untouched and unmoved—but it need not be. The sort of engagement I am interested in here is the sort that causes a reader to question profoundly her basic understandings and attitudes. As with friendship, the potential for epistemic and emotional growth within the scene of reading will not always be realized—much depends on the quality of the reader's intellectual and emotional engagement with the novel and the "fit" between the reader's interpretive schemas and the schemas that structure that novel. A reader's engagement with a literary text can thus replicate the situation of voluntarism that one finds in friendships. This is because a reader has the power to control her exposure to materials that challenge her. She can take up books that are a good "fit" for her capacity for engagement, and refuse those that are either too challenging or that fail to offer enough pleasure to keep her reading.

Central to an understanding of how and why literature holds out the potential for epistemic and emotional growth is a proper appreciation of the semantic open-endedness of (especially) long and complex works of literature. According to the literary critic M. M. Bakhtin, who famously theorized the constitutive *heteroglossia* of the novel form, the "novel can be defined as a diversity of social speech types (sometimes even diversity of languages) and a diversity of individual voices, artistically organized" (262).[12] It is the multi-voicedness he describes in his definition of a novel—a multivoicedness that is accomplished artistically in any given novel through the characters' dialogue, the authorial voice(s), and the incorporation of other genres such as letters, news articles, poems, and so forth, all of which bring with them their own schemas—that Bakhtin refers to with the concept of heteroglossia. The novel form's constitutive heteroglossia is what ensures that any given novel will open out differently into the consciousnesses of its various readers. It is, moreover, what accounts for the fact that the same novel will open out differently within the consciousness of the same reader over time.

By insisting on its fundamental heterogeneity and multivoicedness, Bakhtin in no way suggests that the novel form lacks unity or artistry. He explains: "The novel orchestrates all its themes, the totality of the world of objects and ideas depicted and expressed in it, by means of the social diversity of speech types and by the differing individual voices that flourish under such conditions" (263). Through his use of the term "orchestrates," Bakhtin implicitly and helpfully imagines the novel as a kind of linguistic symphony in which a variety of speech types, discourses, literary styles, and incorporated genres are arranged into a stylistic unity. Insofar as one compares the novel to a symphony, one can imagine the various voices, discourses, and genres that together make up a given novel as so many different melodies, rhythms, and instruments that sound in concert to make up an orchestrated whole. And just as the different melodies, rhythms, and instruments resonate differently for the various listeners of a symphony—some of whom will focus on the melodic line, others of whom will listen hard for the bass undertones, and others who will feel a thrill of pleasure upon detecting the strains of an incorporated folk song with which they are familiar—so will the different elements of the novel resonate variously for diverse readers. While Bakhtin focused his theorizing on the novel, his insights can be usefully extended to other genres, many of which have been, as he notes, "novelized."

The concept of heteroglossia is thus helpful for understanding how and why a truly complex, multilanguaged, multiperspectival work of literature will change for a reader over time and will, in a non-trivial sense, be a different work for different readers. This is not to suggest that any particular work of literature is not structured by the schemas embedded within it, or that its author does not have a meaning or message that she wants to convey and that one would do well as a responsible reader to try to discern. Rather, the concept of heteroglossia shows why the meaning of a novel is not exhausted either by the author's intention or by the schemas that power its plot, shape its characters, and construct its chronotope. Insofar as meaning only ever comes into existence through the interpretive process, that meaning can never be absolutely fixed. So, while on one level heteroglossia must be there *in* the text, on another level the disparate elements of that heteroglossia must be recognized and *actively interpreted* for meaning to come into being in the consciousness of the individual reader. A reader's experience of a novel will depend to a significant extent on her past experiences, her formal training, her cultural exposure, and the circumstances in which she reads the novel—all of which together form her schemas and so condition her readerly practices and expectations.[13] And because people change over time—because they have additional experiences, sometimes receive more formal training, and occasionally develop or alter their schemas—their experience of a given novel will also change over time and with subsequent re-readings. I have modified my interpretation of Toni Morrison's novel *Sula* several times as my attitudes about the dynamics of female friendship, the implications of marital infidelity, and the desire for security vis-à-vis self-exploration have altered over the years. I still love the novel, I still think it is a great work of art, but my experience of the novel and my judgment about its "meaning" have changed over the course of many re-readings and in light of several significant changes in the circumstances of my life.[14] Sometimes a novel will seem to get "better," as a reader discovers ever-new subtleties and meanings. Other times, however, a novel will seem to get "worse," as a reader becomes bored with the thinness of the narrative or is newly offended by the themes and attitudes the novel conveys. Literary critic Wayne Booth describes something of this sort in his excellent argument for a serious reconsideration of the way literary critics think about ethical criticism. He writes: "the 'very same' *Count of Monte Cristo* that at sixteen I thought the greatest novel ever written is now for me almost unreadable" (34–35).

The richness of any particular novel is due to a great deal more, of course, than the novel form's constitutive heteroglossia. Much depends on the theme of the novel and the treatment its author has given to that theme. It is important to note here that the process of writing a novel involves a lot more than plotting out a narrative that merely confirms the author's preexisting ethical or political commitments. Certainly, there may be some authors who compose novels that way—authors who have political or ethical agendas and who will force the details of a plot to conform to their preexisting vision. But others, such as Toni Morrison, approach writing as a process of exploration. Indeed, Morrison writes as a way of delving into a question or situation that she finds intriguing or troubling. In a 1985 interview conducted by Bessie Jones, Morrison formulated the question that motivated the novel *Sula*: "If you say you are somebody's friend as in *Sula*, now what does that mean? What are the lines that you do not step across?" (138). Elsewhere in that same interview, Morrison explains that she views writing as a way of testing out the moral fiber of her characters in order to see how they respond to difficult situations. She says: "Well, I think my goal is to see really and truly of what these people are made, and I put them in situations of great duress and pain, you know, I 'call their hand.' And, then when I see them in life threatening circumstances or see their hands called, then I know who they are" (141). In another interview, with Nellie McKay, she explains: "It's the complexity of how people behave under duress that is of interest to me—the qualities they show at the end of an event when their backs are up against the wall" (420). Moreover, because Morrison regards writing as a process of moral and epistemic investigation, she does not write about ordinary, everyday people or events. Instead, she plumbs the hard cases—the situations where "something really terrible happens." She explains: "that's the way I find out what is heroic. That's the way I know why such people survive, who went under, who didn't, what the civilization was, because quiet as it's kept much of our business, our existence here, has been grotesque" (Morrison, "Interview," by Jones 141). The process of writing a novel can thus be a process of exploration in which the "answer" surprises even the author. In the following chapter, I turn to a close reading of *Sula* to explore, in company with the novel, the questions Morrison poses about the nature of friendship.

Conclusion

A central claim of this chapter has been that literature written by racial and cultural minorities can play a crucial role in the expansion of people's epistemic and emotional horizons. The semantic open-endedness of all good literature, including works that treat racial and cultural difference in interesting and complex ways, might seem to pose a difficulty for my argument that multicultural literature can contribute to better and more accurate racial schemas. But that would be the case only if I were arguing that reading a work of multicultural literature *always* or *directly* has the effect of making its reader less racist and more knowledgeable about her implication in structures of racial inequality. My claim is more limited. Instead, I argue that literature's constitutive heteroglossia enables an author and a reader to engage dialogically at a deep emotional and epistemic level with the difficult questions around race, culture, and inequality that are inevitably raised by a good multicultural work of literature. Such a dialogic interaction can, I suggest, prompt a reader to question and then revise some of her assumptions about structures of racial and economic inequality and how they are sustained. And while questioning does not lead ipso facto to epistemic and emotional growth, the former is at least a precondition for the latter.[15]

The Cervantes poem with which I began this chapter demonstrates the failure of understanding that occurs when the elements of friendship and dialogism I have been extolling as necessary for learning about the dynamics of race are missing from a conversation about race. The question implied by the title—"You are an intelligent, well-read person. All such persons understand that racism is silly and illogical. As an intelligent, well-read person myself, *I* do not believe in racial discord. How, then, can *you*?"—introduces the less than ideal terms under which the exchange between the poet and the young white man is taking place. Because the young man's question implies a challenge to, rather than a sincere interest in, the poet's perspective—because he sees her with an arrogant eye—he begins the exchange by denying her interpretive capacity. He fails to extend to her the friendly presumption that she will bear reliable moral witness and so cannot consider the possibility that she may know something that he does not know about the way race works in their shared world. His arrogant stance toward the poet is what allows him to make an appeal to their sameness at the expense of the racial difference that she insists must be acknowledged if her experiences are to make any sense. Thus, the poem is an answer to the young man's question and a passionate defense of the poet's race-conscious perspective on their shared social world. Finally, it is an anguished appeal for understanding that simultaneously acknowledges the far greater possibility of misunderstanding: "(I know you don't believe this. / You think this is nothing / but faddish exaggeration. But they / are not shooting at you.)" (35). With this last line, the poet further demonstrates her recognition that the young man's social location inhibits his ability to recognize the existence of a racial order that affects them each very differently; she perceives that as a white man in a social order that overvalues both whiteness and maleness, he has never been targeted by the "bullets" of racism that are "discrete and designed to kill slowly" (36). So, although she makes several appeals of her own that acknowledge her potential sameness to him,[16] the poet finally refuses to uphold the young man's arrogant perception of their shared social world—to do so would be to gloss over the racial difference that shapes her very experience of it. She tells him that despite her best efforts to shut out the "sounds of blasting and muffled outrage" that disrupt her poetic reverie, she finally cannot ignore the daily "slaps on the face" that racism, unbidden, brings to her (36).

In a heteroglossic statement near the end of the poem that is at once subtly ironic and heart-wrenchingly sincere, the poet assures her young white male interlocutor, "I am a poet / who yearns to dance on rooftops, / to whisper delicate lines about joy / and the blessings of human understanding" (36). The sincerity of the statement stems from the fact that she envisions a world in which "[t]he barbed wire politics of oppression / have been torn down long ago" and in which "[t]he only reminder / of past battles, lost or won, is a slight / rutting in the fertile fields" (35). The irony stems from the fact that this is finally a poem about racial *misunderstanding*. Unless the young white man starts to care about the poet enough to risk "trying on" her interpretive claim and its implications for his own epistemic and emotional growth, and until he enters into a dialogue that acknowledges her as a worthy interlocutor who might have something to teach him about the social world he lives in, "the blessings of human understanding" will remain frustratingly out of reach for them both.

NOT ONE AND THE SAME THING

The Ethical Relationship of Selves to Others in Toni Morrison's *Sula*

She had clung to Nel as the closest thing to both an other and a self, only
to discover that she and Nel were not one and the same thing.

Toni Morrison, *Sula*

For without friends no one would choose to live, though he had all other goods.

Aristotle, *Nicomachean Ethics*

Paradox and Interpretation

The novel *Sula* begins with a paradox. The novel's first sentence invites the reader to invest emotionally in something that no longer exists: "In that place, where they tore the nightshade and blackberry patches from their roots to make room for the Medallion City Golf Course, there was once a neighborhood" (3).[1] The reader finds out that a neighborhood has been obliterated before she is told what the neighborhood was like, what it was called, or that "black people lived there." This paradox is only one of several contradictions Morrison incorporates into the novel's opening section (McDowell 60; Hunt).[2] Another appears when the narrator conjures a visitor (a white "valley man") who hears the people's laughter but fails to perceive the "adult pain" that "rested somewhere under the eyelids, somewhere under their head rags and soft felt hats, somewhere in the palm of the hand, somewhere behind the frayed lapels, somewhere in the sinew's curve" (4). Shortly thereafter, the narrator points to a nominal inversion by noting that the place was called the "Bottom" even though it was located geographically *above* Medallion in the hills on the outskirts of the town. The reader is told that this came about as a result of a "nigger joke"—a cruel joke that nevertheless provides to the Bottom's black residents "a little comfort somehow" (4–5). A narrative reversal, the juxtaposition of opposites, laughter that hides pain, a cruel joke that provides comfort, and the replacement of the top with the Bottom. Before the characters are properly introduced, before the story even begins, the narrative signals to the reader that she will have to look under, behind, and beyond the surface if she hopes to understand the meaning of the phenomena she confronts.

Paradox turns out to be the key structuring element of *Sula*, with the central paradox being the missing "self" at the core of the novel's title character.[3] A kind of anti-*Bildungsroman*, Morrison's second novel aggressively denies to its readers an ego-centered main character around whose emotional and physical growth and adventures the narrative is organized.[4] It does so in two ways. First, with respect to Sula's life trajectory, the novel is missing its middle. The novel proper is divided into two sections: the first ends in 1927 with Sula's departure from the Bottom, while the second begins in 1937 with her return. Precisely what Sula was doing during those intervening ten years, whatever she might have experienced or felt or learned, is left out of the narrative. Second, Sula is not the undisputed protagonist of the novel despite being its title character. Although she is briefly mentioned in the opening section of the book, the reader does not learn very much about her until the third chapter (McDowell 61). The first chapter, "1919," takes as its primary focalized object the character of Shadrack, while the second chapter, "1920," introduces us to the character of Nel.[5] Sula's status as protagonist is further destabilized by Nel's centrality to the novel's character-system.[6] Apart from being the first of the novel's central duo to be properly introduced, Nel is the only character in the novel to focalize and narrate any part of the narrative (105–06).[7] Nel is, moreover, the one who brings the novel to a close. Finally, it is Nel, rather than Sula, who comes the closest to learning the hard lesson posed by the novel—the lesson of who she is in relation to those around her. Together, these various plot devices and formal features call into question our readerly desire for a single protagonist—our novel-reading habit of elevating one character above the others as the focus of our attention. Moreover, in moving the focus of the story away from individuality (Sula) toward relationality (Sula and Nel), the novel reminds us that people only become selves in relation to other selves (Gillespie and Kubitschek).

These proliferating paradoxes have several implications for how a reader might approach the task of interpreting the novel.[8] For one, the focus on hidden meanings in the first few pages suggests that the novel's embedded schemas may not be perceptible on the surface of the text. Understanding why and how the "laughter" of the Bottom's residents covers over an "adult pain" requires a reader to know something about the history of race relations in mid-twentieth-century Ohio. Such a history cannot be found within the text of the novel; rather, it is contextual information that an attentive reader must seek out for herself and incorporate into her own readerly schemas.[9] Moreover, the focus on the novel's dual-protagonist structure that arises from the pairing of Sula's missing "self" with Nel's narrative centrality highlights the issue of relationality in a way that points outward to the relationship between the reader and the text (McDowell 69). Motivating the novel's paradoxes are questions about the nature of the relationship that will be created by the reader's interpretive activity. Implicitly, the novel asks: "What kind of reader are you going to be?" "Are you available to absorb what I am going to show you?" and, "Will you consider that what you initially perceive may in fact be otherwise?"

In the previous chapter, I argued that reading and teaching literature written by racial and cultural others creates a situation that is rich in dialogic potential. Doing so can give a reader access to a way of conceptualizing the world that she might otherwise never be exposed to. I suggested that in the case of a long, complex narrative like a novel, the engagement a reader might have with a literary work could be epistemically and emotionally significant. In some cases, the "friendship" the reader forms with a novel or a story will subtly or radically shift the schemas she subsequently uses to perceive and interpret—not just the literary work, but even the extra-textual "real" social world in which she lives. I further noted that realizing the dialogic potential of multicultural literature depends on the quality of engagement a reader brings to the text. When a reader approaches the text with an arrogant eye, when she fails to "consult something other than [her] own will and interests and fears and imagination," then the potential for growth and learning will be greatly diminished. To really learn from an other, whether that other is a text or a person, one must be attentive to the schemas the other is using to interpret the worlds the self and other share. In the words of Marilyn Frye: "One must look and listen and check and question" (Frye 75).

In this chapter, I deepen the argument I made in the last chapter about the dialogic potential of multicultural literature. I pay close attention to what the novel shows us about the relationship between Sula and Nel, and to the implications of the novel's paradoxical logic for my own reading practice. In general, I am drawn to Morrison's oeuvre because she approaches writing as a mode of inquiry. As previously noted, the question that motivated *Sula* is fundamentally concerned with the nature of friendship: "If you say you are somebody's friend as in *Sula*, now what does that mean? What are the lines that you do not step across?" (Morrison, "Interview," by Jones). An ethicist in her own right, Morrison explores the dynamics that emerge when a self fails to recognize the other *as* other, as a unique individual with legitimate needs and desires separate from one's own.[10] Because she conducts her investigation in a fictional, rather than a logical, form, she presents her reader less with an analysis than with a dilemma—albeit one that she works through and to which she offers some provisional answers at the conclusion of the novel. But I am also interested in *Sula* as an exemplary work of specifically *multicultural* literature. Morrison's fictional argument is historically and culturally situated, even as it has implications for those who do not share the novel's particular historical and cultural situation. *Sula* exemplifies the way that literature is brilliantly suited to the exploration of what it means to be an (inescapably-situated) ethical human being.

Not One and the Same Thing

In her interrogation of the "lines you do not step across" in *Sula*, Morrison depicts a number of relationships, some of which are more or less successful, others of which are twisted—even grotesque. The most important relationship in the novel is the friendship between Nel and Sula, two "solitary little girls whose loneliness was so profound it intoxicated them and sent them stumbling into Technicolored visions that always included a presence, a someone, who, quite like the dreamer, shared the delight of the dream" (51). Given that friendship is constituted as a particular type of relationship of a self to an other, it is significant that Sula has difficulty with the project of being a self. Having developed, as a girl, "no self to count on," no "center, no speck around which to grow," Sula becomes, as an adult, experimental and mercurial—more process than essence (119).[11] In part, this observation merely says about Sula what is at least partly true for all of us. We humans are all subjects-in-process; our selves are always already in the process of being made and remade through our interactions with the people and objects that make up the world(s) in which we live. But Sula is figured as more than just an ordinary, evolving Heideggerian *Dasein*. She stands apart from her community, even as she is a part of it. As a consequence of having "no ego," and of being "free of ambition, with no affection for money, property or things, no greed, no desire to command attention or compliments,"

Sula feels no responsibility to "be consistent with herself" or with others (119). This mutability is elegantly figured in the novel through the floating significance of the birthmark Sula bears over her eye. With no meaning apart from what its perceivers attribute to it, the mark functions like a fun-house mirror in which characters see magnified aspects of themselves: Nel sees a rose (96), Nel's children see a scary black thing (97–98), Jude sees a copperhead (103), and Shadrack sees a tadpole (156).[12]

The portrait of Sula that emerges from the novel is that of a traumatized but immensely creative woman whose inquisitive orientation toward the world has been frustrated by the particular circumstances of her life as well as by the limited options for creative expression afforded to a person of her race, gender, and class in pre–civil rights America. In the wake of a childhood incident in which she unintentionally causes the drowning death of a young neighbor boy, Sula is portrayed as being emotionally and intellectually freed from social convention in a way that makes her "dangerous" to those around her. Described as an "artist with no art form," she is figured as creativity run amuck (121). Constantly making and remaking herself, Sula turns her "tremendous curiosity and her gift for metaphor" toward an exploration of "her own thoughts and emotions, giving them full rein, feeling no obligation to please anybody unless their pleasure pleased her" (121; 118). Sula's disregard for others' feelings is most obvious when their presence facilitates or frustrates her project of self-exploration:

> As willing to feel pain as to give pain, to feel pleasure as to give pleasure, hers was an experimental life—ever since her mother's remarks sent her flying up those stairs, ever since her one major feeling of responsibility had been exorcised on the bank of a river with a closed place in the middle. The first experience taught her there was no other that you could count on; the second that there was no self to count on either. (118–119)

The reference to selves and others in this key passage points to the way Sula's personality has been shaped by her interactions with others. Just before Sula and Nel go out to the river on the day Chicken Little is drowned, Sula overhears her mother, Hannah, tell a couple of friends that while she loves her daughter, she does not "like her." Sula, having "only heard Hannah's words," is stung and bewildered by her mother's pronouncement (57). The implication is that Sula lacks a schema that would enable her to perceive the parental love and care that motivated those words; she is unable to understand how and why a mother might say that about a prepubescent daughter about whom she worries and for whom she is responsible. Had the accident of Chicken Little's drowning not occurred on that same day, had Hannah not burned to death in a freak accident only a year later, then perhaps time and experience could have intervened such that Hannah's words might not have had such a lasting effect on the formation of Sula's character.

Ironically, Sula's lack of a consistent self encourages her to behave in ways that are distinctly *selfish* according to the mores of the community in which she lives. When her grandmother, Eva, criticizes Sula for her ten-year absence, Sula ignores her. When Eva complains that Sula has not acknowledged the debts she owes to her, Sula turns her back and refuses to engage. When Eva ups the ante by telling Sula to settle down and have some babies, Sula retorts, "I don't want to make somebody else. I want to make myself" (92). When Eva accuses Sula of having "hellfire" burning in her, she declares, "Whatever's burning in me is mine!" (93). And finally, when Eva tells Sula that she has thrown her life away, she retorts, "It's mine to throw," before threatening to burn Eva alive (93). Within a month of that conversation, Sula has herself declared Eva's legal guardian, puts Eva away in an old folks' home, and then takes up residence in Eva's house.

Morrison thus builds for her a reader a schema by which to understand how Sula's frustrated creativity, combined with her idiosyncratic disregard for others stemming from the two traumatic childhood experiences, makes her indifferent to the lines and boundaries that constitute the norms of the society in which she lives. Deprived of a socially-sanctioned art form that could fully engage her "idle imagination," Sula turns to her own sexuality as a medium within which to "find what she was looking for: misery and the ability to feel deep sorrow" (121–22). From Sula's own perspective, her sexuality is not located in the realm of moral abstractions; she neither bothers to legitimate it by expressing it within the institution of marriage nor does she derive pleasure from the fact that her sexual relations are extramarital. Rather, Sula locates her sexuality "in the realm of sensory experience" (McDowell 64). She has sex with men not because she is looking for a connection with another human being, but for "the postcoital privateness in which she met herself, welcomed herself, and joined herself in matchless harmony" (123). That Sula's search for self is conducted by way of having indiscriminate sexual relations with the community's husbands, fathers, sons, and brothers is immaterial for her—if not for the community of people among whom she lives.

The one person with whom Sula comes closest to forming a sustaining "complete" or "perfect" friendship is, of course, Nel. As it plays itself out over the course of the novel, the friendship between the two women ultimately fails not because Sula does not care about Nel, but because she confuses her own interests with those of Nel.[13] Even as a young girl, Sula "could hardly be counted on to sustain any emotion for more than three minutes"; the only time she was able to hold onto a mood was "in defense of Nel" (53). Indeed, Sula's attachment to Nel is so strong that she thinks of the two of them as "two throats and one eye" (147). Consequently, when as an adult Sula has sex with Nel's husband, Jude, she does so without shame or malice. It is only *after* Sula has sex with Jude—only *after* Nel refuses to forgive Sula the trespass on her marriage and her feelings—that Sula recognizes that she has overstepped a boundary that exists between them:

> [Sula] had clung to Nel as the closest thing to both an other and a self, only to discover that she and Nel were not one and the same thing. She had no thought at all of causing Nel pain when she bedded down with Jude. They had always shared the affection of other people: compared how a boy kissed, what line he used with one and then the other. Marriage, apparently, had changed all that, but having had no intimate knowledge of marriage, having lived in a house with women who thought all men available, and selected from among them with a care only for their tastes, she was ill prepared for the possessiveness of the one person she felt close to. (119)

That Sula does not understand her fault in overstepping Nel's boundaries is indicated by her reaction to Nel's sense of betrayal: "Now Nel was one of *them*. . . . It surprised her a little and saddened her a good deal when Nel behaved the way the others would have" (120). In other words, instead of looking, and listening, and checking, and questioning her own motivations and actions, Sula simply blames Nel for not sharing her own perspective on the situation.

Thus, one can think of Morrison's question—"What are the lines you do not step across?"—as referring not just to ethical imperatives such the one contained within the statement, "A friend never sleeps with her friend's husband," but also to the lines that constitute us and make us self and other. Because Sula fails to "consult something other than [her] own will and interests and fears and imagination" in her interaction with others, she exhibits a curiously solipsistic form of self-lessness (Frye 120). Because she pays insufficient attention to the "scope and boundary of the self" in her relationship with Nel, she inadvertently regards her friend with an arrogant eye.

Sula, of course, is not the only character in the novel to regard Nel with an arrogant eye. Jude does so as well, although he is warranted less by childhood trauma and an artistic temperament than by a sense of racial injury to the socially-prescribed role afforded him by his male gender.[14] Having been passed over for a desirable job because of his race, "it was rage, rage and a determination to take on a man's role anyhow that made [Jude] press Nel about settling down." Although before their marriage Jude likes Nel well enough, his reasons for wanting to marry her are driven by *his* needs and desires: "He needed some of his appetites filled, some posture of adulthood recognized, but mostly he wanted someone to care about his hurt, to care very deeply" (82). What is missing here is a concern for what Nel, as the particular person she is, might want or need. It is not that Jude does not recognize any responsibility toward the woman who would be his wife; rather, it is that his relationship to a wife is highly abstract, normatively gendered, and unperceiving of her particularity—her likes, her dislikes, who *she* is. He is not even able to perceive that she will be a separate Being after their marriage. In return for his sheltering, loving, and growing old with her, Jude imagines that Nel would become the "hem" to "his garment," the "tuck and fold that hid his raveling edges." According to him, the "two of them together would make one Jude" (83). In their arrogant perception of Nel, Jude and Sula share a conception of *love as aggregate of the self.*

Nel's Tiny Life

Sula and Jude are not solely responsible for the failures that attend their separate relationships with Nel. To imagine that they are would be to ignore the many paradoxes that structure the narrative. As is typical of Morrison's novels, *Sula* lets no character off the hook—especially those who might imagine themselves as blameless. The characters are all implicated, albeit unequally, in their eventual fates. Although Nel spends the greater part of her life assuming that she is the "good" one, the one unfairly wronged by husband and friend alike, the novel's paradoxical logic ensures that her assumptions will also be upset. In fact, Nel's retreat into conventional morality after she walks in on Jude and Sula having sex proves as detrimental to the flourishing of her self—as well as to her friendship with Sula—as is Sula's thoughtless boundary-crossing (Gillespie and Kubitschek 43). But just as Sula's solipsism was a contingent result of the interaction between her childhood traumas, her individual proclivities, and her sociocultural and historical contexts, so Nel's "tiny life" was never a foregone conclusion (165). Nel's friendship with Sula had opened to her the possibility that her life might have turned out differently. The chapter in which the reader first meets Nel, "1920," sets up the familiar Christian dichotomy between the asexual maternal "good" woman and the sexual non-maternal "bad" one (Freud). The first is personified by Helene Wright, Nel's mother, while the second is personified by Rochelle, the creole whore who is Helene's estranged mother and Nel's grandmother. Helene, who has been raised by her own grandmother under the "dolesome eyes" of the Virgin Mary, is represented as a devoted mother and dutiful wife whose sexuality is subordinated to her maternity (17, 25). It took nine years before Helene's marriage produced a child, and the reader is told that the long absences of her ship's cook husband were "quite bearable" to her, particularly after Nel's birth. Rochelle, conversely, is a prostitute and neglectful mother whose unconventional morality is signaled by the canary yellow dress and gardenia perfume she wears to the home of her own, recently deceased, mother (25–26). The importance of Rochelle for Nel is that she presents Nel with an alternative model of womanhood. Prior to the trip to New Orleans to attend her great-grandmother's funeral, Nel had no reason to question her mother's authority and values. But after being embarrassed by her mother's too-anxious-to-please response to a racist white train conductor, and after meeting her alluring gardenia-scented grandmother, Nel comes to several important and related realizations. The first is that there are other ways to be a woman in the world; the second is that her mother is fallible and limited in her influence on the social world that Nel will have to live in. The last is that Nel is a "me"—a Being related to, but apart from, other Beings. It is this "new found me-ness" that allows Nel to spite her mother's wishes, and to cultivate the friendship of Sula, who is the daughter of a woman of whom Nel's mother disapproves (29).

For Nel, the friendship with Sula is enabling, rewarding, freeing. Although when she was a child Nel's parents "had succeeded in rubbing down to a dull glow any sparkle or splutter she had," her friendship with Sula gives that quality "free reign" (83). When after a ten-year absence Sula comes back into Nel's life, it feels to her like "getting the use of an eye back, having a cataract removed" (95). Sula "made [Nel] laugh," "made her see old things with new eyes," and made her feel "clever, gentle and a little raunchy" (95). Whereas other aspects of Nel's life worked to shut her down, Sula—"whose past she had lived through and with whom the present was a constant sharing of perceptions"—

opened her up. Under Sula's influence, Nel's world becomes brighter, easier, more playful: "Was there anyone else before whom she could never be foolish? In whose view inadequacy was mere idiosyncrasy, a character trait rather than a deficiency? Anyone who left behind that aura of fun and complicity?" (95). Importantly, Nel is not represented as being a different person when she is with Sula; rather, she is drawn as being more fully, deeply, and satisfyingly herself.

The focus on the friendship between Nel and Sula suggests that although Morrison views pair bonding as central to the development of the human self, in *Sula* she is less interested in the type of pair bonding associated with sexual or romantic partnerships than she is with the type of relationship produced through friendship. After all, more important to Nel's childhood self than the dream of the "fiery prince" is the imagined friend with "smiling sympathetic eyes" who shares her dream (51).[15] The novel does not refuse the possibility that a complete friendship might include a sexual relationship; it does, though, remind its reader that they are not one and the same thing. Nel's inability to forgive Sula for having sex with Jude suggests that a self's ability to perceive an other with a loving eye—the ability, that is, "to tell one's own interests from those of others and of knowing where one's self leaves off and another be-gins"—can be difficult when sexuality enters the picture. So, while Nel does perceive Jude as a separate Being, and does not attempt to aggregate his self to her own in the way he does to her, her relationship to him is predicated on a concept of *love as possession*. Just before Sula dies, Nel confronts her friend in a way that reveals her belief that she owns Jude—if not the whole of him, at least the part of him that involves sexual activity.[16] She demands of Sula: "*What did you take him for* if you didn't love him and why didn't you think about me?" (144, emphasis added). When Nel does not get the answer from Sula that she is looking for, she tries again: "And you didn't love me enough to leave him alone. . . . *You had to take him away*" (145, emphasis added). Jude here is figured as an object possessed by Nel and stolen by Sula. His agency in the infidelity is obliterated; his subjectivity, desires, and fault are emphatically denied. Lest the reader miss the crucial point being made in this passage, the novel repeats the message via the trajectory of Sula's relationship with Ajax. The narrator tells us that in the beginning of their relationship, "it was not the presents that made [Sula] wrap [Ajax] up in her thighs. They were charm-ing, of course . . . but her real pleasure was the fact that he talked to her. They had genuine conversations" (127). The implication is that Sula's sexual relation-ship with Ajax is predicated, at first, on a complete friendship. However, once

Sula begins to "discover what possession was" so that her behavior shifts in a way that signals to Ajax that she wants to own his time and sexual attributes, Ajax regretfully ends the relationship (131–33). Thus, according to the ideal self schema that is developed over the course of the novel but never fully realized by any of the characters, perceiving with a loving eye is incompatible with the idea that a self can ever "own" any part of an other, even the other's time or sexual attributes. In conceiving of *love as possession*, Nel is equally guilty of regarding Jude with an arrogant eye.

Through the character of Eva, the novel sets up a key distinction between "watching" and "seeing" that turns out to be central to Nel's eventual acceptance of partial responsibility for the rift that developed between herself and Sula. After years of loneliness, and in the course of enacting her role as a "good" woman, Nel visits Sula's grandmother, Eva, in the nursing home. When Eva says to Nel, "[t]ell me how you killed that little boy," Nel protests that it was Sula, and not herself, who threw Chicken Little into the water. Eva, though, refuses the distinction between them: "You. Sula. What's the difference?" (168). When Nel protests that she did not have anything to do with Chicken Little's death, Eva insists on Nel's culpability: "You was there. You watched, didn't you? Me, I never would've watched" (168). When Eva pushes the point—"How did you get him to go in the water?"—Nel is thrust out of her accustomed self-righteousness and forced to defend herself. Upset at the accusation, and disturbed by Eva's confusing her with Sula, Nel flees the room and then ruminates on the exchange: "What did old Eva mean by *you watched*? How could she help seeing it? She was right there. But Eva didn't say *see*, she said *watched*. 'I did not watch it. I just saw it.' But it was there anyway, as it had always been, the old feeling and the old question. The good feeling she had had when Chicken's hand slipped" (170). Under this scenario, watching involves involvement while seeing does not.

After the visit with Eva, Nel is compelled, for the first time in her life, to reach down into that "*deep place of knowledge inside herself and touch that terror and loathing of any difference that lives there*" in order to "*see whose face it wears*" (Lorde, "Master's Tools"). She remembers the "contentment" that had "washed over her enjoyment" as she watched the water close peacefully over the turbulence of Chicken Little's body. She realizes that what she had passed off to herself for years as "maturity" and "serenity" was only "the tranquillity that follows a joyful stimulation" (170). Acknowledging the "good feeling" she had had when Chicken Little's hands slipped—a feeling not unlike the "postcoital privateness" Sula experiences after sex—obliges Nel to see herself as having had an active part in Chicken Little's death and as being more similar to Sula than she had wanted to admit (170). Nel's shock thus comes not only from recognizing her own implication in Chicken Little's death—she had in fact *watched*, and not merely *seen*—but also from newly perceiving herself as like the person against whom she has defined herself for the previous twenty-five years. Not only is Nel pushed to reevaluate Sula, but also her own sense of self is at risk of being radically upended. Even though Nel tries to push away the new truth with which she is confronted—"Eva *was* mean"—the shock of self-recognition sends her stumbling to the cemetery and to Sula's grave (171). Once there she comes face to face with Shadrack, who had also been witness to Chicken Little's drowning. As they encounter one another for the first time in years, both Nel and Shadrack are forced to remember—and in Nel's case to reevaluate—"gone things" (174).

The complex of associations evoked for Nel by Chicken Little's death, Jude's betrayal, and the loss of Sula's friendship overwhelms Nel's senses, setting the stage for her incipient transformation. Calling out Sula's name, looking upward as if she might glimpse her friend in the treetops above, Nel's self-schema finally breaks apart. This event is nicely figured by the reworking of a metaphor that had appeared in the novel at the time of Nel's abandonment by Jude. At the time, alongside the stirring of leaves, the shifting of mud, and the smell of overripe green things, Nel had acquired, off to the right and just outside her line of sight, a "[q]uiet, gray, dirty" "ball of muddy strings, but without weight, fluffy but terrible in its malevolence" (109). At the time, Nel not only cannot look at the dirty gray ball, but she works hard at *not* looking at it. To do so, presumably, would have been too threatening to the fragile self that she was barely holding together. And in fact, Nel is described at that point in the novel as being in danger of coming physically apart: "For now her thighs were truly empty and dead too, and it was Sula who had taken the life from them and Jude who smashed her heart and the both of them who left her with no thighs and no heart just her brain raveling away" (110–11). Now, though, "[l]eaves stirred; mud shifted; there was the smell of overripe green things. A soft ball of fur broke and scattered like dandelion spores in the breeze" (174). As Nel brings together and looks at these three significant moments in her life, Nel finally realizes that it was Sula, and not Jude, whom she had been missing all along. The novel's final paradox, anticipated throughout by the novel's many other structural and thematic paradoxes, is here finally revealed.

The reader who has borne faithful witness to Nel is now in a position to understand how Nel's self-schema as the "good" one allowed her to pin "herself into a tiny life" (165).[17] She realizes that Nel had accepted as the truth of her life a culturally-sanctioned narrative in which a romantic relationship with her husband would be the most important relationship she could ever have. Within that narrative, Jude's decision to have sex with another woman compels Nel to occupy the role of the betrayed and victimized wife. It is only after Nel looks below the surface of that truth, only after she accepts her implication in the consequential events of her life in which she, Sula, Chicken Little, and Jude all participated, that she can begin to free herself from the prison of goodness, blamelessness, and loneliness to which she had consigned herself so many years before. Once Nel is able to accept partial responsibility for what has happened to her, then she is able to cry the cry that had eluded her so many years before— the "deeply personal cry for [her] own pain" (108). Only then is she able to mourn the loss both of Sula's friendship and of the self that she might herself have been if she had not shut Sula out of her life: "It was a fine cry—loud and long—but it had no bottom and it had no top, just circles and circles of sorrow" (174). In the end, Nel learns the hard lesson of who she is in relation to those around her—including her relation to her self *as* other.

Loving Perception and Complete Friendship

Over the course of the novel, Morrison builds an argument, through fiction, about the role of complete friendship for the full development of the human self. She does this primarily but not solely through her depiction of the development, and then failure, of Nel's and Sula's friendship. The incipient complete friendship shared by Nel and Sula opens for them both the possibility that their lives might have turned out differently. By being for each other companions, interlocutors, and true allies, Sula and Nel create for each other the possibility of being a fully realized individual-yet-relational self. "Like" enough to share the kinds of experiences and attitudes common to young black girls living in Medallion, Ohio, during the interwar years, they are "other" enough to provide an escape from the loneliness and disempowerment of their solitary childhoods. Having discovered that "they were neither white nor male, and that all freedom and triumph was forbidden to them, they had set about creating something else to be" (52). The unrealized alternative implied by the novel is that Sula and Nel might have remained friends—to the benefit of both. Perhaps if Sula had understood that she and Nel were not "two throats and one eye," but rather two mutually-constituting but separate Beings, perhaps if Nel had been able to see that her friendship with Sula was more important to the development of her fully-realized self than was her marriage to Jude so that she could forgive Sula's unintentional trespass of the boundary between their two selves, then perhaps both of their lives might have ended up deeper, richer, and fuller as a result.

Morrison's implied imperative to perceive others with a loving eye is reinforced by other relationships in the novel. One of the most striking, and the one that communicates most starkly the deforming effects of racial perception, is the relationship dynamic associated with the characters of "the deweys." The deweys are three boys who are adopted by Eva within the space of one year. The boys are several years apart in age and very different in ancestry and physical aspect. The first child is described as "a deeply black boy with a beautiful head and the golden eyes of chronic jaundice." The second is "light-skinned with freckles everywhere and a head of tight red hair." Finally, the third is "half Mexican with chocolate skin and black bangs" (38). Despite the manifest differences between them, Eva refers to each of them as Dewey, refusing to differentiate one from the other. In part, Morrison uses the deweys to make a point about the genetic and physiognomic variation that occurs regularly in the population of people who are frequently referred to as simply "black." But their physical differences also serve to emphasize the perversity of Eva's nomenclature. As a result of being regarded as a unit rather than as three separate individuals, they all become "in fact as well as in name a dewey—joining with the other two to become a trinity with a plural name" (38).[18] The case of the deweys illustrates the extreme example of what happens when an individual is not recognized as an individual, but is instead forced by others (for those others' benefit or convenience) to embody a type. Not only do the deweys fail to individuate as they age, but also their physical, emotional, and mental growth remains stunted. Attaining a height of only forty-eight inches tall, the deweys remain until their death "boys in mind" (84). Described by the narrator as "[m]ischievous, cunning, private and completely unhousebroken," with the interests and pursuits of first-graders, the deweys representationally embody the "grotesque" to which Morrison refers in her observation that "quiet as it's kept much of our business, our existence here, has been grotesque" (84–85; Morrison, "Interview," by Jones 141). As such, the deweys figure Morrison's scathing indictment of the practice of seeing and treating diverse people as all alike—a practice central to the doing of race and to arrogant perception generally.

The Dialogic Potential of Multicultural Literature Redux

While a good multicultural novel might succeed in teaching us a great deal about the dynamics of subordination, it is never exhausted by that project. *Sula*, for example, pushes racial and gendered conflict to the margins of the story in favor of a sustained focus on relationships—in particular, the relationship between two female friends.[19] Of course, Morrison's historically- and culturally-specific late-twentieth-century African American social world grounds her inquiry, just as the novel's fictional early-to-mid-twentieth-century African American social world provides the materials with which she undertakes her investigations. Both social worlds—the fictional world represented in the novel and the real world from within which Morrison is writing—are what enable some kinds of relationships to emerge as visible, desirable, and possible, while rendering others invisible, undesirable, and forbidden. Nel has trouble realizing and acting on the strength of her attachment to Sula not because she lacks insight and intelligence, but because her society's dominant ideas and institutions have socialized her to believe that her primary relationship in life should be romantic, sexual, and with a man of her own race. Thus, the "lines" between self and other that one must "not step across" in the novel are—like other ethical and moral imperatives—historically and culturally particular; they are not universal. Moreover, those boundaries are historically and culturally particular at least in part because human selves are historically and culturally particular. As social psychologists Hazel Rose Markus and Shinobu Kitayama have demonstrated, there are several different cultural models of the human self, some of which are more independent and others of which are more interdependent (see also Markus and Conner). What this means is that an action that might constitute a grievous infringement on someone's autonomy in one sociocultural context might be perceived as acceptable or even desirable in another. Consider the practice of arranging your child's marriage; although arranged marriages are not seen as desirable or appropriate in the United States today, the practice has been common in many different cultures around the world in several historical eras. The argument here is that if Nel had lived in another time and place, then she might have been able to perceive her friendship with Sula as being the most important relationship in her life. She might have been able to do this even as she accepted and acted on her desire for sexual relationships with men. Of course, none of what I have argued so far implies that what one learns from the novel is so hopelessly particular that it lacks relevance for those people who exist outside Nel's and Sula's cultural and historical context—people, like myself, who are not black females living in mid-century Ohio. On the contrary, *all* relationships take place within particular historical and cultural contexts. For this reason, the context within which Morrison situates her ethical exploration of the relationship of selves to others is as "particular" or as "universal" as any other.

Let me be very clear here. Unlike some of Morrison's other novels—such as *A Mercy*, which Morrison herself describes as an exploration of how race and slavery came to be "married," and which I discuss at length in Chapter 5— *Sula* is not primarily "about" race. It is, rather, a novel about friendship. At a very basic level, *Sula* is no more about the dynamics of (black) race or (female) gender than a novel written by John Updike is about the dynamics of (white) race and (male) gender. Only someone accustomed to thinking of anything that focuses on the lives of black women as being always already *primarily* about race and gender while simultaneously ignoring the whiteness and maleness of novels written by white men would be able to imagine that it is. *Sula*'s focus on black and female characters—its status as a "multicultural" novel—inflects but does not diminish its value as a forum within which to undertake an ethical investigation about the nature of friendship. The novel as a whole sensitively registers the way race and gender shape its characters, and their relationships with each other, even as it conducts an investigation that has ethical implications for people who are gendered and racialized differently from its characters or its author. What makes Morrison's novel potentially *more* valuable for understanding the dynamics of racialized gender in mid-twentieth-century America than a novel that focuses on the lives of white male characters is, simply, the novel's relative rarity. Insofar as there are fewer novels that treat the lives of black female characters in interesting and complex ways, *Sula* provides something that few other cultural products do—namely, access to a set of experiences, events, and schemas that most of us rarely encounter in fiction, on television, or in film.

Rather than diminishing Morrison's achievement, the fact of sociocultural variability serves to enhance the value of her ethical project. How else is one to locate the boundary between human selves that one ought not to violate in any given situation—unless one explores and probes? How better to conduct that exploration than through literature? A researcher could round up actual people and run experiments; she could put them in "situations in which something really terrible happens" in order to find out "what's heroic" (Morrison, "Interview, by Jones). But such is not ethically permissible in our society. For now, literature remains the most significant venue through which authors and readers alike can examine the myriad and complicated reasons that a wide variety of people who are inescapably situated Beings think and behave the way they do—not for the sake of finding the one right answer, but for facilitating our ongoing ethical investigations regarding how best to live with each other (Wu). As an exemplary multicultural novel, *Sula* has something important to teach us about the way race and gender shape selves, about the kinds of relationships that are possible in different situations, and about the nature of human selves. Beyond that, the novel's paradoxical logic pushes the reader to read carefully, finally offering a kind of friendship to a careful reader willing to bear faithful witness to the interests, fears, and imagination of the various characters in the book. In the course of providing my own interpretation, I have striven to be the careful and attentive reader for which the novel implicitly asks—a reader that has, over time, allowed the novel to challenge and even change her ideas about what it means to be someone's friend.

3

ANOTHER WAY TO BE

Vestigial Schemas in Helena María Viramontes's "The Moths" and Manuel Muñoz's "Zigzagger"

Something important was happening and she was part of it. Something
bigger than the two-plus-two way everybody else lived from day to day
was going on and she was right there and part of it. Whatever it was that
had fallen away was showing her another way to be in the world.
Toni Cade Bambara, *The Salt Eaters*

We need different ideas because we need different relationships.
Raymond Williams, "Ideas of Nature"

Literary Criticism as an Act of Friendship

When a reader picks up a novel or sits down to read a short story, she brings with her a set of schemas through which she interprets the work's structure, theme, plot, and symbolism. Crucially, her schemas are not essential or immutable. Rather, they are self-relevant constructs that come into being and are sustained or changed through her interactions with the individuals, institutions, and ideas she encounters in her world.[1] For this reason, how a reader reads a work of literature reveals a great deal about who she is in relation to the various social worlds or worlds of sense opened up to her by that text. These worlds might include the real world she lives in, the world or worlds represented in the text, and the worlds from which the work of literature has emerged. A reader's schemas are simultaneously revealed and shaped by the activity of reading.

Importantly, a reader's interpretation of a text always stands in relation to the prior act of interpretation enacted by the work itself. As an aesthetic object whose author has selected, ordered, obscured, emphasized, and figured a variety of genres, themes, characters, symbols, and plot details, a work of literature never represents "what actually happened" or shows characters "as they really are." Having originated in the mind of a creator and been rendered into language before being transformed into a set of material objects that are distributed across a wide swath of time and space, a work of literature always refers back in a complexly-mediated way to the schemas operative for its author at the time of its writing. Genre, theme, characterization, plot, and symbolism can be considered as the most visible aspects of that literary mediation; they re-present an author's schemas as embedded into the form of the narrative itself.

Understanding a work of literature as one interpretive link in a longer chain of prior (and future) interpretations clarifies why close attention to a text's contexts is good interpretive practice. Exemplifying the act of caring for the relationship that is created between the text and its reader, placing a text into its historical context can demonstrate a willingness to listen to, and be transported by, a way of thinking and understanding that might be other than one's own. It can be a way of recognizing that others always influence one's interpretive perspective—of acknowledging that, as the literary critic Mikhail Bakhtin has noted, the word half belongs to someone else (294). When done well, the literary critic's historical contextualization promotes attentiveness to the textual clues through which an author's schemas are embedded into the story. And when a reader checks her own schemas against those of the author, she is better able to perceive what Derek Attridge calls the author's "idioculture," the "internal, singular manifestation of the broader cultural field, registered as a complex of particular preferences, capabilities, memories, desires, physical habits, and emotional tendencies" of that artist. Much like my "set of schemas," Attridge's idiocultures are particular to a person and are constantly changing in response to her "exposure to a variety of cultural phenomena" (682–83).

Contextualization can go wrong when a literary critic imagines that a text has only *one* context (a historical one), or that historical contextualization must either reveal the text's blind spots or fix its true meaning.[2] Because the meaning of a work is only fully realized in the interaction between a text and its readers (and because no reader is ever identical to herself), every act of reading stands alone. As a consequence, the number of meanings a text can have is limited only by the number of times it is read.[3] In his introduction to the special issue of *New Literary History* devoted to context, Herbert Tucker sagely observes that, "objects worth studying exist in multiple contexts, of multiple kinds" (ix). As several of the contributors note, contending contexts have a way of proliferating, and the effect of summoning any given context will be uncertain (Jay 560–61; Levenson 677). The task of a critic, then, is to recognize the constitutive heteroglossia of the text, and, in choosing to discuss some contexts rather than others, "vindicate [her] choice of specific contexts" as a "condition of critical scholarship" (Tucker ix).[4]

In what follows, I model my socioformal close reading method through analyses of two exemplary short stories. I start with Helena María Viramontes's short story "The Moths" in part because a reader does not need the specialized tools or schemas of the literary critic to read it. She can enjoy this oft-anthologized story as a tale of mother-daughter reconciliation without knowing very much about the sociocultural and historical contexts from which it emerged. Given the state of public education in the United States, together with the active suppression of knowledge about people of Mexican descent who live in this country, it is unlikely that the majority of the readers who encounter it will have access to a full range of schemas with which to appreciate it. Fortunately, one of the advantages of good literature—one of the ways a literary critic can judge it to be good in the first place—is that will open up to a number of readings on several different levels. Even so, the more one knows about the text's various contexts, the more profound and informative one's interpretation can be. Similarly, a reader can appreciate Manuel Muñoz's "Zigzagger" without knowing the Mexican American folktale of which the story is an inspired revision. But the critic who knows the source tale can better appreciate the story's zigzagging deviations from its origin text. By bringing that knowledge to bear in her interpretation of the story, a critic can draw a more perceptive and persuasive picture of Muñoz's challenge to the heteronormativity and masculinism of American society.

By combining a formalist analysis of the narrative features of each story with attention to the historical and sociocultural contexts from which they emerged, I wish to display the productive role of the literary critic in interpreting works of literature. Additionally, I want to demonstrate the falseness of the dichotomy that has been posed by Stephen Best and Sharon Marcus between literary critical approaches that refuse contextualist approaches to a literary text (i.e., surface readings) and those that attend to the often obscured consequences of racial, gender, sexual, and class identities on the creation of literary texts (so-called symptomatic approaches). Finally, I hope to shine light on

Viramontes's and Muñoz's efforts to imagine and represent what the African American poet, writer, and critic Toni Cade Bambara looks forward to as "another way to be in the world."

Reading "The Moths"

I begin with a consideration of how one kind of context—the short story genre—frames the possibilities for action in the "The Moths," before doing a close reading of the story's opening paragraph to introduce its narrative perspective and primary themes. Next, I consider the sociocultural and historical contexts within which the story asks to be read, before providing a formalist analysis that examines how the story's distinctive use of verb tenses directs the reader's attention to the prominent symbolism involving the sun and the moon. Bringing this all together, I examine in "The Moths" the traces of a vestigial schema—a schema that is not fully fleshed out, but that operates at the level of the author's sociocultural unconscious. In the process of excavating the schemas, explicit and vestigial, embedded in "The Moths," I show how it critically explores, and attempts to revise, an unjust social world.

As a narrative form, a short story typically has a plot with a buildup, climax, and denouement. But whereas a longer narrative form like a novel is likely to represent the lives-over-time of an interconnected range of characters, the characteristic focus of a short story is "something that happened to someone" (Hills 1). Moreover, an important feature of the short story genre is an internal coherence and a narrative compression that is less characteristic of the novel form. A short story is more tightly organized than a novel; for this reason, the narrative energy of a short story typically goes toward giving the context for and setting up the situation in which something happens to someone. What "happens" to the unnamed narrator in Helena María Viramontes's short story "The Moths" is that her grandmother's death prompts her transition from girlhood to womanhood. She makes the transition by agreeing to care for her dying grandmother, by attending to the body immediately after her grandmother's death, and by *realizing*—both in the sense of "comprehending" and in the sense of "bringing to fruition"—the importance of certain values and practices normally associated with the activity of mothering.

Of course, much more takes place in "The Moths" than what happens at the level of the plot. Theme, structure, and symbolism all work together to set up the plot situation in which the transition from girlhood to womanhood will occur. Taking as my starting point the opening paragraph of the story, I consider each of these in turn:

> I was fourteen years old when Abuelita requested my help. And it seemed only
> fair. Abuelita had pulled me through the rages of scarlet fever by placing, re-
> moving and replacing potato slices on the temples of my forehead; she had seen
> me through several whippings, an arm broken by a dare-jump off Tío Enrique's
> toolshed, puberty, and my first lie. Really, I told Amá, it was only fair. (23)

A wealth of information is contained in this short paragraph. The first word, "I," indicates that the story is told in the first person, from the perspective of this one young woman.[5] The second word, "was," sets us up to expect some kind of change; it cues us to the fact that something important has happened between the time in which the story is set and the time of the telling of the story. Next, we find out that the narrator was fourteen years old when the story takes place. She is on the brink of adulthood, standing on the border between girlhood and womanhood. This sense of being on the boundary is reinforced by the narrator's reference to puberty, and to a loss of innocence implied by a "first lie." Additionally, we might note the use of Spanish names—Abuelita, Tío Enrique, Amá—in a story that is written in English. The linguistic code-switching in this paragraph situates the story in a particular cultural context even as it points to a border line between Spanish and English—the transgression of which is an intimate part of the everyday life of this young Mexican American female character.

Other significant aspects of the first paragraph are the theme of reciprocity and an emphasis on female interdependence that is contrasted, over the course of the story, with non-reciprocal male authoritarianism. The narrator tells us that "it seemed only fair" and then again that "it was only fair" that she be asked to care for her grandmother, while the reference to "whippings" hints at the physical violence with which that male authoritarianism is enforced. The repeated use of the phrase "only fair" in this first paragraph emphasizes the justice of being expected to respond in kind; the narrator's grandmother had cared for her, and now it is time for her to repay the favor. Moreover, the repeated use of the phrase "only fair" indicates that reciprocity is—for the narrator, at least—an important value; it constitutes for her what is good, right, beautiful, and just (all traditional connotations of the word *fair*). It is important for us as readers to note this emphasis on reciprocity, because it sensitizes us to see in the narrated events of the story the reality of the fact that the society in which the narrator lives is *not* a fair one; it does not treat this young girl kindly, nor does it operate according to an ethic of reciprocity.

Historical and Cultural Contexts for "The Moths"

To understand why fairness and female interdependence are so central to "The Moths," it helps to consider several important contexts within which the story should be situated. I begin with some basic biographical facts. Helena María Viramontes was born in 1954 and raised in the Mexican barrios of Los Angeles. She did her undergraduate work at Immaculate Heart College in Los Angeles before entering the MFA program at the University of California, Irvine in 1981. While she was there, one of her teachers—a white man—complained about her tendency to write about Mexican Americans; she should, he explained, write about "people" instead (Viramontes "Conversation"). Viramontes's response to the implicit racism of her teacher's valuation of her characters was to remove herself from his supervision; she left the program. Only after the publication of her collection *The Moths and Other Stories* (Arte Publico Press, 1985) did Viramontes return to the program; she finally received her MFA degree in 1994. Currently, she is a professor of English and creative writing at Cornell University, and the author of several books including two novels: *Under the Feet of Jesus* (1995) and *Their Dogs Came with Them* (2007).

Viramontes's teacher's insensitive remark points to the first context within which this story must be understood—that of Mexican-origin people as a racialized minority group within the United States. The point is not just that Mexican Americans were a numerical minority, but rather than that they faced pervasive discrimination as a result of being identified with that group—to the extent that Viramontes's teacher was unable, apparently, to perceive Mexican-origin people as worthy protagonists of the human experience. Especially during the time in which this story is set, limited employment opportunities, residential segregation, underfunded schools, inadequate services, and unmerited disrespect were all "identity contingencies" that Mexican Americans faced as a result of their racial and ethnic identities (Steele; Steele, Spencer, and Aronson).[6] In "The Moths," we see allusions to the material conditions and disrespect faced by Mexican Americans in Los Angeles in the narrator's interaction with Jay, the proprietor of the grocery store she visits to buy supplies. The narrator tells us that "[m]ost of the time Jay didn't have much of anything. The tomatoes were always soft and the cans of Campbell soups had rusted spots on them. There was dust on the tops of cereal boxes" (26). We see, moreover, that the narrator is subject to a kind of irrational disrespect from Jay resulting from a momentary confusion on her part: "At first Jay got mad because I thought I had forgotten the money" (26). But, we might ask ourselves, why should he be mad? If, in the story, the narrator-character *were* to have forgotten the money, then *she* would have been the one inconvenienced by having to go home to get it. The most the Jay character would have had to do is hold the groceries aside for her. It is hard for us to know whether the narrator is subject to this unmerited disrespect because of her age, her race, or her gender—or a combination of all three. Nonetheless, it is clear that Jay feels entitled to treat her poorly; he feels no compunction about taking out his aggression, resentment, and frustration—whatever their true source—on her.

A second important context for this story is Mexican Catholicism. The great majority of Mexican-origin people are Catholic, for the historical reason that the Spanish Monarchy made the conversion of indigenous people a central aspect of its colonial project. In fact, Catholicism has historically been such an integral part of Mexican life that it is sometimes hard to separate the culture from the religion. In "The Moths," Mexican Catholicism appears most obviously in the narrator's father's insistence that she attend mass every Sunday: "He would pound his hands on the table, rocking the sugar dish or spilling a cup of coffee and scream that if I didn't go to mass every Sunday to save my goddamn sinning soul, then I had no reason to go out of the house, period. Punto final" (25). The father's insistence that the narrator go to mass also nicely indicates a third context—that of the patriarchal gender norms of both Mexican and American culture.

The story shows us, through the narrator's inability to accept or conform to them, the pervasive gender norms of the society in which the story is set; this is the third important context for this story. As we saw in the opening paragraph, the narrator has difficulty embodying the culturally prescribed ideal of 1950s Mexican American womanhood. The second paragraph reinforces the point, telling us that she isn't "even pretty or nice like [her] older sisters"; she couldn't do the "girl things" they could do (23). Instead, she is a "tomboy" with "bull hands" that are "too big to handle the fineries of crocheting or embroidery" (27). She isn't "respectful" because she questions authority, and she reacts (inappropriately according to the standards of her society) with anger and violence to being made fun of for being outside this ideal feminine type (23). A feature of patriarchy is that women are assigned the role of "culture bearer." This appears in "The Moths" in the way the narrator's mother is held responsible by the father for the mother's "lousy ways of bringing up daughters, being disrespectful and unbelieving" (25). Additionally, the narrator's older sisters are drawn into the drama, as they are socialized to participate in the disciplining of the young girl. The consequences of all this for the narrator are painful; she is subjected to her sisters' ridicule as well as to her father's physical abuse.

As a young woman growing up in East Los Angeles in the 1960s, Viramontes responded to her sociocultural and historical situation by participating actively in the left social movements that were sweeping the country, especially the Chicano Movement and the women of color feminist movement. The Chicano Movement was an ethnic civil rights movement that emerged in the 1960s alongside other ethnic civil rights and left liberation movements (C. Muñoz; García). Mexican Americans throughout the country, but especially in the West and Southwest, asserted a newfound pride in their previously denigrated racial and linguistic heritage, and created for themselves an oppositional identity that they called "Chicano." An integral part of the Chicano Movement was the reclamation of Mexican cultural icons such as Pancho Villa or Emiliano Zapata and the use of indigenous (primarily Aztec) mythology and symbolism. The turn toward the indigenous that was apparent in Chicano Movement art and literature should be understood as an explicit rejection of the ideas and practices associated with Eurocentric notions of European racial or cultural supremacy.[7]

As Viramontes was beginning her writing career in the late 1970s, Chicana, black, American Indian, and Asian American women began to organize together around a new and historically-specific activist identity that they called "woman of color" (Moraga and Anzaldúa; Anzaldúa, *Making*).[8] Feminists of color created this new social movement in response to ethnic nationalist (and sexist) civil rights movements run primarily by minority men as well as to gender-universalist (and race-blind) feminist organizations run primarily by middle-class white women. Women of color activists, including many artists and writers, such as Toni Cade Bambara, Barbara Smith, Cherríe Moraga, Gloria Anzaldúa, Mitsuye Yamada, and Audre Lorde, began to share ideas about what it meant to be non-white women living, loving, and working in late-twentieth-century America. In the process, they developed a political identity as "women of color" as well as a distinct "woman of color consciousness." At the heart of a woman of color feminist consciousness is a conviction regarding the knowledge-generating significance of identity—a belief that knowledge can be linked to "our skin color, the land or concrete we grew up on, [and] our sexual longings" without being uniformly determined by them. Women of color believe that the "physical realities of our lives" will profoundly *inform without necessarily limiting* the contours and the contexts of both our theories and our knowledge (Moraga and Anzaldúa 23).[9] A woman of color consciousness has been central to the interpretive perspectives and representational practices that authors such as Helena María Viramontes employ in their writings.

Temporality in "The Moths"

There are three distinct temporalities in "The Moths," each of which refers to a distinct phase in the narrator's emergence into womanhood. They are the *situational past*, the *time of the past self*, and the *time of the possible self* (see Figure 3).

These three temporalities can be distinguished by the verb tenses through which they are created. So, for example, Viramontes makes effective use of flashbacks to provide the context for the transition that is about to happen. These flashbacks occur at the point where the narrator switches to the *would always* verb tense. The *would always* verb tense refers to an old habit that stopped sometime in the undifferentiated past; it denotes something often repeated in the past, but no longer done. This verb tense appears for the first time in the third paragraph of the story, just after the narrator tells us about the incident in which her abuelita shaped her hands back to size using a balm of moths' wings and Vicks. After that event, she tells us, her amá "would always" send her over to her grandmother's house. The would always verb tense is used

Verb Tense	Temporal Mode
Past continuous • Simple past • Past perfect	**Situational past** • The temporality in which the story is set
Would always	**Time of the past self** • The temporality in which the narrator has the most significant interaction with her abuelita
Prophetic or mythic time	**Time of the possible self** • The temporality in which the dreams, hopes, and illusions of the narrator are expressed

FIGURE 3. Temporal modes in Viramontes's "The Moths."

frequently in the next two paragraphs, although the "always" is more often implied than present in the text. It creates in "The Moths" a temporality we might call the *time of the past self*. It refers to the way the narrator used to be, before that way of being was interrupted by the events in the story that will lead to the transition we are given to expect. It is the temporal mode in which the protagonist has the most significant interaction with her grandmother.

Three other past verb tenses, used in combination, create the situational past. The *situational past* is the temporal mode in which most of the events in the story take place. This temporality is framed by the *past continuous* verb tense ("was dying"), indicating that a longer action in the past has been interrupted—usually in the form of a completed action set in either the *simple past* ("Abuelita snapped"; "she died") or else the *past perfect* ("had pulled"; "has seen"; "had forgotten").[10] As the temporal mode in which the story is situated, the situational past includes the actual event of Mama Luna's death.

The final verb tense in the story is not a past tense, but rather transforms the present into a mythic temporality that is both timeless and prophetic. It does this through the use of a formulaic phrase that is repeated twice, each time with a slight difference: "there comes a time," and then, "there comes an illumination." It appears in only one paragraph—the paragraph that signals the beginning of the event (the grandmother's death) that "happens" to the story's narrator. It is, moreover, the temporal mode in which the dreams, hopes, and illusions of the narrator begin to be expressed.

The *time of the possible self* is the temporality to which an attentive reader will pay the most attention in interpreting this story. Why? Because the paragraph in which it occurs prepares the way for the transition that is at the heart of this beautifully crafted story:

> There comes a time when the sun is defiant. Just about the time when moods change, inevitable seasons of a day, transitions from one color to another, that hour or minute or second when the sun is finally defeated, finally sinks into the realization that it cannot with all its power to heal or burn, exist forever, there comes an illumination where the sun and earth meet, a final burst of burning red orange fury reminding us that although endings are inevitable, they are necessary for rebirths, and when that time came, just when I switched on the light in the kitchen to open Abuelita's can of soup, it was probably then that she died. (27)

At the level of discourse, the paragraph accumulates images of transition: from one mood to another, one season to another, one color to another, day to night, life to death, light to dark, death to rebirth, defiance to resignation, natural to artificial light, closed to open. These multiple transitions signal the move into the realm of possibility. As engaged readers of the story we move away from the painful past to enter a temporal imaginary in which it might be possible for the young girl to leave behind her past self and become a different kind of woman—a self with agency, a woman who nurtures and is nurtured in turn, a person not at the mercy of an unkind society that treats her with casual, or concentrated, disdain.

The shift in verb tense (from past tense to mythic time) is one signal to the reader that something is about to happen. Consider now how naming works in this story. As readers, we never learn the name of the narrator, and with the exception of brief references to Tío Enrique and Teresa, everyone is identified by their social roles: Amá, Apá, granddaughter, older sisters. This indicates that the characters in the story do not represent individuals as much as they represent subject positions within a prevailing social order. So, it is notable that the narrator's grandmother is named, and that her name is Mama Luna. Her name, when set in the context of the tendency among movement-era Chicanos and Chicanas to draw upon indigenous (primarily Aztec) mythology for inspiration, and of Viramontes's demonstrated commitment to a woman of color feminist consciousness, suggests a link to the story of Coyolxauhqui, an ancient Mesoamerican goddess who is associated with the moon. The Coyolxauhqui story comes from a powerful Mexica legend that has survived in various (weakened) forms for over 500 years. Most Mexicans and Mexican Americans know aspects of this legend—such as the belief that the full moon is a malevolent force that can harm unborn children—even if they are unfamiliar with the goddess, or unaware of how their beliefs connect with her story.

My purpose in excavating the legend of Coyolxauhqui is to show how schemas can survive over time and can shape our approach to an issue—even if we are unaware, at a conscious level, of the myths that have given birth to them.[11] The Coyolxauhqui legend is a formative myth that operates at a conscious or unconscious level for many Mexican Americans in a way that people who are wholly unfamiliar with Mexico's history and culture may need help—in the form of additional information—to understand. As a result of our hybrid cultural history, Mexican Americans are heir to a Mesoamerican mythic system, just as we are heir to the several mythic systems that have come down to us through Western culture. Most Americans easily recognize how Greek and Judeo-Christian myths have informed the images and narratives of much of

Western literature. The difference in this case is that "The Moths" is drawing in an oblique way on a schema that most Americans (including some Mexican Americans) do not share.

Coyolxauhqui:
An Aztec Story of Dismemberment and Mother-Daughter Betrayal
The story of Coyolxauhqui's military defeat and bodily dismemberment at the hands of her brother Huitzilopochtli was collected and recorded by Fray Bernardino de Sahagún in the mid-1500s as one among a number of legends, tales, and histories related to him by indigenous scribes in the years after the fall of the Mexica (or Aztec) empire. De Sahagún collected the material into twelve books, referred to today as *The Florentine Codex*, that are the major source of documentary information we have about the indigenous cultures of Mesoamerica prior to Spanish conquest.

Like that of other societies in other places and other times, the religious worldview of the Aztecs at the time of the Spanish conquest was a syncretic one. In the older Otomi tradition, Coyolxauhqui was the moon goddess. In the relatively more recent Mexica tradition, she was the daughter of Coatlicue and sister of the Centzonuitznaua, or 400 stars, and of Huitzilopochtli, the god of war and a manifestation of the sun god. Importantly, Huitzilopochtli was the principal god of the Mexica, who, prior to their ascendance to power over the various tribes living in the valley of Mexico, were a "ragtag" tribe of warriors (Brotherston).

The story begins with Coyolxauhqui's mother, Coatlicue, doing penance at Coatepec. As Coatlicue sweeps the temple, a ball of feathers appears and falls on or touches her. Coatlicue tucks it into her bosom or waist for safekeeping and goes on with her task. When she is finished, she looks for the ball of feathers. But it has disappeared, and she is pregnant. When Coatlicue's daughter, Coyolxauhqui, and her 400 sons, the Centzonuitznaua, find out about this unexpected and shameful pregnancy, they become infuriated and decide to kill their mother. The infant in her womb, who is Huitzilopochtli, hears the commotion, and calls out to his mother that he will protect her. At this point, everyone stops and girds for battle. Then, at the decisive moment, Huitzilopochtli is born and appears fully armed with the fire serpent Xiuhcoatl, with which he strikes his sister: "Then he pierced Coyolxauhqui, and then quickly struck off her head. It stopped there at the edge of Coatepetl. And her body came falling below; it fell breaking to pieces; in various places her arms, her legs, her body each fell" (de Sahagún 4). After Coyolxauhqui's murder and dismemberment, Huitzilopochtli pursues the Centzonuitznaua, making them flee into the southern sky while he remains victorious.

At an allegorical level, the Coyolxauhqui myth represents the daily struggle between the moon and stars and the sun, in which every morning the sun once again wins the battle, banishing the moon and the stars to the southern sky. It also provides an explanation for why the moon appears and disappears in fragments, waxing and waning in phases every month (Instituto Nacional). But the story is a story of parthenogenesis as well as a story of kinship relations. Apart from its obvious importance as the origin story of the sun and war god, Huitzilopochtli, we can interpret it as a story of a mother who betrays her daughter, by giving birth to her murderer, or of a daughter who betrays her mother by attempting to control, through matricide, her mother's fecundity and/or unsanctioned sexuality. Either way, the rift between the mother and the daughter in this story symbolized the inauguration of Aztec warrior society (represented by the birth of Huitzilopochtli), and affirmed an ideology of male dominance (represented by Huitzilopochtli's decisive defeat of the powerful daughter Coyolxauhqui and the collective of sons, the 400 stars, who were allied with her). And, in fact, the story of Coyolxauhqui's defeat was very important to the Mexica. According to Mesoamerican specialist Gordon Brotherston, the story of Coyolxauhqui's dismemberment by Huitzilopochtli was an origin story for the Mexica, serving both to explain and to justify their ascendance to power over the other tribes residing in pre-Columbian Mesoamerica.

Coyolxauhqui's defeat and dismemberment is represented and memorialized in the huge and imposing Coyolxauhqui stone, a round disc that weighs eight tons and is 10.66 feet in diameter (see Figure 4). The stone was discovered in 1978 by electric grid workers who were doing maintenance work in the center of present-day Mexico City (Instituto Nacional). The unearthing of the stone sparked a major archeological project at the site of what turned out to have been the ceremonial center of the ancient Mexica city of Tenochtitlán. Archeologists have since determined that the stone was discovered in the original location where the Mexica had placed it, at the foot of the south stair of the fourth rebuilding (c. 1469–81) of the major Aztec temple, known today as El Templo Mayor (see Figure 5).

The significance for the Mexica of the Coyolxauhqui stone, and of where they placed it, becomes evident when we consider that a representation of

FIGURE 4. The Coyolxauhqui stone.

SOURCE: Wikimedia Commons. Author: Thelmadatter. <http://commons.wikimedia.org/wiki/File:CoyolxauhquiDisk.JPG>. This work has been released into the public domain.

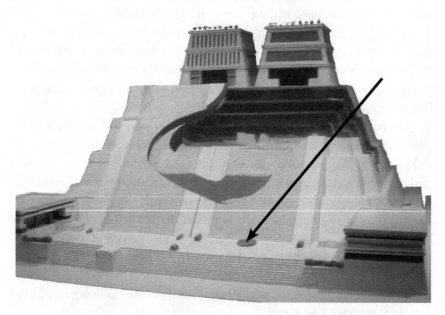

FIGURE 5. Scale model of El Templo Mayor; arrow points to the location of the Coyolxauhqui stone.

SOURCE: Wikimedia Commons. Author: Thelmadattter. <http://commons.wikimedia.org/wiki/File:ScaleModelTemploMayor.JPG#filehistory>. This work has been released into the public domain.

Huitzilopochtli (in the form of the stone of the Fifth Sun) would most likely have been housed *inside and at the top* of the same temple (see Figure 6).

This stone, more commonly and mistakenly known to many people as the Aztec or Mayan Calendar stone, is similar to the Coyolxauhqui stone in that it is a circular carving. However, it differs significantly in that it represents the sun god as both all-powerful (his tongue is in the form of a sacrificial knife) and at the center of the cosmos. The stone of the Fifth Sun was carved around the same time as the Coyolxauhqui stone (est. 1479) and is somewhat larger; it weighs twenty-four tons and is twelve feet in diameter. The Coyolxauhqui stone was thus prominently displayed by the Mexica in proximity to the stone of the Fifth Sun so as to be a graphic and highly visible reminder of Huitzilopochtli's birth and most important victory.

So, while Coyolxauhqui herself may not have been an important deity for the Mexica, the story of her defeat and dismemberment appears to have been at the very core of Mexica cultural and political identity. It is not surprising, then, that aspects of the Coyolxauhqui legend have survived into the present day

FIGURE 6. The stone of the Fifth Sun.
Source: Wikimedia Commons. Author: Anagoria. <http://commons.wikimedia.org/wiki/
File:1479_Stein_der_fünften_Sonne,_sog._Aztekenkalender,_Ollin_Tonatiuh_anagoria.JPG>.
This file is licensed under the Creative Commons license.

within the not-always-conscious cultural memories of Mexican and Mexican American people. When the Spaniards succeeded in overthrowing the Mexica in 1521, they tore down the Aztec temples and built Catholic churches out of the stones that had fallen down. They burned the codices, killed the priests, outlawed indigenous religions, and enforced the native people's conversion to Catholicism. But the Spanish conquerors were not able to completely erase the people's minds, as the survival of this vestigial schema in a twentieth-century story written by one of their descendants so beautifully demonstrates. So, while there is no explicit allusion to the Coyolxauhqui legend in the story, an understanding of the symbolism behind this formative origin myth shows how a Chicana/o cultural context influences the schemas that are embedded deep within the story.

The Symbolic Re-membering of Coyolxauhqui:
The Rebirth of the Daughter as Mother

I return to the story now to show how "The Moths" presents a critique of the Catholic religion through the substitution of a patriarchal male god with a matriarchal alternative, explaining how this works before tying the story back to the Coyolxauhqui legend. Remember that it is the father who insists that the young girl go to mass, and who digs his nails into her arm to make sure she understands "the importance of catechism" (25). Despite the fact that the young girl puts on her best shoes and grabs her missal and veil before heading out the door, she does not go to mass. Instead, she takes the sinister route, turning left and going to her grandmother's house. The grandmother, with her gray eye that makes the narrator feel "safe and guarded and not alone," takes the place of God, who is "supposed" to do this, but does not (24). Organized religion, represented by the chapel with the "frozen statues" with "blank eyes," is not a sacred place for the young girl. She leaves the chapel without blessing herself.

The grandmother's house, in marked contrast to the chapel, is a woman-centered sanctuary where the young girl participates in the making of an alternative female sociality. In the grandmother's house, women's everyday chores are transformed into sacred practices full of meaning. The young girl nurtures her grandmother's plants, and is nurtured in return by gaining a sense of worth, efficacy, and power (24). The grandmother's house is a place of refuge where the young girl's "bull hands" can be put to productive use. It is there that we see her working through her pain and anger as she uses her hands in a healing ritual to crush the tomatoes and chiles in a *molcajete* for her own and her grandmother's nourishment (26). She and her abuelita communicate not through words (or the Word)—textual or oral—but through touch, household chores, and everyday actions. And finally, although displaying affection in a conventional way is difficult for the narrator—she does not kiss her grandmother—she finds a way to care for her grandmother by rubbing her body with alcohol and marihuana and by ministering to her when she is ill. These scenes with the grandmother involving the narrator's hands offer a noticeable contrast to the scene where she stands in front of her mother with her "hands just hanging helplessly by [her] side" (26). Those helplessly hanging hands capture beautifully the young girl's discomfort with the gendered, racial, sexual, and ethnic identity scripts that have been thrust upon her by the people she lives among. Thus, by representing the grandmother's house as a sacred refuge, and the young girl's interactions with her grandmother as the means by which she participates in an alternative female sociality, the story anticipates the possibility that the narrator may yet find another way to be in the world.

The prominent symbolism involving the sun and the moon links the Coyolxauhqui legend to the story's critique of a patriarchal Catholic worldview. Recall from my earlier discussion that the story moves into the *time of the possible self* just as the sun goes down and the grandmother passes away. In a nod to a Mesoamerican cyclical cosmology, the story prompts the reader to remember that endings are both inevitable and necessary for rebirths (27). The fact that this temporal shift occurs at the moment of the sun's setting serves to remind the reader that just as the sun is victorious every morning against the moon and the stars, so do these same antagonists defeat him, every evening. The climax of the story comes right after the young girl uses her hands for the tender undressing and sacramental bathing of her abuelita following Mama Luna's dying of stomach cancer. In her reconstructed religion, the young girl plays the role of priest. She goes to the linen closet, takes out bleached white towels, and "[w]ith the sacredness of a priest preparing his vestments, [she] unfolded the towels one by one on [her] shoulders" (27). By reconnecting the feminine with the sacred, the story opens up the possibility that the young girl may be able to create for herself a new, more affirming, identity through her participation in an alternative matriarchal spirituality.

The end of the story enacts a rebirth in which the young girl plays the part of both mother and child. Stepping into the bathtub with her dead grandmother, she symbolically re-enters the waters of the womb and begins to heal herself in communion with her mother and grandmother. Part of this process

involves learning to mother as well as to be mothered. As she holds her grandmother in the water, the young girl smooths her grandmother's hair, and con-
soles her—much in the way a mother soothes a small child. Amid multiple
images of boundary confusion—the bath water overflows the tub onto the tile;
the grandmother's soul is released in the form of hundreds of small gray moths;
and the narrator imagines accompanying her grandmother on her journey toward death with chayote vines that "crawl up [the grandmother's] fingers and
into the clouds"—the narrator is to finally able to enact a rebirth that will lead
to a reconciliation (32). Using a grammatical formulation that mimics the hic-
cup that is part of a sob, she is finally free to express her great desire for her
mother: "I wanted. I wanted my Amá." Once the narrator is able to acknowledge this need, once she is able to acknowledge the hurt and the love she feels—
for herself, for her grandmother, and for her mother—only then is she able to
cry. She becomes simultaneously the woman who is being born and, in a sense,
the mother of the newborn woman that she is. She is born anew as a woman
in a context that affirms interdependence, reciprocity, and physical as well as
emotional care (28). By taking us back to the moment of birth to rewrite the
origin story, "The Moths" symbolically repairs the mother-daughter bond and
enacts a re-membering of that long ago daughter, Coyolxauhqui. But instead of
the son, it is the daughter who is (re)birthed, and instead of dismemberment,
separation, and violence, what comes out of *this* birth is forgiveness, reunion,
remembrance, and love figured as interdependence and care.

When the Mexica depicted Coyolxauhqui as broken and dismembered at
the base of their great pyramid, they undeified the moon and the stars in favor
of the glorification of the sun god, Huitzilopochtli. In destroying the divinity
of the female principle, they inadvertently set the stage for Huitzilopochtli's
replacement, as one god among several, by the singular male Judeo-Christian
God. But the memory of women as both powerful and divine lives on in the
vestigial schema that organizes "The Moths"; it gives us a glimpse into a way
of being in the world that goes back even further than the conquest of Mexico by the Spanish. "The Moths" looks back to a profoundly different way of
conceptualizing the world that existed coevally (albeit in a different space)
with the emergent European idea of nature as singular, man as an abstraction,
and monotheism as the only possible divine order (Williams, *Culture* 67–85).
By bringing Mexican Americans' pre-Western past into our mid-twentieth-
century colonized present, Viramontes engages in the kind of "border thinking" described by Walter Mignolo in *Local Histories/Global Designs* (49–88).

Not a form of hybridity or syncretism, border thinking is an epistemological stance taken by those who are open to the "unforeseeable diversity of the world" and "unheard and unexpected" forms of knowledge (81). For Mignolo, border thinking involves, at a minimum, the recognition of the colonial difference from a subaltern perspective (6). Shaped by the irreducible difference of those who are thinking from what the Argentinian philosopher Enrique Dussel calls the "underside of modernity," border thinking challenges hegemonic forms of knowledge that conceptualize time as linear and unidirectional, modernity as distinct from coloniality, and history and knowledge as exclusive properties of the West. Insofar as it is an epistemological stance that allows for a spatial confrontation between at least two radically different concepts of history, it enables a "double critique" that reveals the limits of both (81).

In my reading of Helena María Viramontes's tightly woven and beautifully written short story "The Moths," I show that the different verb tenses in the story correspond to different temporalities, and that shifts among the verb tenses set the reader up to expect shifts in perspective. I further demonstrate that the shift into mythic time, what I call the *time of the possible self*, cues the reader to interpret the events in terms of what might be, rather than what is. At the level of the story, Viramontes depicts the grandmother's house as a woman-centered sanctuary in which the young girl participates in the making of an alternative female sociality that valorizes interdependence, reciprocity, and physical as well as emotional care. At a symbolic level, Viramontes evokes the Coyolxauhqui story through references to (1) the ongoing battle between the sun and the moon, (2) the cycle of death and rebirth, and (3) the importance of repairing the shattered mother-daughter relationship. By moving the story into the time of the possible self, Viramontes imagines a world in which it might be possible for the young girl to reconcile with her mother, leave behind her split self, and become a different kind of woman—a woman who can construct for herself a more life-affirming world than the one she lives in.

Reading "Zigzagger"

I turn now to Manuel Muñoz's rewriting of a Mexican American cautionary folk tale to further my argument about how an excavation of a text's contexts can highlight its imaginative and critical potential. In his beautifully crafted short story "Zigzagger," Muñoz imagines what a non-normative masculinity might look like.[12] The masculinity he figures does not depend on the denigration of

women, but rather has an affirmative relationship to both women and femininity. As such, the story provides a fictional representation of an alternative way of
being in the world that has liberating potential for men and women of all sexualities. Because my own analysis builds on his, I begin with a précis of literary
critic Ernesto Martínez's reading of Muñoz before turning to the Dancing with
the Devil folktale and its implications for the short story in question.

In his analysis of Muñoz's short story collection *Zigzagger*, Martínez discusses the challenges of representing—speaking for, depicting, or embodying—
queer people and their interests in a work of literature. According to Martínez,
Muñoz takes a "provocative, multifocal narrative approach" to representing
queer experience and identity in *Zigzagger* (113). Rather than always having his
gay characters narrate or focalize those events in their lives that pertain to their
nonnormative sexuality, Muñoz spreads the responsibility for representing the
lives of his gay characters to other characters in the collection—to Nicky's sister, Vero, in "Good as Yesterday"; to the father of the dead gay man in "The
Unimportant Lila Parr"; and to the mother of the boy who has his first sexual
experience with the devil in "Zigzagger."

By asking what is at stake for Muñoz in "shifting the site of queer enuncia-
tion," Martínez's reading of Muñoz's stories helpfully exposes the minute social
mechanisms by which queer identity and experience are produced—by queer
and straight people alike—in everyday life and in literary works. Martínez
argues that when Muñoz assigns to nonqueer characters the burden of representing queerness, he exposes the "web of relationships and discourses that
constitute queer experience and queer identity in any given context" (113). His
stories demonstrate, on both a thematic and a structural level, how deeply *all
of us*, queer and nonqueer alike, are implicated in the ongoing production and
reproduction of queer identity and experience. Moreover, because Muñoz's stories take a fictional approach to the constitution of queer subjectivity—because,
that is, the stories represent gay characters and their straight family members
in ways that make us care about them *as if they were real people*—the stories are
able to demonstrate what is at stake when we accept or refuse our own involvement in the lives of the queer people who exist within our own (nonfictional)
discursive and relational webs.

Martínez includes in his analysis of Muñoz's stories an astute, if brief, discussion of the title story, "Zigzagger." He notes that the young gay Chicano
character whose sexual awakening is at the center of the story has a painfully
ambivalent relationship to his community that is registered at several levels of

the story. He further argues that by using an omniscient narrative style while focalizing the narrative perspectives through both the boy and his mother, Muñoz "provides a collective account of what it means [for a gay Chicano] to be a part of, as opposed to *apart from*, the values, experiences, and concerns of a small Mexican and Mexican American community" (129). Martínez's careful formalist analysis of the collection's narrative perspective is crucial for understanding the ideological intervention the story is attempting to make. However, Martínez does not explicitly engage with the Mexican American folktale of which the story is an imaginative re-visioning. To further demonstrate how understanding a story's context deepens our appreciation for the ideological intervention(s) a story is attempting to make, I turn to that folktale now.

Dancing with the Devil—When the Devil Is Gay

For those unfamiliar with the Dancing with the Devil folktale, the basic outline is this: the scene is a Mexican American dance hall in south Texas (or the California central valley, or sometimes even a discotheque in Tijuana, Mexico). At one of the tables is a young Mexican American woman whose conservative and strict parents have expressly forbidden her to be there. In defiance of their authority, and with a girlish desire to have fun, the young woman has snuck out of her house to join her girlfriends at the dance. Once the dance is in full swing and couples are gliding counterclockwise around the dance floor to *conjunto* polka music, in walks a good-looking, strong, tall, and sharply dressed man. He is different from the usual kind of man who comes to these dances; he is expensively dressed, maybe in a suit with expensive boots, and he may even be Anglo. All the single women in the dance hall, especially the young woman, notice him and immediately desire to dance with him. Eventually he asks our rebellious (but still innocent) young woman to dance. She happily agrees to do so and finds him to be everything she has ever dreamed of: charming, suave, a skilled dancer. But then she looks down and sees that his expensive boots have disappeared, and where his feet should be are either chicken feet or hooves. At this point she recognizes that she is dancing with the devil; she screams in terror and falls down in a dead faint. The devil, having failed in his attempt at seduction, then disappears in a puff of smoke.

In his book *Dancing with the Devil*, the anthropologist and literary critic José Limón notes that this cautionary folktale is a woman's tale; it is typically narrated by and told to women (168–86).[13] Limón interprets the devil's presence in the tale as "a register of the society's initial and shocking encounter with the cultural logic of late capitalism" (179). He suggests that for its narrators it is a "text with a very proximate relationship to the Real of their lived historical experience, though now rewritten symbolically" (184). In other words, the tale of the dancing devil represents women's desire for escape from the choices they face: a life of economic struggle or domestic tedium, or both. The handsome stranger, unlike the lower-class Mexican American men these women normally have to choose among, has both money and cultural (racial) capital that, as their proper provider, he will necessarily share with them. Moreover, because the devil is both charming and attentive, he represents the possibility of romance and sexual satisfaction. Importantly, however, the devil disappears before any of these desires can be fulfilled. For Limón, then, the dancing devil represents both women's desire and the limits of that desire—the implacability of the race, class, and gender struggles these women face every day of their lives. According to Limón, the ultimate significance of the tale resides in the fact that it is collectively authored. He argues that the women who participate in its telling and retelling are "active artisans of language" who transform the Real of their existence through a creative and critical reaction to the shared circumstance of their lives. They delight in the making and sharing of the story with one another, thus enhancing their collectivity and nurturing a particularly Mexican American form of solidarity we call *confianza* (184).

There are of course other meanings we might give to the tale depending on who is telling it and to whom it is being told (see, e.g., Herrera-Sobek). In the version recalled by the literary critic Sonia Saldívar-Hull from her own adolescence, perhaps the most significant element of the fable is the fact that the young woman who dances with the devil is at the dance *sin permiso* (without the permission of her parents). Given this emphasis, the young girl's brush with the devil would stand first and foremost as a warning to all other young girls who would consider similar kinds of adolescent misbehavior.

Importantly, Muñoz's rewriting of this woman's tale changes some of its key elements, most notably by making it about *gay* and *male* sexuality. Just as crucial, though, is the fact that Muñoz's version can be fully appreciated only when it is placed in the context of the values, taboos, and symbolism of a larger Mexican American community. Moreover the cautionary aspect of the folktale that Saldívar-Hull insists upon is crucial to my reading of Muñoz's version. By depicting heterosexual and homosexual relations within the Mexican American community as they are (with all their attendant homophobia and violence), as well as how they might be (with the possibility of more equal and respectful relations between men and women), Muñoz effectively provides a cautionary tale for those who would cling—even to their own emotional detriment—to officially sanctioned and hierarchical heterosexual social roles.

According to the ideology of Mexican American heterosexuality, there are starkly drawn differences in the gender roles of men and women. Men are breadwinners; women are homemakers. Men take care of women; women are taken care of, but are thereby at the mercy of men's immense physicality, both sexually and in terms of physical violence. Unlike the straight male characters that embody the heterosexual norm, the young gay male characters that populate Muñoz's stories have a different relationship to women and to femininity. In "The Unimportant Lila Parr," for example, the relationship between the mother and her gay son is characterized by identification and sharing. The story is focalized by the father, and so we are privy to the father's intensely emotional and private response to the brutal murder of his son in a roadside motel. We find out that the father felt excluded from and threatened by the closeness between the mother and the son: "The man walked into the house one day to see his wife and son sifting through [some] old clothes and laughing." He is disturbed to see his son participating in what he characterizes as a "weakness" signaled by his wife's careful cultivation of mementos from her past (40). What the father in this story fails to realize, of course, is that his inability to identify with and share in the lives of both his (gay) son and his (female) wife traps them all, as well as Lila Parr, into living lonely and parallel lives in which the possibility of comfort in the face of tragedy is notably absent.

The short story "Zigzagger" opens at dawn on a Sunday morning with a mother and father keeping vigil at the bedside of their son, who came home violently ill the night before. Through a braided narrative structure that interweaves present time with flashbacks from the day before—and that is narrated from the perspectives of both mother and son—we learn that the boy had gone out to a dance with a group of his friends, both boys and girls. There he meets a handsome stranger with whom he has his first sexual encounter. After his friends find him sick outside the dance hall, they bring him home and leave him raging and cursing like a man possessed, with red welts and deep scratches all over his body. The mother and father tend to their son, communicating with each other as much through silence as with words, until he sleeps peacefully and the welts and scratches disappear. The story ends when the boy's friends come by to check on him and he wakes up psychologically and emotionally transformed. The manner of the story's narration suggests that the story is at least as much about *if* and *how* the community (represented by the mother and father and the boy's friends) will assimilate this disruptive happening into their everyday reality as it is about the boy's newfound sexual self-acceptance.

Muñoz's gay characters' alternative relationship to femininity is revealed in part by the way the women characters mediate the gay male characters' relationships *to* their objects of desire without *being* the objects of desire. In "Zigzagger," for example, two different women facilitate the boy's access to the dancing devil. As in the standard version of the tale, the handsome stranger/devil approaches a young girl, in this case one of the boy's friends. However, in Muñoz's version of the tale the girl is not impressed. She dismisses the stranger/devil with a flick of her pink-braceleted wrist while the boy watches as if he "were the only one watching." Unlike in the standard tale, where all the women notice the handsome stranger's entrance, in this version "[t]he boy felt as if he had been the only person to notice the man with the plain silver buckle . . . [a] plain silver buckle that gleamed like a cold eye, open and watching." As the handsome stranger/devil talks to the girl, the boy notices his posture, his hips, his seductive arrogance; he sees "the silver buckle blink at him, as if it watched back, as if it knew where the boy was looking" (13). When the girl subsequently complains to the boy about the man's unwanted attention, she gives the boy the excuse he needs to approach the man who wears the knowing silver belt buckle. Later a different woman stands talking to the handsome stranger/devil, thus giving him the pretext he needs to stand around waiting for the boy to approach. Conveniently, this woman disappears from the scene (and from the narrative) just as the boy approaches.

The focus on male physicality in Muñoz's stories further figures the male body, as opposed to the female body, as the object of sexual desire. In "Zigzagger," for instance, we learn that the father is a man who makes "the doorways in their house look narrow and small, his shoulders threatening to brush the jambs" (5). Curiously we get no corresponding description of the mother; we have no idea what her shape and size might be. This is not to say that the mother is not important to the story. She is. She is the character that focalizes the largest part of the narrative. However, what is interesting in Muñoz's version of the tale is that it is the mother's *subjectivity* that matters in the story, not her *sexuality or physicality*. Thus the story upends the standard heterosexual structure of power/knowledge: instead of a male subject and a female (or feminized) sexual object, these stories figure a female (or feminized) subject and a male sexual object.

At the heart of almost all the stories in the collection, and certainly of this one, is the ambivalent desire for different forms of openness. For the gay male characters this openness is figured both as the bringing of family secrets—many, but not all, involving sexuality—out into the open, and as penetration by the male sexual organ. As strong as these intertwined desires are, however, they are understood by the characters as threatening to the families' physical and spiritual well-being. Non-communication, accomplished through silence and obfuscation about matters too painful to face, allows the three main characters in "Zigzagger"—father, mother, and son—to coexist in their common solitude. Thus, the gay male is represented as being a part of the larger Mexican American community; his actions and behaviors take their meaning from the same set of values, taboos, and symbols that those around him espouse. But his membership in that community is represented as ambivalent and subject to certain conditions.

The non-communication imposed on the gay son as the price for his membership in the larger Mexican American community is enforced, albeit differently, by the mother, the father, and the friends. On the morning after the dance, when her son awakens and comes out of his bedroom to greet his friends, the mother imagines that if no one, especially her son, talks about what happened, she can refuse its reality:

> The mother sees him, the look in his eye, and she wants to say nothing at all. She believes, as she always has, that talking aloud brings moments to light, and she has refused to speak of her mother's death, of her husband's cheating, of the hatred of her brothers and sisters. She sees her son at the doorway and wants to tell him not to speak. (18)

For his part, the father actively intervenes to prevent the disclosure that is threatening to burst forth. As "[t]hey all stand and wait for the boy to talk, the doors and windows open as wide as possible and every last secret of their home ready to make an easy break to the outside," the father moves to prevent the boy's speech. He walks toward the boy and says, "You're awake," before turning to his son's friends and saying, "See? He's fine. Now go home," while motioning them away from the porch. The boy's friends meanwhile "leave without asking [the boy] anything at all" (18). We see dramatized in this scene what Martínez has pointed out as the socially produced and deliberate "estrangement from queer experience" on the part of heteronormative Mexican and Mexican American communities (124).

This brings us back to the devil motif and how it works in this short story, as well as in the collection as a whole. As noted earlier the paradoxical desire for openness in these stories is also expressed as a desire for penetration by the male sexual organ, a desire always accompanied by the fear of being possessed by something dangerous and possibly evil. In "The Third Myth," for example, the gay male protagonist is tormented by the fear that he will be punished for his gay sexual practices. He says, "I . . . worry and fear what I might be made of. What is in me and how it gets out" (30). Similarly the penetration experienced by the boy at the climactic moment (climactic both narratologically and sexually) of "Zigzagger" is simultaneously a moment of transcendent experience and fantastic fear. Into what has been up to this moment a realistic narrative comes an irruption of *lo real maravilloso*:

> And though he felt he was in air, he saw a flash of the man's feet entrenched in the ground—long, hard hooves digging into the soil, the height of horses when they charge—it was then that the boy remembers seeing and feeling at the same time—the hooves, then a piercing in the depth of his belly that made his eyes flash a whole battalion of stars, shooting and brilliant, more and more of them, until he had no choice but to scream out. (17)

This paragraph shows as well as any that for Muñoz's gay Mexican American characters, the act of opening oneself up—whether to honest communication about taboo subjects, the possibility of feminine subjectivity, or gay male sexuality—is simultaneously frightening, painful, thrilling, and mind-blowingly beautiful.

The epigraph to Muñoz's short story collection foreshadows the devil motif that is central to the title story and encapsulates the ambivalent rewards offered to a gay Chicano who wants to bring his sexual self out into the open. The epigraph—"The exit is through Satan's mouth"—is a line from the title poem of *Satan Says*, a book of poetry by Sharon Olds. The poem speaks to a writer's powerful desire to write about, as a way of escaping from, familial bonds woven from memories that are both constraining and painful. At the same time the poem evokes the guilt, shame, and sorrow a writer feels when she betrays her family's dirty secrets by exposing them to the world in the process of achieving her own escape (and of creating her art). The lyric "I" in Olds's poem ultimately appears to resist the devil's lure; she accepts her imprisonment even as she warms herself at the fire of the love (presumably for her family) that she discovers at the end of the poem. Muñoz seems to have chosen the scarier, but possibly more rewarding, option. For one thing, his epigraph is drawn from the *middle* of Olds's poem; it does not endorse the conclusion as much as capture the moment at which the "I" in the poem realizes that the only way out of her private hell will necessarily involve a deal with the devil. Muñoz, we come to understand, has made his deal with the devil; he embraces the devil with fear, makes love to the devil with pleasure, and in the process, exposes the dirty secrets of the Mexican American family (and the larger Mexican American community) to the view of the reader. But this exposure is not without its rewards. By opening up the pathological tangle of lies, silences, and shame that denies the reality of life-affirming sexual and emotional love between men—as well as of satisfying nonsexual love and identification between men and women—Muñoz creates the possibility that men and women of all sexualities might be able to communicate with each other in ways that will relieve their painful isolation, thus giving them alternative modes of being in the world.

Importantly, Muñoz's rewriting of the Dancing with the Devil fable does not end with the sighting of the devil's feet. The story continues on through the act of sexual union and ends only after the boy and his mother, father, and friends have gained (an as yet unspoken) knowledge of the boy's homosexuality. In Muñoz's revision of the classic folktale, its moral points not to the limits of Mexican American female desire and agency in a race-, class-, and gender-stratified world, but rather to a whole world of transformational possibilities—of alternative forms of Chicano masculinity; of the acceptance of homosexuality in Mexican American communities; of honest, open, and loving communication between family members of all genders and sexualities; and of gay Chicana/o self-love. The story further speaks to the importance of challenging our society's assumptions about what is good and what is evil. Like Toni Morrison's *Sula*, "Zigzagger" questions the idea that hewing close to society's norms is a good thing. In *Sula*, Nel is likened to a spider who is so terrified of the "free fall" that accepting Sula's unconventional sexuality might bring that she is "blind to the cobalt" on her own back and to the "moonshine fighting to pierce" her corners (120). Ruled by fear and seeking the safety that convention can offer, Nel pins herself into a "tiny life," accepting a kind of death-in-life until she is pushed to examine her lifelong assumptions about "who was good" (165, 146). In "Zigzagger," the boy protagonist is able to accept and act on the force of his deep desire. He refuses society's judgment that men must resist penetration—whether by shutting themselves off emotionally from other people or by viewing the behaviors associated with homosexuality as evil. For

his courage, he is rewarded with life—wild, grand, dangerous life—figured in
this story through "a whole battalion of stars, shooting and brilliant, more and
more of them" that come flashing out of his eyes and give him "no choice but
to scream out" (17).

Conclusion

By situating "The Moths" and "Zigzagger" in relation to their various sociocultural and historical contexts, and by attending to the theme, symbolism, and
narrative structure of each, I show how the former is expressed through the
latter. I contextualize each story historically not to condemn it as blind to the
ideologies of its era, but rather to enhance my own ability to listen to what
each story might be trying to communicate to me as its reader. Even as I recognize the text's agency—it is, itself, an act of interpretation of the world(s) from
which it emerges—I appreciate each text as a made thing, one that has been
intentionally and creatively constructed by its author. And so, in bringing to
bear several key sociocultural and historical contexts, I understand myself to
be excavating some important schemas that are embedded into the literary text
and that were operative as conscious or unconscious schemas for its author at
the time of its making. Finally, I acknowledge that the messages I take from
these stories depend, in part, on who I am—that is, on the schemas I bring with
me to my act of interpretation.

While conceiving of my relationship to a literary text as a kind of dialogic
friendship, I also realize that other critics will form different kinds of relationships with the same text, and so will hear different messages. I accept this. Because any interpretive approach will reveal some features of the literary work
but not others, I embrace methodological pluralism as a disciplinary imperative. But my acceptance does not imply that I think all kinds of relationships
between reader and text are dialogic and caring, or that all interpreters will be
able to hear as well as some others what the "text itself is saying." Thus, I have
sought to vindicate *my* choice of contexts through careful explication of how
they are embedded, and how they work, in the stories under consideration.

What I find valuable about "The Moths" and "Zigzagger" is the way they
represent the minute day-to-day interpersonal interactions that give rise to specific racial, gender, and sexual (Mexican American) identities without fixing,
flattening, condemning, or celebrating those identities. But I find even more
valuable the way they also represent alternative ways of being in the world—

ways that remain within a Mexican American cultural context but that are more reciprocal, more forgiving, and more loving than the ways bequeathed to the descendants of the original inhabitants of the Americas by modernity/coloniality. As border thinkers, Viramontes and Muñoz are actively generating different ideas so that we might have different relationships. They are fashioning what the Mexican poet, essayist, and novelist Rosario Castellanos yearned for as "another way to be human and free" (111).

DISMANTLING THE MASTER'S HOUSE
The Search for Decolonial Love in Junot Díaz's
"How to Date a Browngirl, Blackgirl, Whitegirl, or Halfie"

I urge each one of us here to reach down into that deep place of
knowledge inside herself and touch that terror and loathing of
any difference that lives there. See whose face it wears.
Audre Lorde, "The Master's Tools"

Consider the title of Junot Díaz's short story "How to Date a Browngirl, Black-girl, White Girl, or Halfie." The reader who approaches this story without reading it through the intersecting lenses of race, class, gender, and sexuality is perverse indeed. In suggesting that the story will provide guidelines for how to date a girl, the title makes a direct second-person address to the reader who is, after all, the putative recipient of the proffered advice. Like Althusser's police-man who subjects the passing pedestrian to the authority of the state ("Hey, you there!"), so does the title of the story hail the reader-as-learner, seeking to interpellate her into its system of racial understanding. The title further in-forms its reader that the girl will be a type—a racial type. Through its prolif-eration of female racial types who are apparently available to be dated, it nixes the notion that there might be a generic (that is, a non-racialized) ideal called "girl." Finally, the title invokes the commonly accepted, but less openly ac-knowledged, practice of treating people differently according to the race, class, gender, and sexuality with which they are associated. All this before the reader even begins to read the story itself.

But who *is* the intended addressee of this story? And what is the story's racial understanding? As we begin reading the story, we notice that the "you" of the story is very specific. "You" turns out to be someone whose mother and brother have gone for a visit to Union City, who has an aunt who likes to "squeeze your nuts," whose family keeps government cheese in the refrigerator, and whose mother displays a picture of him with an Afro (143). What becomes increasingly apparent—a fact confirmed when "your nemesis, Howie," addresses him directly—is that the story's narratee, its "you," is none other than Díaz's fictional alter-ego and most frequently recurring character, Yunior (146). With the exception of two stories in *Drown* ("Aurora" and "No Face"), and one in *This Is How You Lose Her* ("Otravida, Otravez"), Yunior appears as the protagonist or narrator (or both) of every narrative in each of Díaz's first three books—including his Pulitzer Prize–winning novel, *The Brief Wondrous Life of Oscar Wao*.[1] Understanding the character of Yunior, and especially Yunior's attitudes about race, class, gender, and sexuality, is thus central to an understanding of Díaz's oeuvre as a whole.

In this chapter, I approach the task of understanding Yunior's attitudes about racialized gender by reading Junot Díaz alongside the black lesbian feminist poet and essayist Audre Lorde. To many, reading Díaz with Lorde might seem like an odd move. Currently, Díaz is as mainstream as Lorde is marginal. Díaz's literary star is in ascendance with his receipt in October 2012 of a MacArthur "Genius" Fellowship, the nomination of his collection *This Is How You Lose Her* (October 2012) for the National Book Award, and the publication of a tantalizing excerpt from his latest novel-in-progress, *Monstro*, in the special science fiction issue of the *New Yorker* (June 2012). Erudite in the ways of the literary intelligentsia (but also street-smart), hip (but unabashedly nerdy), and well-versed in genre-blending twenty-first-century eclecticism, Díaz would seem, on the surface, to have little in common with the kind of protest feminism associated with women of color such as Lorde. Lorde's theoretical insights, by contrast, have lately been neglected within literary criticism, consigned by many literary scholars to the dustbin of recent history as an exemplar of the kind of "identity politics" they are grateful to move beyond.[2]

Yet there is a cost, I contend, to turning away from the insights about identity given to us by women of color writers. Turning away from identity has meant turning away from an acknowledgment of what literature does best—which is to provide us access to the thoughts, feelings, experiences, and stories of implied persons, those "others" whose fictional lives challenge, provoke, amuse, and inform our own. As I have argued over the last three chapters, a work of literature and its interpretation always point back to those who read it. Readers are revealed as Beings in the world by the meanings they pull from the texts they choose to read and to explicate. For the literary critic, incorporating into one's critical method a nuanced and trained awareness of the epistemic consequences of identity is thus a necessary aspect of interpreting all works of literature—and especially those works written by an author whose perspective is substantially different from, or challenging to, one's own. This is why tracing Díaz's indebtedness to the tradition of thinking about identity functions as a dual intervention; I am able to contextualize Díaz as a writer and thinker while also recognizing the ongoing relevance, scope, and reach of the writings of women of color.

In what follows, I trace the continuity between Díaz's fiction and the writings of late-twentieth-century women of color writers to claim him as a writer who is thinking in a complex materialist way about the dynamics of racial identity. I focus on Díaz's short story "How to Date a Browngirl, Blackgirl, Whitegirl, or Halfie" because the story has a tight focus on the character of Yunior, and especially on Yunior's attitudes about racialized gender. In the course of arguing against a recent characterization of Díaz as a "postrace" writer, I set out the racial context within which the story asks to be situated. I then lay out the features of women of color feminist theory—with Lorde as the exemplary figure—in order to limn Díaz's indebtedness to the set of schemas they developed collectively during the 1980s and early 1990s. I end with a close reading of the short story to illustrate Díaz's courage in challenging hegemonic racial schemas as he searches for the self-acceptance that comes with decolonial love.

Speaking Voldemort's Name: A Challenge for Our Times

In his essay "Historical Fantasy, Speculative Realism, and Postrace Aesthetics in Contemporary American Literature," literary critic Ramón Saldívar declares that "a new generation of minority writers has come to prominence whose work signals a radical turn to a postrace era in American literature" (574). His intention in identifying this cohort of minority writers is to describe their role in the emergence of a new literary genre—one he calls speculative realism or historical fantasy—that is characterized by the contact of fantasy and metafiction with history and the racialized imagination, vernacular cultures, and stories of figures from the Global South. This new genre's imaginary, by Saldívar's accounting, is comparatively less heroic and more jaded than the one produced by Civil Rights–era writers of color, but it is equally possessed of a strong, even utopic, aspiration for substantive social justice. Its authorial representatives, in his seminal essay in *American Literary History*, are Salvador Plascencia and Junot Díaz.

Saldívar is insightful in his recognition of this new literary genre, and in his identification of metafiction, parabasis, and generic hybridity as its primary constitutive formal features. Indeed, his analyses have shifted my understanding of the authors and texts he examines, and his ideas inform my current research and teaching. I take issue only with Saldívar's designation of this era and genre as being "postrace," in the sense of "signaling a conceptual shift to the question of what meaning the idea of 'race' carries in our own times" ("Historical Fantasy" 575). Like the black/white binary that he suggests "postrace" writers are attempting to move beyond, the designation of contemporary racial meanings as "post" to a prior idea called "race" conceives of the latter in too stable a fashion. Just as an understanding of race that adheres to a black/white binary signals a parochial perspective on a local expression of a globalized modern/colonial world-system, so does a bifurcation of historical eras into "race" and "postrace" set up a false binary—as if there were one racial logic prior to a significant point in time (say 9/11), and now there is another.

Race has never been a stable social formation. Instead, it is a dynamic system of historically-derived and institutionalized ideas and practices that takes different forms in various times and places. Race, in other words, is a *doing* (Moya and Markus). Rather than the expression of a biological or cultural essence located inside the culture or the body of the racialized person (as most people believe it to be), race is a system of social distinction that emerges as a result of the ongoing interactions of individuals who are associated, by themselves or others, with a multiplicity of competing ancestral, ethnic, and religious groups. Because race is one of the fundamental organizing features of capitalism, it shares that economic system's prodigious flexibility, morphing in appearance and expression according to the demands of capital, labor, raw materials, manufacturing capacity, and market demand. What distinguishes race *as such* in its various guises over time and across space is that it involves creating and maintaining ethnoracial groups based on perceived physical and behavioral characteristics usually linked to an individual's biogeographical ancestry. It then associates differential power and privilege with these characteristics for the purpose of justifying the resulting group inequalities.[3] This dynamic process—this *doing* of race—has not abated or changed in a fundamental way over the past several decades.

Certainly, the way U.S. Americans talk about race has changed. But this signals a shift in how race manifests rather than a break in its underlying logic. As a system of social distinction, race tracks society-wide contests over the ideological and ethical norms regarding the meaning and salience of group-based ethnic and religious human difference. The horrors wrought by the genocide of European Jews during World War II by the Nazi party and its collaborators woke up the world to the dangers of race-based thinking. As a result, and in the wake of the U.S. American ethnic pride movements of the 1960s and 1970s, outright and explicit racism became déclassé. This set the stage for the emergence of what sociologists like Eduardo Bonilla-Silva have termed "symbolic" or "colorblind" racism. Expressions of blatant racism were forced underground, and politicians who wanted to appeal to racial resentment as a way of motivating electoral behavior were forced to rely on coded messages that allowed them to preserve plausible deniability that they were referring to race. Richard Nixon provides an early and illustrative example; he pioneered the coded racial appeal with his Southern Strategy in 1968, in which he lured white voters away from the Democratic to the Republican Party by using the rhetoric of "states' rights" and "law and order." The phrase "states' rights" evoked for white Southern voters the key justification for Southern hostilities leading to the American Civil War even as it implied contemporary opposition to federally mandated desegregation efforts such as the forced busing of both black and white students to districts outside their neighborhoods for the purpose of achieving racial mixing in the schools. Similarly, Nixon's use of the phrase "law and order" signaled an impatience with the widespread civil unrest and changing social mores of the era—an impatience that had as its base fear and hostility to changes signaled by the burgeoning political power of African Americans, Latina/os, and Native Americans (J. Boyd; Johnson). Importantly, neither phrase openly addressed the issue of race. Political consultant Lee Atwater subsequently perfected the coded racial appeal, first as political advisor to Ronald Reagan, then as George H. W. Bush's presidential campaign manager in 1988, and finally as the Republican Party Chairman. In a 1981 interview, Atwater acknowledged that the point of the strategy was to reach the racist white Southern voter without alienating other U.S. Americans who might be offended by explicit racism. He explained:

> As to the whole Southern strategy that Harry Dent and others put together in 1968, opposition to the Voting Rights Act would have been a central part of keeping the South. . . . You start out in 1954 by saying "Nigger, nigger, nigger." By 1968 you can't say "nigger"—that hurts you. Backfires. So you say stuff like forced busing, states' rights, and all that stuff. (Lamis, *Two-Party* 7–8)[4]

The result of this mid-twentieth-century shift in strategy on the part of those, like Atwater, who were actively working to maintain white racial hegemony is that, by the 1970s and '80s, explicit discussions about race in the public sphere were dominated by anti-racist activists intent on exposing and rectifying the 500-year legacy of white supremacy. As a consequence, by the 1990s, there was a marked increase in attacks by commentators across the political spectrum on all discussions about race (Alcoff, *Visible* 11–19; Li 1–7).[5] Critics of so-called "identity politics" have been so successful in their efforts that even politicians of color—President Obama being the prime example here—often employ "race-specific, race-free language" in the performance of what literary critic Stephanie Li has elegantly termed, in her book of the same name, "signifying without specifying."

As the idea of race itself came to be equated with racism, so that even refer- ring to or noticing race could be taken as evidence that one was being racist, speaking explicitly about race has become more difficult and potentially explo- sive. This fact is illustrated by a number of media incidents in which conserva- tive pundits accused high-profile individuals who commented about race of being racist.[6] A particularly egregious example involved the former Georgia State Director of Rural Development for the United States Department of Agri- culture, Shirley Sherrod. After a highly-edited and out-of-context excerpt from a video of a speech on her struggles to *overcome* racial resentment was posted online by conservative blogger Andrew Breitbart, Sherrod was pressured by the NAACP and the U.S. Department of Agriculture to resign her position.[7] Although Sherrod was quickly exonerated of racism both by the media and the court of public opinion, the immediacy with which her fault was assumed speaks to the dangers faced by anyone who dares to, in Junot Díaz's memorable phrase, "speak Voldemort's name" ("Dark America").

Such is the sociocultural context within which we must consider contem- porary non-ironic claims that we live in a postracial age. These claims, I con- tend, are a logical development in the doing of race, rather than a break in the underlying racial logic. Given the amount of work that still needs to be done before race ceases to be a structuring force in U.S. Americans' daily lives, efforts like Breitbart's to shut down any and all conversations about race are merely a way of ensuring that current structures of power remain undisturbed. And while I recognize that Saldívar's use of "postrace" is *not* intended to shut down conversations about race but is instead intended to point to ironic uses of the term by literary figures such as Colson Whitehead, I argue that the provenance and common meaning of the word often obscures its recuperation as a critical term. Hence, I see a need to be explicit about the ideological and institutional contexts within which the word is deployed, as well as to clearly register the multiple ways in which it can be interpreted, whenever it is used.

Finally, I would not want Saldívar's identification of a postracial, postmagical, post-postmodern hybrid novelistic genre to translate into a disregard or dismissal of Civil Rights–era writers with a deficit of "posts" to their name—writers whose work might subsequently be deemed too mimetic, too serious, not hip or fun enough. Nor would I want a focus on the difference between Civil Rights–era and post–Civil Rights–era writers to obscure the extent to which authors like Díaz are heirs to the writers of color on whose shoulders they stand and whose lessons they took even as they developed the new novelistic genre Saldívar describes. Although writers such as Díaz and Plascencia address the struggle for social justice from their particular historical vantage point, and although they use the aesthetic tools and generic resources available to them in innovative ways that are consonant with the work of other writers of their generational cohort, I argue that their work represents a shift in strategy rather than a radical break in the ongoing effort to represent and comment on social, and especially racial, injustice. The insights and writings of women of color helped shape the intellectual milieu within which Díaz was educated; he himself understands his decolonizing epistemology and practice as existing within a genealogy of activist women of color writers like Lorde.

Bearing Witness to Ourselves

Audre Lorde was one of a group of non-white women writers (many of whom identified as lesbian) who came of age in the United States during a time of intense political activism around three issues that most activists saw as separate political concerns: race, gender, and sexuality. What distinguishes these women from the activists who advocated on behalf of a single issue is that they came to understand—as a result of their daily lived experience and their political involvement with feminist, lesbian and gay, anti-war, anti-poverty, and anti-racist social movements—that such purportedly separate vectors of oppression were in fact mutually-constituted. Over time, they found that male-run nationalist movements, white-run feminist organizations, and lesbian separatist groups of whatever race or ethnicity were not conducive either to their personal liberation or to significant social change. As a result, in the late 1970s, women such as Gloria Anzaldúa, Maxine Baca Zinn, Toni Cade Bambara, Joy Harjo, bell hooks, Cherríe Moraga, Aurora Levins Morales, Rosario Morales, María Lugones, Barbara Smith, Juanita Ramos, Bernice Johnson Reagon, Nellie Wong, Merle Woo, Mitsuye Yamada, and Lorde (among others), began to share ideas about what it meant to be non-white women living, loving, and working in late-twentieth-century America. In the process, they developed—alongside specific group identities such as Chicana feminist, or black feminist or Asian American feminist—the political identity "women of color," as well as a distinct theoretical framework and practice associated with the same.[8] Not only did women of color forever alter the trajectory of critical thinking about the dynamics of social inequality, but also they remain at the forefront of thinking about how the mutual constitution of race, gender, class, and sexuality affects a person's experience of his or her most intimate self.

Although the women of color who were writing from the late 1970s through the mid-1990s only occasionally set out in academic fashion the features of what others and I recognize as women of color theory, those features are nevertheless remarkably consistent across a wide range of writers. At the theory's heart is a conviction regarding the knowledge-generating significance of identity. Beyond that are three fundamental features: a central thesis regarding the multiplicity of identity, a specific conception of the human self as embodied and embedded, and a guiding ethos regarding the necessity of sustained and brutally honest self-examination.

First, the central thesis is what, following the literary critic Michael Hames-García, I call the *multiplicity thesis* (Hames-García, *Identity* 4–7). The basic idea that human identity is multiple—it is raced, gendered, sexed, and classed, all at once. It follows from this that any analysis of a person's relation to society must take into account all of these aspects as intermeshing, constitutive aspects of her self.

Second, women of color forged a conception of the human self as embodied and as embedded within a complex web of overlapping systems of social relations. The human self as figured by women of color signals their rejection of the Western neoliberal individual subject that first splits, and then privileges, mind over body, the spiritual over the material, white over black, and male over female. It is a self that moves through the world as a thinking body with weight, shape, color, and texture; it is a creative entity that cognizes abstract concepts and feels pain and pleasure, while also loving, hungering, eating, and excreting.[9] And while an understanding of the self as an embodied/thinking/feeling

Being may no longer be revelatory in light of recent neurological studies as-
serting the same, it is worth noting that women of color figured the self as such
in the decades *preceding* the scientific studies that made this idea consecrated
knowledge (see, e.g., Damasio). Finally, the woman of color self does not come
into being as an autonomous, agential, individual bearer of personal attributes;
it is highly interdependent and constituted through its interactions with other
selves and with institutionalized ideologies of race, gender, and sexuality.[10]

Third, women of color share a guiding ethos that is readily apparent in the
performative nature of their writings. This ethos involves the imperative to undertake difficult and sustained self-examination in the service of personal and
social change. At the core of the impulse women of color have toward brutal
self-examination is a trenchant understanding of the way in which their self-
concepts have been negatively shaped by the social structures in which they
live. As persons who were *multiply* positioned as "outsiders" to a putative and
idealized "norm" (commonly understood in U.S. society to be a propertied,
able-bodied, heterosexual European man),[11] women of color comprehended
that a close examination of their personal experiences with, and intimate feelings about, those aspects of themselves that caused them to be positioned as
outsiders could provide important information about the complex way in
which our society is organized (Moya, *Learning* 23–101).

The difficulties presented, and opportunities afforded, by being constitutive
outsiders meant that, in their essays, stories, and novels, women of color frequently performed the ceremonies required for their own healing. Sometimes
that healing is thematized, as in Leslie Marmon Silko's novel *Ceremony*, Joy
Harjo's poem "I Give You Back," or Toni Cade Bambara's novel *The Salt Eaters*.
Other times it emerges over the course of the story or essay as the author simultaneously describes and performs the actions required for healing the wounds
inflicted by the racism, classism, sexism, and homophobia to which women of
color are subjected. This is the case with Lorde's "Eye to Eye: Black Women, Hatred, and Anger," to which I turn as an illustrative example.[12] The essay discovers,
describes, and analyzes the anger that is manifest in relationships between black
women, but it is also a painful working-through of the destructive effects that
racism and sexism had on Lorde's self-concept. Finally, it is an instructive narrative example of an intentional journey toward self-acceptance and self-love.

Lorde begins "Eye to Eye" by acknowledging the power of the "Black
woman's anger" that is unleashed "most tellingly against another Black woman
at the least excuse" (145). According to Lorde, this anger has its "root cause" in

"Hatred, that societal deathwish" that she faces a result of having been "born Black and female in America" (145, 146). She notes that black women are not the source of her anger, merely its most frequent recipients. Having made this observation, she then asks two questions, the answers to which require the kind of self-examination implied by the guiding ethos of women of color: "Why do I judge [another Black woman] in a more critical light than any other, becoming enraged when she does not measure up? And if behind the object of my attack should lie the face of my own self, unaccepted, then what could possibly quench a fire fueled by such reciprocating passions?" (145–46). Answering these two questions required Lorde to scrutinize her "own expectations of other Black women, by following the threads of [her] own rage at Blackwomanness back into the hatred and despisal that embroidered [her] own life with fire long before [she] knew where that hatred came from, or why it was being heaped upon [her]" (146). Only by examining and dismantling the barrier created by "America's measurement" of her, "piece by painful piece," would she be able to use her "energies fully and creatively." Only by accepting as beautiful and worthy and undiminished that about her which others find contemptible— her Blackwomanness—could Lorde effectively "remove the source of that pain" from her "enemies' arsenals" and lessen their power over her (146–47).

Lorde begins her narrative examination by recounting some of her most painful childhood encounters with racism—on the subway train, at the eye doctor's office, at school, and even in her lighter-skinned mother's preferential evaluation of Lorde's lighter-skinned siblings (147–49): "Did *bad* mean *Black*? The endless scrubbing with lemon juice in the cracks and crevices of my ripening, darkening, body" (149). She notes that because childhood experiences of racist hatred are absorbed without being understood, the anger they generate can be corrosive— Lorde's own anger is "like a pool of acid deep inside [her]" (150). Echoes of that hatred subsequently return as anger and cruelty in black women's dealings with each other because they see themselves reflected in each other's visage: "For each of us bears the face that hatred seeks, and we have each learned to be at home with cruelty because we have survived so much of it within our own lives" (146).[13] Getting over "America's measurement" of her is thus a necessary step in Lorde's difficult journey toward self-acceptance and a decolonial love.

To move past the pain and suffering caused by that measurement, Lorde turns to the "Black woman's anger [that] is a molten pond at the core of [her]" (145). Like any powerful force, anger has uses and effects that are both constructive and destructive. In this essay, as in "The Uses of Anger: Women Responding to Racism," Lorde evokes anger's redemptive potential; she does so by recount-ing a wide variety of incidents and experiences to which she and other black woman throughout the world and over time have been privy. They range from the banal (the casual rudeness of a black woman clerk at the public library to-ward another black woman) to the truly horrific (the spectacle of a black woman in labor whose legs have been tied together by white doctors "out of a curiosity masquerading as science" so that her baby dies in the course of trying to be born) (150). As Lorde conjures anger for herself and for us through the fearless lyricism of her prose, she urges us to pay attention to and learn from that anger, to harness its power in the service of personal and institutional transformation. She does this even as she acknowledges that anger is "an incomplete form of human knowledge" (152). She explains: "My anger has meant pain to me but it has also meant survival, and before I give it up I'm going to be sure that there is something at least as powerful to replace it on the road to clarity" ("Uses" 132).

Recognizing Lorde's narrative trajectory in "Eye to Eye" involves appreciat-ing the distinction she makes in the essay between suffering and pain. Suffering, she explains, "is the nightmare reliving of unscrutinized and unmetabolized pain." By contrast, "[p]ain is an event, an experience that must be recognized, named, and then used in some way in order for the experience to change, to be transformed into something else, strength or knowledge or action" (171). Of the two, only pain can generate the anger that might lead to clarity and positive action. Thus, Lorde's re-immersion into the pain and anger generated by past (and present) hatred is done deliberately and with the intent of moving her own personal story beyond suffering, pain, and anger to the self-love and other-love that may be found on the other side. What Lorde seeks to demonstrate through the course of her narrative is that, as difficult as it is to come away undimin-ished from the experience of looking full face into the eyes of someone who despises you for something that is not in itself despicable, the cost of *not* doing so is much greater. The cost for black women, Lorde suggests, is nothing less than a diminution of their profound worth and genuine possibility, as well as the loss of their ability to fully love themselves and those in whom they see themselves (169–74). Speaking directly to black women, Lorde writes: "I have to learn to love myself before I can love you or accept your loving. You have to learn to love yourself before you can love me or accept my loving. Know we are worthy of touch before we can reach out for each other" (174–75).

"Eye to Eye" is thus performative in the following way: Lorde confronts the hatred, which caused the suffering, experiencing it anew as pain, and transforming it into anger. She then uses that anger to gain clarity about her situation for the sake of gaining knowledge about herself and the world she lives in. All this is prior to taking some kind of positive action toward changing her sense of self and the world she lives in. By learning to love herself, she can, without fear, reach out and love the other who is most like her. And while "Eye to Eye" is a particularly powerful example of its genre, it is not unique. In conception and execution it is of a piece with similar writings by other—black and non-black—women of color who have also had to confront their internalized racism, sexism, and homophobia in order to learn to love themselves and others like them. Notable examples include Nellie Wong's poem "When I Was Growing Up"; Merle Woo's epistolary essay "Letter to Ma"; Moraga's essays "La Güera" (Moraga and Anzaldúa) and "A Long Line of Vendidas" (*Loving*); and Gloria Anzaldúa's several essays in *Borderlands/La Frontera: The New Mestiza*, especially "How to Tame a Wild Tongue" and "*La conciencia de la mestiza*: Towards a New Consciousness."

Díaz was a student in the 1980s and '90s, during the time when women of color's writings were being published and taught in the academy. Their influence on him has been significant. In an interview I did with him for the *Boston Review*, Díaz acknowledges that women of color were "producing in knowledge" "something that [he] needed to hear in order to understand [himself] in the world." Key to women of color's "genius," he notes, was the fact that this knowledge had been "cultivated *out of* their raced, gendered, sexualized subjectivities":

> To me these women were not only forging in the smithies of their body-logos radical emancipatory epistemologies—the source code of our future liberation—but also they were fundamentally rewriting Fanon's final call in *Black Skin, White Masks*, transforming it [from "O my body, make me always a man who questions!"] into "O my body, make me always a woman who questions . . . my body" (both its oppressions and interpellations *and* its liberatory counter-strategies). (Díaz, "Search")

Here we see Díaz's characteristic and deft interweaving of scholarly, literary, and popular culture references: Franz Fanon, *Black Skin, White Masks*; James Joyce, *Portrait of the Artist as a Young Man*; and Duncan Jones's 2011 movie *Source Code*. We also witness how he transmutes into his own richly allusive language all three features of women of color theory: first, he acknowledges the mutual constitution of race, gender, and sexuality in the shaping of subjectivity (cf. the multiplicity thesis); second, he figures the embodied self as constituted by, and embedded within, a web of relations; and third, he pays tribute to the importance of examining one's own embodied self as a locus of oppression and a source for radical emancipatory epistemology and practice.

I turn now to one of Lorde's most quoted (and misunderstood) passages in her celebrated essay "The Master's Tools Will Never Dismantle the Master's House" as a way of highlighting what was at stake for Díaz as he embarked on his career as a writer of African descent growing up on "the sharp end of the stick" of racial meaning in America ("Dark America"). Lorde writes:

> [T]hose of us who have been forged in the crucibles of difference—those of us who are poor, who are lesbians, who are Black, who are older—know that *survival is not an academic skill*. It is learning how to stand alone, unpopular and sometimes reviled, and how to make common cause with those others identified as outside the structures in order to define and seek a world in which we can all flourish. It is learning how to take our differences and make them strengths. *For the master's tools will never dismantle the master's house.* They may temporarily beat him at his own game, but they will never enable us to bring about genuine change. (112)

We should be clear about what Lorde is saying here. First, she is *not* saying, let me make a world where black lesbians who are poor and older get to wield power over the white former master. Nor is she asking for those who live comfortably within current structures of power to open up the door and let her in. Rather, she is hoping to define and build "a world in which we can all flourish." Hers would be a world where differences can be generative rather than something to be feared, avoided, denigrated, and rendered shameful. It would be a world in which black does not mean "bad," and being lighter-skinned is not better just because those who were lighter at a certain point in history had the military power to create the institutional structures and ideological systems that continue, even today, to make those ideas into a commonly accepted "truth" of our social reality.

But what exactly are the tools that won't dismantle the master's house? Hames-García, drawing on the work of María Lugones, has answered this question by arguing that the master's tools are the tools of purity and separation: the impulse to split subject from object; mind from body; sex from gender; and race from class, gender, sexuality, and ability (*Identity* 1–37). All aspects of the self, Hames-García reminds us, are mutually constituted: "they blend, constantly and differently, like the colors of a photograph," and how any one aspect manifests in a given case will depend on how it is constituted in combination with all the other aspects (*Identity* 6). Díaz adds to this by pointing to a lesson he learned from women of color regarding what he describes as the "true source of the power" of the regimes that imprison people of color as neocolonial subjects in the twenty-first century—namely, "*our* consent, *our* participation." He explains:

> Why these sisters struck me as the most dangerous of artists was because in the work of, say, Morrison, or Octavia Butler, we are shown the awful radiant truth of how profoundly constituted we are of our oppressions. . . . These sisters not only describe the grim labyrinth of power that we are in as neocolonial subjects, but they also point out that we play both Theseus and the Minotaur in this nightmare drama. (Díaz, "Search")

Díaz here suggests that the necessity of finding one's way out of the racial labyrinth, or of dismantling the master's house, has not diminished in our contemporary moment. He understands, moreover, that the pain and work involved remains significant. In a May 2012 lecture at Stanford University, Díaz responded to a young Caribbean American woman's question about the difficulties of psychic and emotional decolonization by asking the audience to consider the agonizing emotional work involved in "bearing witness to ourselves":

> For me to actually say: You know what? My mother did like me a lot less because she preferred my racially-lighter siblings. Who the hell wants to say that about their parent? And who the hell wants to not just think that that's a delusion, that's just because I think I wasn't loved enough. Who wants to actually plant that? And who wants to say that, like, I've always like super-envied my older brother who passes for white because I've envied his privilege and because I wanted the attention he had. Who wants to *really* embrace that, and integrate that in? And who wants to say that I felt fucked-up and poor and weak and ugly and stupid for most of my fucking life? Who wants to integrate that? And that I made as many people around me pay for that as I could, except the people who should've paid, and the structure that should've paid. Who wants to integrate that? Who wants to integrate that? Or say this: I date who I date because I was told that people who look lighter are better. ("Dark America")

For an aware person of color living in post–Civil Rights–era America, the difficulty of admitting that one has integrated into one's self-concept Eurocentric racial values involves multiple layers of complexity. First is admitting that one does not see oneself as beautiful. In an American culture that values self-affirmation above all else, it is a shameful thing in itself to admit to feeling ugly. Second is the discomfort involved in recognizing a disjunction between the decolonizing imperative to perceive non-white people as beautiful and the truth that one might prefer people with European-origin features. Third is the shame generated by the fact of having learned those preferences from one's own parents. And finally, there is the resistance to giving up whatever privilege one might have accrued as a result of incorporating into one's life prevailing mainstream values and practices.[14] Indeed, given the implications for changes to his practice that such a witness would call for, Díaz says, it took "more courage and more work for [him] to bear witness to [himself] as a Caribbean person" than to face the violence of the crack epidemic that so terrified him when he was growing up in the 1980s and '90s as a poor young immigrant boy in New Jersey ("Dark America").

It is in "How to Date a Browngirl, Blackgirl, Whitegirl, or Halfie" that Díaz undertakes the project of bearing witness to himself in order to confront *his own* racial self-loathing. It is there that he heeds Lorde's call to reach "down into that deep place of knowledge inside [himself]," touch the "terror and loathing of any difference that lives there," and "[s]ee whose face it wears." In my reading of the story, I show that critics and readers who seize on the sexism and racism encoded in lines in the story such as, "If she's a white girl, you know you'll at least get a hand job," and who then subsequently marshal such lines as evidence that the story itself endorses sexism and racism, fail to consider these sentiments in the context of the story and of Díaz's oeuvre as a whole. Such statements are admittedly upsetting. But a perceptive reader will ask: Why is that statement there? Why does this young Dominican American character think that about white girls? And more crucially, does the story as a whole endorse that statement? Moving too fast to the condemnation of a representation in a work of fiction can obscure an understanding of how a fictional work might be structured to bring to light the dynamics around difficult issues like race, class, gender, and sexuality without necessarily either endorsing or resolving the logic behind those dynamics.

The Search for Decolonial Love

"How to Date" presents a scenario in which a thirteen-year-old Yunior, having finally succeeded in getting the family's apartment to himself for the night, talks himself through a hypothetical date with one of several female classmates. Yunior narrates in the imperative mode, as he instructs himself through the process of preparing for, waiting for, entertaining, manipulating, taking leave of, and then regretting his interaction with, the girl who is his date. The second-person narration of "How to Date" makes it anomalous within the context of *Drown*, while giving it a superficial resemblance to three stories in *This Is How You Lose Her*.[15] The difference between "How to Date" and the stories in *This Is How* is that the latter function as retrospective diaristic dispatches from the front lines of a war between the sexes that Yunior is so far losing badly; they do so by probing the "outrageous sinvergüencería" he evinces in his devastatingly failed romantic relationships (48). Their primary focus is thus on the roots and consequences of Yunior's gender politics—particularly as it relates to his inability to control his compulsive promiscuity. "How to Date," by contrast, uses Yunior's present-tense second-person narration to self-reflexively examine his painful implication in the Eurocentric racial logic at work in the Dominican diaspora. What makes the story especially pertinent to an exploration of the constitutive power of race as a system of social distinction interactive with gender and class is that, rather than focusing on a specific romantic relationship, the story presents an ever-shifting scenario in which Yunior's attitude and behavior changes according to the racial type of the girl he ends up dating. Recall that the question implied by the title is not *if* Yunior should date these different girls, but *how* he is to interact with them. How, given a girl's race and class status, is she likely to regard him? What will she want from him? How should he treat her to maximize his chances of getting what he wants from her? Is what he wants the same if she is a browngirl or a blackgirl as it would be if she is a whitegirl or halfie? Given all the possible identity contingencies Yunior is likely to face, what is a poor boy supposed to do?[16]

To make the story work at a narrative level, Díaz employs an unusual syntax, one that combines present-tense conditional sentences with the imperative mode. The resulting sentence structure takes the form of "if she is X, do Y," as in, "If the girl's from the Terrace stack the boxes behind the milk," or, "If she's a halfie don't be surprised that her mother is white" (143, 145). When the issue under consideration is the girl's (rather than Yunior's) behavior and attitude, Díaz alters the syntax slightly. In that case, he drops the imperative mode and the sentence structure becomes a true conditional, in the form of "if she is X, then she will do Y," as in, "If the girl's an outsider she will hiss now and say, What a fucking asshole" (146). The overall effect is to place the reader inside the narrative, allowing him or her to explore the possible outcomes of the hypothetical date alongside Yunior as it progresses.

What becomes evident as we move with Yunior through the story is that he lives in a world whose values are not of his choosing, and the mechanisms of which are largely out of his control. Even so, he angles to position himself most advantageously—given his available resources—to influence those mechanisms in his favor. Yunior is acutely aware that his ability to get what he wants depends on who the girl is—what a girl of "her type" might want from a boy of "his type." He is further cognizant of the fact that the girl's perception of him will differ according to *her* positioning within the socioeconomic and racial order, as well as how she understands that positioning—even in those cases where *his* behavior remains constant. So, for example, while at dinner at El Cibao, Yunior commands himself to "Order everything in your busted-up Spanish," reminding himself to "Let her correct you if she's Latina and amaze her if she's black" (145). In the way that light passing through a prism produces a dazzlingly full spectrum of colors, so does perception refracted through identity in this story produce a wide and varied range of interactional dynamics. What Díaz's syntactically odd sentences make clear, is that, as the specific factors involved in setting the scene proliferate, the identity contingencies multiply correspondingly. Du Boisian double-consciousness here opens up into Díazian multiple-consciousness.

Part of Yunior's difficulty is figuring out which combination of type of girl and sort of behavior will bring him the satisfaction he seeks. Possessing little money or status other than what being young and male gives him, and burdened by a shaming sense of racial inferiority, Yunior possesses a few resources: intelligence, charm, and a watchful sense of behavioral restraint.[17] Demonstrating the sensitivity to relational dynamics that will make him such a successful seducer in subsequent Díazian narratives, Yunior is careful to take his cues from his date; he rightly intuits that when resources are limited, not missing or thwarting an opportunity might be the best way to succeed. Escaping Yunior's control entirely, however, are the basic contours of his sexual and aesthetic desire—formed as they have been by the coloniality of power:

> She might kiss you and then go, or she might, if she's reckless, give it up, but that's rare. Kissing will suffice. A whitegirl might just give it up right then. Don't stop her. She'll take her gum out of her mouth, stick it to the plastic sofa covers and then will move close to you. You have nice eyes, she might say.
>
> Tell her that you love her hair, that you love her skin, her lips, because, in truth, you love them more than you love your own. (147)

Statements like this last one amount to what Díaz refers to as a "speaking of Voldemort's name" in fictional form.[18] For Díaz, as for the women of color who came before him, saying the shameful thing out loud is the first step to escaping its power. Making a belief manifest renders it available to be confronted, examined, contextualized, and evaluated, in order that it may be rejected, destroyed, or altered through a transformation of the underlying ideas and practices that give it vitality. Having Yunior admit his preference for European-origin features over his own African-origin features is thus Díaz's fictional way of pushing Yunior (and the reader) forward in the journey toward epistemic and emotional decolonization. He is thus doing in fictional form what Lorde did so well in the form of the personal essay.

A distinctive feature of Díaz's fiction is an emphasis on the embodiment of his characters—their skin color, hair texture, height, body shape, and abundance or lack of flesh. At a basic narrative level, this serves to characterize the fictional individuals who inhabit his stories. But it is also Díaz's way of representing his characters as Beings whose habitus has been formed by the particular structures of race, class, and gender through which they come into being. It also recalls the second feature of women of color theory, which is a conception of the human self as embodied and embedded within a complex web of overlapping systems of relations. For Díaz, attending to the embodiment of his characters is preliminary to interrogating the meanings physical features like hair texture and skin color have been made to bear.

When Díaz includes lines such as "Hide the picture of yourself with an Afro" or "Run a hand through your hair like the whiteboys do even though the only thing that runs easily through your hair is Africa," he is referencing and commenting on a peculiarly Dominican attitude about the relationship between hair texture and race (143, 145).[19] In *Black behind the Ears: Dominican Racial Identity from Museums to Beauty Shops*, sociologist Ginetta Candelario describes the importance of beauty culture and hair texture to Dominican attitudes about their ancestry and relationship to whiteness. For historical reasons having to do as much with the fact that the Dominican Republic shares the island of Hispaniola with Haiti (whose citizens, in the Dominican imagination, are indisputably "black" and of African descent), as with the fact that the country was ruled for decades by a dictator whose interests were aligned with the military and political-economic interests of the United States, Dominicans tend not to identify themselves in ways that acknowledge their African ancestry.[20] They distance themselves from the legacy of slavery and anti-black racism through a variety of linguistic, behavioral, and ideological practices. One such practice involves describing themselves with language that "affirms their 'Indian' heritage—*Indio, Indio oscuro, Indio claro, Trigueño*"—thus facilitating the construction of a non-black Indo-Hispanic Dominican identity (5). Another involves focusing on those aspects of their physical beings that are in crucial ways "alterable" and so subject to the long-term process of encoding whiteness on the body referred to as *blanqueamiento* (Candelario, "Hair Race-ing" 138). For Dominicans, whiteness is less a matter of skin color than an "explicitly achieved (and achievable) status with connotations of social, political, and economic privilege" (131).

According to Candelario, a central aspect of Dominican beauty culture turns on the racial meanings assigned to what is referred to as *pelo malo* (bad hair) and what is considered *pelo bueno* (good hair):

> *Pelo malo* is hair that is perceived to be tightly curled, coarse, and kinky. *Pelo bueno* is hair that is soft and silky, straight, wavy, or loosely curled. There are clearly racial connotations to each category: the notion of *pelo malo* implies an outright denigration of African-origin hair textures, while *pelo bueno* exalts European, Asian, and indigenous hair textures. Moreover, those with good hair are, by definition, "not black," skin color notwithstanding. What is instructive about the Dominican case is the seeming possibility of racial transformation through hair care. (*Black Behind the Ears* 182)

Given Dominicans' historically-derived habit of distancing themselves from blackness, discounting dark skin color as a signifier of African ancestry, and equating African-origin hair with blackness, the setting, curling, drying, and taming of hair becomes the focus of considerable time and attention of Dominican women. For Dominicans, Candelario explains, hair serves as an "alterable sign" that is the "principle bodily signifier of race" (252, 223).

Note that I am not making a negative judgment regarding Dominicans' "mystified" understanding about their "true" racial identity. Race has no being outside a specific community of meaning; its bodily and behavioral signifiers are historically-determined and variable rather than natural and unchanging. For instance, there is no reason why skin color, rather than hair texture, should be the primary (although not sole) determinant of racial identity in the United States—other than that this is the way racial distinction has evolved here. One possible explanation may be that hair texture alone is insufficient to distinguish between people of European descent and the wide variety of peoples of non-European descent (including people indigenous to the Americas) whose presence has been foundational to the development of this country's racial imaginary. Over the course of U.S. history, people from many different ethnic and religious backgrounds, with varying phenotypes, have been in continuous contact with each other. In such a context, skin color and facial physiognomy taken together are more consistently reliable as "racial" markers than hair texture alone would be. My point is that race—as a system of social distinction parasitic upon perceived physical and behavioral bodily characteristics—is both opportunistic and somewhat arbitrary. Consequently, individuals and institutions that "do race" will seize on and make much of whatever physical or behavioral differences allow them to most effectively distinguish between putatively "superior" and supposedly "inferior" groups in any given social context. If in the Dominican Republic what gets seized on is hair texture, then in the United States it is skin color and facial physiognomy. It is a difference without a distinction.

I am, however, less sanguine about Dominicans' attitude about their putatively non-African Indo-Hispanic biogeographical ancestry, or about the association some might assume between non-African ancestry and human beauty. In itself, a person's biogeographical ancestry is an empirical matter devoid of aesthetic, intellectual, or cultural significance. It is only because race works as the schema through which Dominicans and U.S. Americans alike perceive biogeographical ancestry, that being of European descent is believed by many people in both the United States and the Dominican Republic to be more desirable than being of African, Asian, or Indigenous-American descent. Given the legacy of European colonialism, rejecting one's African (or Asian or Indigenous) ancestry is tantamount to actively participating in and reproducing the racialized logic that sustains white supremacy. This doing of race is precisely what Díaz works against in his remarkable short story.

"How to Date," with its references to Africa and Afros, thus performatively claims for Yunior his African ancestry even as it stages a critical consideration of the way Dominican attitudes about hair as a racial signifier affect Dominican men and boys. Importantly, the most salient difference between Dominican and U.S. American attitudes about the relationship between African ancestry and race derives from the fact that the United States has undergone a civil rights movement, a crucial part of which was the Black Pride movement. As a result, African Americans as an ethnoracial group in the United States have done important decolonizing work through their sustained efforts to delink African ancestry from notions of biological inferiority. Díaz, as a Dominican

American of African descent has benefited from this delinking, and my effort in this chapter is to demonstrate how it shows up, both thematically and formally, in his fiction.

Consider, in this sociocultural and political context, Yunior's use of the term "Afro" to describe his younger self's pictured hairstyle. Although the term has become naturalized for us today as a neutral descriptor of a particular hairstyle featuring long, thick, tightly-curled hair combed away from the scalp into a large, rounded shape, it crucially references the Black Power political movement of the 1960s. Despite the fact that variations of the style have been worn in other times and places, the hairstyle's designation in the mid-'60s as an "Afro" (a name that derives from "Afro-American") was an intentionally political act (Mercer; Kelley). And even though the Afro's political significance has been obscured by its commodification as "revolutionary glamour" in the 1990s, most of the young people who chose to wear Afros during the '60s were making anti-establishment, anti-authoritarian, anti-war, and often anti-white political statements (Davis). As the most iconic symbol of the "Black is Beautiful" movement, the Afro hairstyle connoted—especially for the young black men and women who wore it—pride in one's African heritage and resistance to a bodily aesthetic that privileges a European somatic norm (Kelley 348–49). Díaz's decision to have Yunior describe the pictured hairstyle as an Afro activates at the level of the story's political unconscious the ideology of black pride, and enacts a rejection of Yunior's rejection of his own Africanness. The fact that the narrator does so at the same time as he instructs his younger self to *hide the picture away* creates a boomerang movement—simultaneously pointing a way out of the "grim labyrinth of power" in which Yunior remains imprisoned, while also acknowledging the arduousness of escaping the encircling bonds of shame that racial self-hatred can forge.

It is noteworthy that the most troubling and difficult interactions Yunior has during his hypothetical date are with the "halfie," presumably a girl of mixed European and African ancestry whose parents are associated with different races. The "whitegirl" appears untroubled by her own sexual desire; she openly expresses a liking for "Spanish guys" and hums along with the radio as she washes up after her sexual encounter with Yunior (148). By contrast, the "local" or "homegirl" (read Latina or black) "won't be quick about letting you touch" because she "has to live in the same neighborhood" and "has to deal with you being all up in her business" (147). The halfie, though, is represented as being uncomfortable with her racial identity and ambivalent about her sexuality. She expresses a dislike for black people, who, she says, "treat me real bad," and she breaks away from Yunior in the midst of intimate touching by crossing her arms and saying "I hate my tits." She pulls away again when he strokes her hair and says, "I don't like anybody touching my hair." And finally, she complains about the fact that Yunior is "the only kind of guy" who asks her out—him and "the blackboys" (148). The point to be made here is not that this is how halfies *are*. Rather, this is how Díaz represents Yunior as perceiving them to be. The discomfort evinced by the halfie is thus indicative of how Yunior sees himself in relation to another person who, like him, is existentially neither/nor. In the halfie's case, her sense of existential ambiguity is related to being neither black nor white; in Yunior's that sense is related to being neither black nor white, neither American nor Dominican, neither Spanish-speaking nor English-speaking. The epigraph for *Drown*, taken from a poem by the Cuban American poet and scholar Gustavo Pérez Firmat, generalizes this sense of an existential neither/nor to the project of the book as a whole: "My subject: / how to explain to you that I / don't belong to English / though I belong nowhere else." The halfie in "How to Date" functions as the paradigmatic representational mirror for Yunior's developing self. As such, she reflects back to him his as-yet-unconsummated desire for a decolonial love—a love that might emerge only in the wake of the radical acceptance and welcoming home of the formerly racially- and sexually-denigrated non-European self.

Junot Díaz as Audre Lorde's "Man Child"

I close with a meditation by Lorde about the challenges of raising her then-teenage son as a way of figuring Díaz's relationship to her theoretical insights. Lorde writes:

> I wish to raise a Black man who will not be destroyed by nor settle for those corruptions called *power* by the white fathers who mean his destruction as surely as they mean mine. I wish to raise a Black man who will recognize that the legitimate objects of his hostility are not women but the particulars of a structure that programs him to fear and despise women as well as his own Black self.
>
> For me, that task begins with teaching my son that I do not exist to do his feeling for him. ("Man Child" 74)

Díaz, I suggest, is Lorde's political, spiritual, and emotional man child. Having learned the lessons of women of color, he takes responsibility for his own feelings, and advances the project of "forging in the smith[y] of his body-logos" a "radical emancipatory epistemolog[y]." By routing the critique of white supremacy through the body of his fictional alter-ego Yunior, Díaz takes up the "set of strategies and warrior-grammars" mapped out by women of color in the 1980s and '90s (Díaz, "Search"). In so doing, he responds to Moraga's call to come to terms with our own suffering in order to challenge and, if necessary, "change ourselves, even sometimes our most cherished block-hard convictions" (Moraga and Anzaldúa i); to Mitsuye Yamada's call to reject as inevitable the "unnatural disaster" of racism and sexism that results in an inability to see women of color as fully human; to Gloria Anzaldúa's call to put "history through a sieve" in order to winnow out the lies we have inherited about non-European people's supposed racial and cultural inferiority (*Borderlands* 82); to Joy Harjo's call to "release" the "fear to be loved" that is the legacy of European colonialism for Native peoples; and to Audre Lorde's call "*to reach down into that deep place of knowledge inside [ourselves] and touch that terror and loathing of any difference that lives there*" in order to "*[s]ee whose face it wears*" ("Master's Tools" 113). And while Yunior has not yet (and might never) succeed in doing so, Díaz enables himself (and invites us, through his fiction) to reach for "the oldest cry," the "deeply personal cry for one's own pain" (Morrison, *Sula* 108). It is this cry that the character of Nel in Toni Morrison's *Sula* needs to cry in order to understand that the one whose love she really desired was not Jude, but Sula, Nel's own mirror-self. The great tragedy of that novel, of course, is that Nel is only able to cry that cry years after she has lost Sula, first to a misunderstanding bred by the racist and sexist structures that imprisoned her, and then to death.

By holding up a representational mirror to his own broken-by-the-coloniality-of-power self in a story that compellingly invites our emotional and psychic engagement, Díaz reminds us what is at stake for people with subordinated identities who must choose among different epistemological, scholarly, and political alignments as they fashion their critical and artistic practices. He shows us that recognizing the epistemic consequences of identity does not entail reifying present identity categories or elevating them beyond critique. Nor does it prevent the possible reimagining and refiguring of a different kind of present or future. Instead, it makes us more alive to the multifarious insights and perceptions of those whose perspectives are different from ours—insights and perceptions that will affect our present lives and imaginative futures whether or not we want them to. In choosing to confront his own participation in the structures of power that imprison him, Díaz thus joins women of color in writing the "source code of our future liberation." But Díaz, like the women of color who preceded him, cannot write it by himself—Pulitzer Prize, "Genius" grant, and a prodigious intellect notwithstanding. This code is open source, and it is up to us as his readers and interpreters to help him write it. Writing this open source code involves, among other things, understanding what intersectional feminist approaches to race look like in the contemporary moment, particularly in the hands of writers like Díaz. It involves recognizing *the men as well as the women* who have spent time engaging the work of women of color feminists as a step toward, and as an ongoing practice of, epistemic decolonization, and who dare to represent the complex lives they lead in our contemporary "postrace" moment. As much as we need to map the "new" in Díaz's fiction, we also need to rethink what has been cast out as the "old" and ask ourselves why it has been discarded. Finally, we need to identify writings (like those of Díaz) that work as decolonial "wormholes" between worlds—allowing unexpected, time-delayed but necessary cross-fertilizations of creativity between artists and groups often seen as separate or unrelated. This chapter, then, is a kind of time-travel companion piece, if you will, reminding us that Díaz's "new" literary geographies come etched in *tlilli tlapalli*, in a kind of Anzaldúan red and black ink, the symbolic colors of ancient writing and wisdom as passed down and reinterpreted *by* women of color.

THE MISPRISION OF MERCY

Race and Responsible Reading in Toni Morrison's *A Mercy*

One question is who is responsible? Another is can you read?
Toni Morrison, *A Mercy*

The difficulty and urgency of learning to read well is communicated in the opening lines of Toni Morrison's 2008 novel *A Mercy*. The first sentence—"Don't be afraid"—is an injunction that positions us (the reader) as the recipient of an urgent communication (1). Our sense of having blundered onto an obscure but pointed message is reinforced a few sentences later when the first-person narrator hails us with an observation that borders on an accusation: "You know. I know you know" (1). The insistence with which the narrator asserts our prior knowledge implicates us in our role as reader while also highlighting the question of responsibility for the resulting interpretation. This twinned preoccupation with reading and responsibility surfaces again a few sentences later in the two questions that serve as the epigraph for this chapter and around which the novel is structured: "One question is who is responsible? Another is can you read?" (1).

Morrison often writes as a way of exploring a question or problem and *A Mercy* is no exception. In this remarkable novel, she grapples with two phenomena normally perceived as distinct but which she represents as being fundamentally intertwined: (1) race as a system of social classification, and (2) the ethics and activities involved with reading texts—including, but not limited to, the text of the racial other. At stake in Morrison's exploration of race in *A Mercy* is her attempt to do with race what she did with slavery in her magnum opus, *Beloved*; she wants to break it open to examine its origins and find what it does to those who are its victims as well as to those who benefit from its operations.

Accordingly, she looks to a time and place before the color-coded racial schema that many U.S. Americans now perceive as "natural" had fully emerged.

The Origins of Race

Morrison deliberately chose the setting of A Mercy to facilitate her meditations about the origins and consequences of race and racism. In an interview about the writing of the novel, Morrison explains her motivation: "I was looking for a time before slavery and black became married. Before racism became established but when slavery was the most common experience of most people."[1] She goes back in time to imagine what it might have been like, and also to rewrite the narrative that we now have about the origins of our country. She explains: "Dividing the world up ethnically or racially was a deliberate and sustained event that grew. But *before* that, I just wanted to suggest what it could have been like, what it might have been like, *before* the narrative that we have now about the beginnings of this country" (Tanenhaus and Farrell; see also Morrison, "Morrison Discusses 'A Mercy.'"). The events in the novel take place over a period of about eight years from 1682 to 1690. If we consider the life-span of several of the characters, the time frame of the novel is somewhat longer, reaching back into the 1660s. The novel is set in the American colonies of Virginia, Maryland, and what is most likely present-day New York. Although the Vaark farm where much of the novel's action takes place is never explicitly located, a several days' journey taken by the novel's protagonist brings her into contact with settlers who take her dark skin color as evidence that she is the Devil's minion. The implication is that she has stumbled onto the setting for what will be the infamous Salem Witch Trials a couple of years in the narrative future. The novel is thus set at a historical moment before blackness and slavery were indissolubly linked, but in a geographical setting where this linkage was just coming into being (Jennings 645; Waegner 92).

Morrison's first task in seeking to understand how our historical past has turned into our racial present involves investigating the complexity of that past. Contrary to what many Americans believe, slavery was not the default status of all people of African descent in early colonial America. While most Africans who came to the Americas were enslaved, the idea of perpetual servitude for all people of African descent had first to be invented before it could be institutionalized. Historians of American colonialism have long debated the origins of race and its relationship to African slavery, and at least two schools of thought emerged in the second half of the twentieth century (Vaughn, "Origins"; Campbell and Oakes). Oscar and Mary Handlin inaugurated the first school of thought in what became known as the "Handlin-Degler debate"; historians such as Edmund Morgan, T. H. Breen and Stephen Innes, and George Fredrickson subsequently championed it.[2] They posited that socioeconomic forces in seventeenth-century colonial America supported labor stratification along religious and color lines leading, over time, to an ideology of white supremacy. This is known as the socioeconomic thesis. The other school of thought, advanced by historians such as Carl Degler and Alden Vaughn (and to an extent by Winthrop Jordan), argued that xenophobia, ethnocentrism, and English attitudes about the negative connotations of the color black led to "an early and pervasive antipathy toward blacks," which served to justify the enslavement of Africans from almost the beginning of their arrival in the colonies (Vaughn, "Origins" 326).[3] This is known as the proto-racism thesis. Importantly, Morrison's fictional exploration of the emergence of race and racism embraces the principle of multicausality; both the socioeconomic thesis and the proto-racism thesis find support in A Mercy. The novel gives weight to the socioeconomic thesis through its depiction of the consequences of Jacob Vaark's decision to invest in the sugar trade (35), and its reference to the historical event of Bacon's Rebellion (11; see also Jennings 647–48; Waegner 102–04). However, the novel also supports the proto-racism thesis in its depiction of Florens's chance encounter with some Puritans, who are frightened at the sight of an "Afric" and assume that Florens's dark skin is a sign that she is the Devil's minion (131–33). What matters for Morrison's purposes in writing the novel is that what historians James Campbell and James Oakes call "the invention of race" was a "long and agonizing process" that did not fully crystallize in the United States until the late eighteenth century (173; see also Jordan). Race, in the sense of an "innate, ineradicable inferiority, rooted in the body," was not a salient feature of the society in which Morrison set A Mercy (Campbell and Oakes 174).

Most historians agree that, in the decades immediately preceding the events represented in the novel, people of African descent in the colonies had a greater range of freedom and opportunity than they would in the decades that followed. Prior to the 1660s, Africans living in Virginia enjoyed many of the legal rights, liberties, and protections afforded to other colonists. Some were servants, others were free, and some even owned other slaves. Free Africans could earn money on their own, buy and sell goods and livestock, and sue (or be sued) in court. Those who were enslaved sometimes bought their own freedom, or were granted their freedom (Morgan, *American* 154–57). In fact, one of the Africans who arrived in Virginia from Angola in 1621, a man by the name of Anthony Johnson, surfaces in court records in 1654 over a contest of his ownership of another slave, a man by the name of John Casor (Breen and Innes 13–15). This is not to say that the Africans who arrived in the American colonies prior to 1660 were considered by European settlers to be the same as European arrivals. As Florens's encounter with the English Puritans indicates, some Europeans did regard Africans with a sense of fear and revulsion stemming from their relative darkness. It is, however, to say that Africans were not, in the beginning, assumed to be natural slaves who were subject as a matter of course to lifelong bondage. The other side of this same story is that the majority of Englishmen who came to the American colonies in the early seventeenth century arrived as indentured laborers and spent at least part of their lives in conditions of servitude that approximated slavery (Morgan, *American* 215–34). In the early years, some European settlers would have spent their entire lives in bondage, either because their terms of service had been coercively extended or because they died before attaining their freedom (Morgan, *American* 319–24). The characters of Willard Bond and Scully represent in the novel this class of European indentured servant. Furthermore, some Native peoples in colonial America were also enslaved (Morgan, *American* 329–30). The character of Lina stands in the novel as the representative of the non-black slave labor of early colonial America. Here is my point: if the association of blackness with slavery was not immediately obvious to people in the sixteenth and early seventeenth centuries, neither was the association of whiteness with freedom. However powerful and seemingly self-evident these associations are for us now in the wake of Enlightenment ideals of liberty and equality (for whites) and American chattel slavery (for blacks), they are a result of historical contingencies associated with the rise of a capitalist world-system founded on European imperialism and the transatlantic slave trade.

In fact, African slavery was only gradually legalized in the American colonies over the course of the seventeenth century (Jennings 648). Initially, European planters and farmers found it cheaper to purchase the time and labor of European indentured servants than to purchase African slaves. As a result, it took some time for the traffic in enslaved Africans to take hold; for much of the century, blacks remained a small part of the overall population of the American colonies. But as the economy became increasingly reliant on slave labor, and as the dangers associated with large numbers of landless and impoverished freedmen grew, the European traders and colonists who possessed the social, political, and legal power to do so deliberately legislated black slavery into existence.[4] Massachusetts was the first colony to legalize slavery, in 1641 (Whitmore, *Colonial Laws* 91). Virginia legalized slavery in 1661, and a year later passed a statute mandating that children of African slaves follow the condition of the mother (Morgan, *American* 333). In 1664, Maryland passed a law decreeing lifelong servitude for blacks, with the added proviso that any Englishwoman who married a black man would be enslaved for as long as he was alive (Browne 533–34). In 1667, Virginia outlawed baptism as a reason for gaining freedom. In 1669, Virginia passed a law that legalized the killing of a Negro slave by his or her master, and then a year later passed legislation that distinguished non-Christians who arrived "by shipping" (i.e., Africans) from those who entered "by land" (i.e., Indians). The former were to be enslaved for life, while the latter were to serve until age thirty (Morgan, *American* 312, 329). Meanwhile, those blacks who had either arrived free or attained their freedom did their best to hang on to their property and their civil rights: in the Virginia county of Northampton, a county in which full records exist and in which the aforementioned Anthony Johnson lived for most of his life, there remained at least ten free "Negro" households as late as 1668 (Morgan, "Slavery" 17–18). But like a train gathering steam, the laws that institutionalized black slavery became more numerous and more punitive as the century progressed. In 1680, the state of Virginia passed a series of laws prohibiting slaves from arming themselves, leaving their master's property without written permission, or physically attacking "*any* Christian." Blacks who attacked a white man would be subject to thirty lashes, while any white person could, with impunity, kill those blacks who resisted being returned to slavery (Hening 481–82). In 1684, New York made it illegal for slaves to sell goods (New York [Colony] et al. 157). In 1691, South Carolina passed the first comprehensive slave codes (Hadden 270). Also in 1691, Virginia passed one law that outlawed marriages between blacks and whites while punishing other kinds of relationships, and another law that prohibited the manumission of slaves within state borders (Morgan, *American* 335, 337). These statutes, chosen for the sake of illustration, are just a few of the many that legislated black slavery into existence.

As the century came to an end, the transformation of the American colonies into a slave society was almost complete. As the number of enslaved Africans increased to the point where they made up the largest part of the agricultural labor force in the tobacco-producing Southern colonies, and as the laws designed to keep blacks in poverty and enslaved had their desired effect, the fatal link between blackness and slavery was forged. This despite the fact that the fully formed racist ideology of innate African biological inferiority that whites would later use to justify black slavery in the face of eighteenth-century Enlightenment ideals of liberty and human equality was still being invented (Campbell and Oakes; Jordan). The forging of the link between blackness and slavery by the slave codes is why the opening of *A Mercy* is set in 1690 on the Vaark farm in New York. It is also why Jacob Vaark travels to Virginia in 1682 to make the trade with Senhor D'Ortega that will bring Florens under his dominion. Morrison is zeroing in on the precise historical time and place at which the previous social and juridical fluidity that had characterized early American colonial society was beginning to harden.

Can You Read?

Morrison's concern with race is not limited to understanding its origins. She is interested also in how contemporary reading practices are implicated in the historically-derived and institutionalized system of ideas and practices that is race. Her interest in the paired concerns of reading and race can be traced back at least as far as her dismay with the way her first novel, *The Bluest Eye*, was received. In the afterword to the twenty-fifth anniversary edition of that novel, Morrison reflects on the difficulty of her narrative project. In attempting to hold "the despising glance" of "racial self-contempt" on Pecola while also "sabotaging it," she had hoped to "lead readers into an interrogation of themselves for the smashing" of one as vulnerable as Pecola. Her efforts, she reports, were unsuccessful: "many readers remain touched but not moved" (211). Instead of questioning themselves, many readers took "comfort" in "pitying [Pecola]." Morrison ends her reflection on a pessimistic note, concluding that, "[w]ith very few exceptions, the initial publication of *The Bluest Eye* was like Pecola's life: dismissed, trivialized, misread" (216). Morrison blames herself; she perceives others' misreading of Pecola as indicative of her aesthetic failure. I would rather blame her readers. But a more productive response would be to consider how difficult it is for many people to fully appreciate how pervasive our current racial schemas are, and to acknowledge how powerfully they shape our perceptions—of ourselves, of other people, and even of those fictional others we meet between the pages of a book. Morrison's meditations in *A Mercy* on the ethics of, and activities involved in, reading race onto others provides me with an opportunity to explore these issues. Through my reading of *A Mercy*, I travel back to the historical space-time in which race was newly emerging as a system of social distinction and economic control. I do so to imagine, in the company of one of the world's most profound thinkers, how people might have once read—and how they might in the future read—each other and themselves differently.

In *A Mercy*, learning to read well indicates and transcends the usual capacity to decipher alphabetic script. Immediately after asking if we can read, the narrator (who we later find out is Florens) informs us: "If a pea hen refuses to brood I *read* it quickly and, sure enough, that night I see a minha mãe standing hand in hand with her little boy, my shoes jamming the pocket of her apron" (3–4, emphasis added). The novel's first mention of reading thus references a sign that Florens interprets as indicating that she will dream that night about being abandoned by her mother. Later on in the novel, we learn that Florens is able to read and write alphabetic script, so it is noteworthy that her first reference to the activity of reading refers to an animist world shot through with significance.

In highlighting the range of activities and objects involved in "reading" the world, Morrison evokes a notion of literacy that can be traced to the premodern world.[5] Vestiges of this notion are retained in the Spanish verb *leer* (to read), which derives from the Latin verb *legere*. According to literary critic Walter Mignolo in *The Darker Side of the Renaissance*, one of the original meanings of *legere* was "to discern." He argues that with the increasing relevance of alphabetic writing to Western culture, the verb began to be applied more exclusively to discernment of the letters of the alphabet in a written text (105). This allowed European colonizers to reject the variety of forms of non-alphabetic writing and reading that were practiced by the indigenous inhabitants of the Americas at the time of encounter. The literary critic Birgit Brander Rasmussen builds on Mignolo's work in her book *Queequeg's Coffin* to argue that a key site of colonial conflict in the Americas involved the narrowing of the definitions of "writing" and "literacy" to refer solely to communication via alphabetic script. By designating as "literate" only those people who could read and write alphabetic text, European colonizers were able to portray indigenous Americans as lower down in the "hierarchy of humanity," such that alphabetic literacy became a "maker and marker of racial difference." Rasmussen explains:

> As Europeans began to develop a sense of themselves as different from those they colonized, that difference became not only racialized but also linked to the possession of writing, defined narrowly as alphabetism. The persistent use of the possessive in the discourse on writing is notable. Eighteenth-century and nineteenth-century writers repeatedly stressed that Europe *had* history, writing and literature, that others did not *possess* it. This possessive investment in writing

eventually came to underpin white racial identity, particularly in North America, where it was elaborated through anti-literacy slave codes. (29)

Morrison's decision, then, to have Florens open the narrative with a reading of the social world rather than an alphabetic text functions as an important intervention. It undermines the historically-constructed idea that reading refers only to alphabetic literacy, while also rejecting the racialist idea that people who do not read alphabetic texts are illiterate.

There is another dimension to Morrison's figuration of reading in *A Mercy* as discernment. The question Florens poses is not "Can you see?" but "Can you read?" "Reading," rather than "seeing," is the operative metaphor in the novel for the processes involved in interpretation and understanding. The distinction is crucial—it belies the idea that we merely look out and "see" the world "as it really is," while also pointing to the whole range of activities involved in arriving at an interpretation of a situation or a person. Distinguishing "reading" from "seeing" in this way foregrounds interpretation as a *learned* practice that depends on a reader's culturally-competent grasp of the schemas that structure a range of human and non-human interactions: *Can you read?* By emphasizing the fact that schemas are learned, the novel highlights their constructedness—and their contingency. Because they are built up over time as a result of experience, a person might not have had the time, experience, or inclination necessary for building the schema appropriate to a given situation. She might, as a result, impose onto that situation the *wrong* schema, one that fundamentally changes the meaning of the interaction or event, and by so doing make a tragic mistake: *You can't read!* It is not incidental that the entire plot of the novel turns on a misunderstanding—Florens's *misreading* of a text that is social rather than alphabetic, namely the social text of the crucial encounter in which her mother offers her to her future master, the Dutch-English trader Jacob Vaark. In this way, Morrison's notion of literacy is consistent with that used by Lani Guinier and France Winddance Twine in their discussions of racial literacy, which I treat at length in this book's introduction. And while Morrison's concern with literacy encompasses the whole of the social world, she structures *A Mercy* in part to help her readers develop racial literacy.

Morrison's concern with interpretation in *A Mercy* is expressed in the novel's narrative structure as well as in its theme. The literary critic Alex Woloch elaborates a theory of characterization in *The One vs. the Many* that illuminates the significance of Morrison's narrative choices. Through analyses of several nineteenth-century realist novels, including Jane Austen's *Pride and Prejudice* and Charles Dickens's *Great Expectations*, Woloch develops a theory of characterization that builds upon the narrative signification generated through the tension between structure and reference inherent in the literary character (17). Drawing on Marx's theories of utility and alienation, Woloch demonstrates that the omniscient, asymmetric character-systems of the nineteenth-century realist novel create a "formal structure that can imaginatively comprehend the dynamics of alienated labor, and the class structure that underlies this labor" (27). According to Woloch, the dynamic interaction between "flat" and "round" characters in nineteenth-century realist novels "registers the competing pull of inequality and democracy within the nineteenth-century bourgeois imagination," even as it "reflects actual structures of inequitable distribution" (31). He argues that minor characters, insofar as they fulfill their narrative function, are necessarily flattened, distorted, and subordinated in the service of allowing the protagonist to grow, develop, and flourish as a "free human being" (29). When we extend Woloch's insights to the twentieth-century novel, and in particular to novels by minority authors, we are better able to understand the significance of the narrative choices and formal innovations they make. Authors such as Helena María Viramontes, James Baldwin, and Toni Morrison create character-systems and distribute narrative attention and perspective in ways that work against, rather than with, the bourgeois imagination that pervades nineteenth-century realist novels. Their narrative structures reference real-world struggles waged by minoritized communities against the inequitable distribution of material and social resources; these authors' innovations in novelistic form are ways of reconceiving, within the minoritarian imagination, the dynamic interplay that always exists between inequality and democracy, structure and individuality, language and reference (see, e.g., Moya, *Learning* 175–214; Martínez).

Consider, in this context, *A Mercy's* character-system and its anomalous distribution of character-space. The protagonist of *A Mercy* is a young slave woman named Florens. Born in 1682 in Maryland as the result of a gang rape that had been orchestrated to "break" as well as to "mate" her enslaved West African mother, Florens neither knows nor misses her father. Besides Florens, there are seven major characters. They are Jacob Vaark (an Anglo-Dutch trader who owns the farm, all the goods, and most of the people on it); Lina (a Native American slave owned by Jacob Vaark); Rebekka Vaark (the lower-class, English-born wife of Jacob Vaark); Sorrow (a servant to Jacob Vaark who is of mixed ancestry); Willard and Scully (two white indentured servants on lease to Jacob Vaark); and the woman referred to by Florens as "a minha mãe" (Florens's enslaved West African mother). These are major rather than minor characters because they each take a turn focalizing the narrative for the space of one chapter. Lastly, there are several minor characters. These include the Portuguese slave trader Senhor D'Ortega; his wife, Senhora D'Ortega; the rum trader Peter Downes; and a free black man known to the other characters only as Blacksmith. It is a character-system that, in spanning a wide range of types of people in colonial America, aims to represent American colonial society in its totality.

Now consider the novel's overall narrative structure. The first chapter is narrated and focalized by Florens, speaking to a second person. Later in the novel we learn that Florens is writing the text we are reading, and that the intended recipient of her communiqué is Blacksmith. At first, however, Florens's narrative is disorienting. She is speaking to someone—who knows who?—in the present tense. Throughout the first chapter, it is hard to keep track of what has happened in the narrative past versus what is happening in the narrative present. We are aware that something awful has happened since Florens writes: "[m]y telling can't hurt you in spite of what I have done . . . I will never again unfold my limbs to rise up and bare teeth" (3). But we do not know exactly what happened until much later in the novel, and then we get only a glimpse. Because Florens informs us that she will "start with what [she knows] for certain," before telling us that the "beginning begins with the shoes," we know that at least some of what she is describing must have happened in the narrative past (4). There are one or two tense shifts to orient us ("So when I set out"), and a few temporal markers ("Now at last" and "Before this place"), but for the most part we are left to flounder in the temporal vacuum of an eternal present (4, 6). Is this disorientation deliberate? I believe it is. It is Morrison's pointed way of forcing her reader to slow down and consider the difficulty of understanding the unfamiliar world presented in the novel.

The second chapter features an extradiegetic narrative voice speaking in the third person. The primary focalizer of that chapter is Jacob Vaark. It is in this chapter that we are properly introduced to all but one of the characters, and that we get the clearest picture of the society in which they all live. The only character we do not meet is Blacksmith, who does not enter the story until after the time frame of the chapter. Importantly, the perceptions, attitudes, and judgments, as well as the metaphors and stories contained within the Vaark chapter are attributable primarily to him. So, for example, people of the Roman Catholic faith are not invariably represented in the novel as "Papists." However, since that is how Jacob thinks of them, they *are* Papists in the chapter he focalizes.

Together, the first two chapters set the general pattern followed throughout the rest of the novel. Every odd-numbered chapter features Florens's first-person narrative voice writing to Blacksmith. These are interspersed with the even-numbered chapters, each of which is focalized by a different major character but narrated by an extradiegetic narrator speaking in the third person. As with the Vaark chapter, the focalizer of each even chapter supplies the majority of the attitudes, judgments, perceptions, metaphors, and narratives in that chapter. In this way, the reader effectively "reads" the fictional world through the schemas provided by the focalizing major character. Finally, there is only one character besides Florens who both narrates and focalizes a chapter. That character is minha mãe, Florens's mother, and her chapter concludes the novel. For a visual representation of the narrative structure, see Figure 7.

Chapter	Narrator	Focalizer	Temporal Framework
One	Florens (first-person diegetic)	Florens	1682–1690—the narrative present of the novel is set in 1690
Two	Extradiegetic	Jacob	One day in 1682
Three	Florens (first-person diegetic)	Florens	One day and night
Four	Extradiegetic	Lina	Three days
Five	Florens (first-person diegetic)	Florens	One night
Six	Extradiegetic	Rebekka	Three days
Seven	Florens (first-person diegetic)	Florens	One full day, night, and next morning
Eight	Extradiegetic	Sorrow	From the shipwreck to the month following the birth of her daughter
Nine	Florens (first-person diegetic)	Florens	Stay at Blacksmith's—three days and two nights
Ten	Extradiegetic	Willard and Scully	Approximately five months
Eleven	Florens (first-person diegetic)	Florens	Three months
Twelve	Minha mãe (first-person diegetic)	Minha mãe	After Florens is given to Jacob Vaark but before she is taken to his farm in 1682

FIGURE 7. Narrative structure of Toni Morrison's *A Mercy*.

What an examination of the narrative structure of *A Mercy* demonstrates is that there is a mismatch between the power Jacob Vaark has as a member of the colonial society, and the power Florens has as the primary teller of the tale. At the level of the story, Jacob brings together the different characters that populate this novel; he is the only character with the social and economic power to pull this motley assortment of people toward him and compel them to do his will. He possesses this power at the level of the story not because he is the smartest or strongest character (although he is both smart and strong), but because he is the only one who is "backed up" by the strength of the emerging social, legal, religious, and economic institutions represented in the novel. Jacob, then, is relatively powerful in the fictional society represented in *A Mercy*; his interpretive perspective can be assumed to be the hegemonic one. Florens, by contrast, is weak and unimportant from the perspective of those in her society who wield power. But because Morrison accords her nearly half the narrative space, and because she is one of only two characters to speak in the first person, Florens is the most powerful character in the novel at the level of novelistic discourse.

My point in highlighting the disjuncture between the relative power Jacob and Florens each have on the story level versus the discourse level is to suggest that, were it not for Morrison's aesthetic choices, Florens's would remain the untold tale. By giving so much of the character-space to Florens, Morrison is troubling, by calling attention to, the power structure that would have existed in colonial American society. By registering Jacob's social and economic centrality while also distributing the telling of the story across a wide range of major characters, Morrison acknowledges the role that individuals might have in the making of a story versus the role they might have in the making of a society. Rather than reflecting actual structures of inequitable distribution—as was the case in the nineteenth-century bourgeois novel—Morrison's narrative structure enacts a redistribution of narrative space. It is a redistribution that attempts to redress the imbalance of power accorded to Florens and Jacob by the fictional society in which they live. Moreover, by illuminating the multiple and intersecting worldly contexts that provide the content for human consciousness, Morrison reminds us that consciousness presupposes a sociality—a set of values, characteristic ways of interacting, particular persons who actively inhabit specific geographical and psychic spaces. Differently from Díaz in "How to Date," but with similar goals, Morrison elucidates, extends, and deepens the Du Boisian notion of double-consciousness. As she does so, she moves her readers away from us/them binaries (too often figured in terms of black/white, female/male, or worker/capitalist dichotomies) toward a recognition of the fact that wherever there is a social situation involving more than two groups of people, there will be multiple worlds of sense, all of which interact with the others in a somewhat different way. My point here is not to dismiss the importance of Du Bois's insights about the development and existence of double-consciousness. It is, though, to allow for the way contemporary cultural critics such as Díaz and Morrison might be developing important insights that elucidate and build on the insights that came before.

Morrison's multiply-focalized narrative structure has the further effect of emphasizing the fundamentally *interested* nature of interpretation and representation.[6] In a video interview, Morrison likens her narrative structure to the Japanese crime mystery film *Rashomon* (1950), made by Akira Kurosawa ("Morrison Discusses Her Inspiration"). *Rashomon* is built around the recounting by four different people of the same series of events, notably the rape of a woman and the murder of her husband. The rape and murder are cinematically recreated four times, once each from the perspective of the bandit/rapist, the woman who was raped, the dead husband (who speaks through a medium), and the woodcutter, who was a witness to the events and who acts as the narrator for the movie. The accounts all differ wildly from one another, and their difference reveals each narrator's self-interest, particularly about the way each wants to be perceived by others. Morrison explains:

> I toyed with having the other characters on that farm speak from the first-person point of view, but it didn't feel right to me. It didn't feel comfortable. I wanted to say other things that they did not know. I wanted to assert things that they would not know. Also, I wanted it a kind of *Rashomon*, you know, their point of view about things interspersed with Florens's, somebody else speaks, so that the narrative moves like an engine—tchk, tchk, tchk—but interspersed are these static moments of the characters: what they feel, what they know, their relationships to each other, and also their complement to the journey because they're still . . . You can feel the movement, even though you're only with one character, or only with this character. That character is still pushing the story.

A Mercy's *Rashomon*-like structure works beautifully, as illustrated by the way the various characters perceive the character of Blacksmith. Besides being the one recurring character in the novel who does not focalize a chapter, Blacksmith is a free, skilled male artisan of African descent in colonial America. As such, he is unusual enough to excite and threaten the other characters' sense of their own place in society. Accordingly, he functions as a cipher—an empty placeholder onto which the other characters project their desires, anxieties, and judgments. The schemas through which the characters perceive Blacksmith derive from their socioeconomic standing, cultural upbringing, and personal experience. How they perceive Blacksmith tells us much more about them than about him. For Florens, Blacksmith is God made flesh—her savior, her safety, and her lover. For Willard Bond, Blacksmith is evidence of the existence of injustice. Blacksmith's freedom and ability to demand a wage for his labor excites in Willard a resentful desire for increased status. For Lina, Blacksmith is loss personified; as a living embodiment of carnal temptation, Blacksmith reminds Lina of her own loss of freedom, as well as of the possibility of losing Florens. For Rebekka, Blacksmith is the anchor that holds her and her husband together. For as long as Blacksmith and everyone else are working on the new house, Jacob stays by her side. And while Blacksmith presents the most dramatic example of how people might read their own fears and desires onto the body of an other, the multiply-focalized narrative structure of *A Mercy* ensures that all of the characters in effect "change character" depending on which other character focalizes them. The point here is not that any one character is right about the truth of Blacksmith (or any of the other characters) while another is wrong, but rather that Morrison's narrative structure invites us to interrogate the historically- and culturally-situated schemas that guide each character's perception of every other.

The novel's narrative structure does not support a monologic (or even a dialogic) ethos. But neither does it hold that all claims are equal or that truth is irredeemably subjective. The existence of multiple conflicting narrative perspectives in the novel does not imply that specific conflicts that arise between the characters at the level of the story cannot or should not be adjudicated. The novel poses several important questions—the answers to which matter for how a reader is to interpret the novel as a whole. Did Lina kill Sorrow's baby? Did Willard steal the shoat his owner accused him of stealing? Are people of African descent fully human beings with all the inalienable rights and obligations that being fully human implies? In each case, there is something important at stake for how a reader is to understand the character, the issue, or the novel as a whole. The answers matter not only for guiding a reader's interpretation, but also for approaching the question of who is responsible—for what happens to Florens, of course, but also for the emergence and maintenance of race as a world-shaping system of social distinction.

Who Is Responsible?

The question of who is responsible for race is a complicated one, and it takes Morrison the whole of the novel to work through. It would have been easy for her to lay the entirety of the blame on bad actors—to condemn as immoral the European and African slavers who were directly responsible for capturing, enslaving, and transporting Africans in the slave trade, along with the predominantly European landowners who self-interestedly exploited the labor of enslaved Africans while displacing and slaughtering the original people of the Americas. It is tempting to do that. But as the body of work that Morrison has produced attests, she never takes the easy way out. She understands that blaming some people as evil while exonerating others as innocent cannot explain the persistence of race into the present day. Even less would it explain what Junot Díaz has referred to as the "true source" of the power of the regimes that imprison people of color as neocolonial subjects in the twenty-first century—that is, our ongoing participation in the interactions, institutions, and ideas that continue to regard and treat us as inferior human beings (Díaz, "Search"). So I begin with the Jacob Vaark chapter not because as a European American slave owner Jacob is represented in the novel as being uniquely responsible for the emergence of race, but rather because his chapter provides the clearest picture of the social and economic fluidity of late-seventeenth-century colonial American society.

Over the course of that chapter, during which Jacob takes a "long sail in three vessels down three different bodies of water" and a "hard ride over the Lenape trail" to visit Senhor D'Ortega, we learn most of what we need to know about the early American geography and society in which he makes his way (13). Indian villages, fields, hunting grounds, and trails remain a prominent, if diminishing, part of the landscape. Vagabondage is a real threat to colonial landowners, and tribal warfare and European religious sectarian divides are significant shaping forces for the way society is organized. From Jacob's perspective, "land claims were always fluid": "[o]ther than certain natives, to whom [the land] all belonged, from one year to another any stretch might be claimed by a church, controlled by a Company or become the private property of a royal's gift to a son or a favorite" (14). Social relations were also comparatively fluid, as indicated by Jacob's feelings about his interaction with his client/ debtor D'Ortega. On the one hand he is embarrassed at being invited to dine on a Sunday afternoon with a man who is so far above his station; on the other he is contemptuous of D'Ortega for his Catholic religion, his trade in slaves, and his foppish cowardice in the face of Jacob's own superior physical strength. "Where else but in this disorganized world would such an encounter be possible?" muses Jacob (29).

The society in which Jacob lives might be disorganized—but it is far from free. Everyone is expected to work, and those without money or protection are liable to being impressed into involuntary servitude. But in seventeenth-century colonial America servitude was a fact of life; it was not yet the fate of every member of a particular group, nor was it an ineradicable aspect of an enslaved person. This meant that a person could, and many did, move into and out of conditions of servitude. This is represented in the novel by the fact that, of the seven major characters, five are living in conditions of servitude in the novel's present of 1690 even though they were not born into slavery. Lina was captured as a child and eventually sold into slavery after her village was decimated by smallpox and warfare; Rebekka was born free in England and effectively sold into an overseas marriage by her father in order to relieve the family of a mouth to feed (Jennings 647); Sorrow was rescued as a child from the sea by a sawyer and then passed on to Jacob Vaark to work as a servant; Willard is working off his passage from England; and Florens's West African mother was a young woman when she was captured in warfare by a rival African king and sold into slavery to the Portuguese. She survived the harrowing Middle Passage and the rapes by her captors in Barbados before ending up in Maryland as a cook and sex slave to a Portuguese slaver and his wife (Waegner 92–93). The European American Scully is the only character to have inherited his servitude from his mother, while Jacob is the only character to inhabit a position of mastery.

Jacob is presented to us as a prototype of the hard-working, pull-yourself-up-by-your-own-bootstraps, American man. Abandoned by his Dutch father when he was still a baby, Jacob is the son of an English mother of "no consequence" (38). He passed his childhood scrabbling for survival on the streets of England before spending time in an English poorhouse. The importance of Jacob's socioeconomic background resides in the historical fact that the primary way seventeenth-century England solved its problem with excess population was by exporting its poor to the American colonies. While most men of his class would have worked in conditions of servitude in the colonies before meeting an early death, Jacob was spared this unenviable fate as the result of two lucky breaks. The first break came when he was taken on as a runner for a law firm, necessitating that he learn to read; the second came when he inherited land in the American colonies from a long-lost Dutch uncle. Were it not for these contingencies, Jacob might well have ended up, as did Willard and Scully, as a European indentured servant in colonial America.

Jacob is characterized by Morrison as a man of his era, but also as idiosyncratically decent and kind. The novel includes details that show him to be concerned with the well-being of vulnerable living beings, both human and non-human. On his journey to the D'Ortega plantation, Jacob participates in a random act of unobserved and uncompensated kindness when he pauses in his journey to free the bloodied hind leg of a young raccoon stuck in a tree break. Later, he is moved to fury by the "brutal handling" of a horse who is being beaten in the street (33). Most crucially, he is willing to accept responsibility for two young girls (Florens and Sorrow) in part because he believes that they would be better off under his charge. While Jacob does not question the idea of male legal, social, and moral supremacy, he is thoroughly lacking in racial animus. He has an easy fellowship with Blacksmith, to the point of sharing food and eating from the same utensil; he condemns the race-based "lawless laws" that were passed in Virginia following Bacon's Rebellion; and his perceptions of non-European people register an awareness of their shared humanity (11–12).[7] When he is compelled to inspect D'Ortega's slaves for a possible trade, Jacob notices that the women's eyes "looked shockproof" and he is aware that the men being inspected are also "judging the men who judged them" (25). It is noteworthy that the whole experience of being forced to inspect slaves makes Jacob nauseated and angry. This is not to say that Jacob does not have biases. Who among us does not? However, Jacob's biases are religious rather than racial in nature, with his primary bigotry directed at the Catholic "Papists" he had been socialized as a young boy to despise (15). My point is that Jacob's biases are typical for his historical era, and are intended to reflect the significance of religious and national distinctions for people living during that time and place. Because race as a color-coded system of labor stratification and social distinction had not yet fully emerged into being (Quijano; Campbell and Oakes), it could not have the same shaping power on the schemas by which a man like Jacob would interpret his social world were he to have been born even fifty years later.

Over the course of Jacob's chapter, we watch him make two very consequential and seemingly opposed decisions that, together, illustrate the reality of what the historian Edmund Morgan calls "the American Paradox." In his 1972 Presidential Address to the Organization of American Historians, Morgan confronted what was then a key challenge for colonial historians. Having accepted that slavery and oppression are not exceptions to the narrative of American development, Morgan was nonetheless loath to dismiss the rise of liberty and equality in American history as a "mere sham": "The rise of liberty and equality in this country was accompanied by the rise of slavery. That two such contradictory developments were taking place simultaneously over a long period of our history, from the seventeenth century to the nineteenth, is the central paradox of American history" (5–6). The first decision Jacob makes is one that he (and Florens's mother) conceives of as "a mercy"; the second is made as a result of a cold calculation (195). The mercy is to accept Florens in partial repayment of a debt D'Ortega owes to him. The second is the decision to invest in rum, and thus to engage indirectly in the slave trade. How are we to understand the apparent contradiction represented by these two decisions, the effects of which reverberate throughout the narrative? Why would a good man, a man who imagines the "silence" of a "passel of slaves" as an "avalanche seen from a great distance"—that is, an avalanche whose roar he knows is there but cannot hear—why would he turn away from that knowledge to further his desire for money and status (26)? Furthermore, how is *our* evaluation of Jacob's decision to invest in rum central to what Morrison is trying to accomplish in the novel as a whole?

Only Things, not Bloodlines or Character

Like most Americans, both then and now, Jacob chooses not to examine too closely a self-interested decision that might compromise his sense of himself as a good person (Tavris and Aronson). And Jacob is certainly not alone. All of the characters in A *Mercy* are either orphans or have been abandoned by their parents; all of them are hungry for love and status; and all of them, to a greater and lesser extent, behave in supremely self-interested ways. The difference is that, in the nominally egalitarian socioeconomic order that was just then being created, Jacob is the only character who is able to secure the institutional backup he needs to accomplish his self-interested designs. Unlike the characters of Florens or Lina or Sorrow, Jacob's desire for power and status is supported by the emerging institutions of his day. As a European male property owner in late-seventeenth-century colonial America, Jacob does not have to work *against* the attitudes and interests of the people with whom he does business. Nor does he have to work against the operations of the crown, the courts, or the churches. By virtue of his national heritage, his biogeographical ancestry, his religious affiliations, his gender, and his inherited access to capital, he is able to negotiate and work *with* them.

The philosopher María Lugones lays out a theoretical framework useful for thinking about the impact of institutional backup on different people's capacity for agency. In her book *Pilgrimages/Peregrinajes: Theorizing Coalition against Multiple Oppressions*, Lugones is concerned with the "tactical strategist's" ability to enact, as well as to recognize in others, "resistant intentionality" for the purpose of forming political collectivities that can encompass heterogeneity and multiplicity (208–09). Toward that end, she describes our shared social world as being made up of many alternative domains of intelligibility—or "worlds of sense" (20–26, 85–93). These worlds of sense each have their own sociality—their own set of values, characteristic ways of interacting, and particular persons who actively inhabit a specific geographical and psychic space. Lugones's point is that all people live within multiple, contemporaneous, and overlapping worlds of sense. But the different worlds of sense are never equal—neither for the experience of the different individuals who participate in them, nor in their ability to impose their logic onto the individuals for whom they are not the primary or chosen domain of intelligibility. The ability of a given world of sense to make itself legible and influential to those who participate in its sociality depends on the institutional structures and ideological frameworks that provide its backup; only the hegemonic world of sense has the power to define "reality" or to enact "common sense." By contrast, some worlds of sense will be unintelligible to many people who participate in them; insofar as powerful institutional structures and ideological frameworks do not back them up, they may be imperceptible or nonsensical to everyone except for the few people for whom they are primary. The result, Lugones explains, is that there are certain kinds of acts that are accorded intelligibility as "political" within a hegemonic world of sense. In our contemporary society, such acts might include marching in the streets, campaigning for elective office, or organizing and fundraising online. At the same time, there are other acts that lack intelligibility as political within the hegemonic world of sense. These might include the disruptive calling of attention to oneself of the person of low status who is expected to remain invisible, the lack of openness to being "cured" on the part of the person who is labeled mentally ill, or the inattention of the youth whose schooling is inimical to his well-being. Such acts, Lugones argues, should be considered political insofar as they are part of an intentional interfering with, refusal of, or resistance to the reductive and unitary logic of the hegemonic common sense. And while such intentions lack the kind of institutional support, or backup, that would transform them into modernist agency proper,[8] Lugones nevertheless considers such "resistant intentionality" important insofar as it helps subordinated individuals "sustain themselves" by "keeping [them] from being exhausted by oppressive readings" (15).

Bringing Lugones's insights into an analysis of *A Mercy*, one might say that each major character focalizes, and experiences most vividly, his or her own world of sense—even as he or she also lives in and is interpreted by other worlds of sense, including the hegemonic world whose participants have the most power to determine what happens to him or her. Jacob is the character in the novel that exists most comfortably within the emerging hegemonic world of sense. It is for this reason that his actions receive the kind of backup that will turn them into agency—understood as the capacity of a person to act in the world in a way that accomplishes his or her designs. So, for example, when Jacob's disaffection for D'Ortega becomes contempt, his admiration for D'Ortega's fine house converts envy into aspiration. Following the conclusion of the deal that results in his acquisition of Florens, Jacob congratulates himself for having successfully "gone head to head with rich gentry." This, in turn, leads him to realize that "only things, not bloodlines or character, separated them" (31). Thus does Jacob set in motion a determination to have a Protestant version—"without the pagan excess, of course"—of D'Ortega's material success. But Jacob's designs are necessarily cloaked in self-delusion. He imagines that his home will be "pure, noble even because it would not be compromised" by dealings in slavery and a field full of slaves (32). Embodying the prototype of the self-made American man, Jacob is "determined to prove that *his own industry* could amass the fortune, the station, D'Ortega claimed without trading his conscience for coin" (32, emphasis added). Upon deciding to invest in rum, Jacob deceives himself about the "profound difference between the intimacy of slave bodies at [D'Ortega's plantation] and a remote labor force in Barbados" (40). He ignores the fact that it will be the industry of that "remote labor force" that will amass whatever wealth he will be privileged to enjoy (40). Furthermore, both Jacob and the society in which he lives accept as a matter of course—as completely natural—that his wife, Rebekka; his slaves, Lina and Florens; his servant, Sorrow; and his two leased indentured servants, Willard and Scully, will labor without pay to further his interests rather than their own. Thus does Jacob accept as truth the "mirage of individual autonomous action" (Lugones 211). Because he is unable (or unwilling) to perceive how the social, political, and economic institutions of his day back up his interests at the expense of others' interests, Jacob is able to imagine that it is through "his own industry" that he is able to build his fine house.

In contrast to Jacob, Sorrow is the character in *A Mercy* who is most unintelligible within the developing hegemonic world of sense in seventeenth-century colonial America. As the character that remains most obscure to the interpretations of the other characters throughout the novel, Sorrow is also, predictably, the one who can be easily labeled as mentally ill. A young girl of uncertain biogeographical ancestry, Sorrow is the daughter of a ship captain who is killed when his ship is pirated. She is described by Lina as "[v]ixen-eyed" with "black teeth and a head of never groomed wooly hair the color of a setting sun" (59), and by the sawyer as "a bit mongrelized" (142). Having been drugged for minor surgery and thus overlooked during the melee, the prepubescent Sorrow awakens alone after the ruin is over. The trauma of abandonment, hunger, and extreme solitude that Sorrow experiences during the several days and nights she spends alone on the looted ship result in the appearance, in Sorrow's own world of sense, of the character Twin. Like the friend invented by the character of Pecola near the end of Morrison's novel *The Bluest Eye*, Twin is imperceptible to everyone but Sorrow. But Twin is crucial to Sorrow's ability to survive her newfound world. After nearly starving, Sorrow jumps ship and is finally rescued by a sawyer who finds her unconscious and almost drowned on the bank of a river. Housed and fed, but uncared for, by the sawyer and his wife, Sorrow is subject to the emotional abuse of the sawyer's wife and the sexual abuse of the sawyer and his two sons. When Sorrow unknowingly becomes pregnant, the sawyer's wife pushes him to get rid of her. As a result, Sorrow is unceremoniously handed off to Jacob Vaark. Twin answers Sorrow's real human need for recognition and companionship. Twin is Sorrow's "safety, her entertainment, and her guide," and the only one who knows and uses the name given to Sorrow by her ship captain father (141).

Unfortunately, however, Sorrow's silent yet observable commerce with Twin, combined with Sorrow's woeful lack of socialization within the world of colonial landlubbers, make her enigmatic to those with whom she lives. Florens reports that upon first meeting her, Sorrow "flaps her hand in front of her face as though bees are bothering her" (9). Florens interprets this to mean that Sorrow is unhappy about Florens's arrival at the Vaark farm. We find out later, in Sorrow's chapter, that this is not the case. In that chapter, we are told that Sorrow is "curious and happy to see someone new" when Florens shows up. She is "about to step forward just to touch one of the little girl's fat braids" when "Twin stop[s] her, leaning close to Sorrow's face, crying, 'Don't! Don't!'" Attributing Twin's behavior to "jealousy," Sorrow promptly "waved [Twin's] face away" (146). Following this moment of miscommunication, Florens and Sorrow never again have the opportunity to become friends, since both Twin and Lina actively work to prevent it. Translating this back into Lugones's terms, we can say that Sorrow's behavior and motivations lack intelligibility within the hegemonic world of sense of seventeenth-century colonial America. At the same time, those who dwell within Sorrow's own world of sense—which in her case is limited to herself and Twin—sustain her and keep her "from being exhausted by oppressive readings" (Lugones 15). Sorrow is so much more, in other words, than the "natural curse" Lina describes her as; the "slow-witted" girl Rebekka considers her; the "steady female labor" Jacob values her as; or the sexual plaything that the sawyer, his sons, and the Deacon all take her to be (65, 117, 39).

Lugones's concept of backup helps clarify the mechanisms through which *A Mercy*'s narrative structure intervenes in a hegemonic world of sense. In theorizing about the formation of political collectivities that can encompass heterogeneity and multiplicity, Lugones argues that the tactical strategist's ability to recognize resistant intentionality (in oneself and in others) must be central to any political project that wishes to effectively enact change. She suggests that those who struggle against multiple oppressions, and who are therefore rendered unintelligible to those who live within a hegemonic world of sense, must learn to "make social" their own and others' resistant emancipatory intentionality (224–26). By allowing Sorrow to focalize her own chapter—by creating a *Rashomon*-like structure that brings to light Sorrow's world of sense—Morrison does in fact "make social" Sorrow's resistant emancipatory intentionality. It is because Morrison allows us to read Sorrow's world through Sorrow's own schemas that we can understand Sorrow as not lazy, not daft, and not dispensable. When we enter fully into Sorrow's world of sense, then we understand that *her world does make sense!* Instead of perceiving her as stupid and unmotivated, we gain the ability to read Sorrow as deliberately refusing to participate in the sociality, and so uphold the values, of the hegemonic world of sense. We are able to read her as choosing instead to participate in her own world. Having invented Twin to serve a specific human need for comfort and recognition, Sorrow dispenses with Twin once she no longer needs Twin's company. At the end of Sorrow's chapter, after the birth of her baby, Twin disappears completely, "unmissed by the only person who knew her" (158). Meanwhile, Sorrow ceases her wandering—presumably because she only ever wandered off to spend time with Twin. Instead, Sorrow begins attending to "routine duties, organizing them around her infant's needs, impervious to the complaints of others" (158). Unlike Lina, whose need for community paradoxically tightens the bonds that hold her in thrall to her mistress, Rebekka, Sorrow actively refuses to acknowledge the primacy of Rebekka's needs and values. Through her actions, Sorrow calls into question not only the rightness of those needs and values, but also the legitimacy of their claim to primacy over her own.

By contrasting Sorrow's world of sense—not to mention those of Florens, Lina, Rebekka, Willard, and Scully—with that of Jacob, Morrison makes a point about how many people it took to pull him up by his bootstraps. Not to mention how many people it took to make and maintain them. With that in mind, I turn now to an exploration of how Morrison holds Jacob, as the representative European colonialist in the novel, responsible for his role in the emergence of race.

A Plan as Sweet as Sugar

When we first meet Jacob, he emerges from the sea onto land as if he were a *Tiktaalik roseae*[9] crawling out of the primordial ocean: "The man moved through the surf, stepping carefully over pebbles and sand to shore. Fog, Atlantic and reeking of plant life, blanketed the bay and slowed him. He could see his boots sloshing but not his satchel nor his hands" (10). But Morrison is an equal opportunity creationist, and her imagination is not secular. Through imagery that evokes the earth without form and the face of the waters upon which God moves as he creates heaven and earth, she links Jacob also to the Judeo-Christian creation story. In the first chapter of Genesis, verses 1–5, God is described as moving over the undifferentiated void as he separates the land from the waters, the light from the dark, and the day from the night. During the ensuing six days, he brings the rest of creation into being by dividing it up into ever more specific entities. Each time he divides it, he names it and gives it a function. He creates the world by separating, ordering, naming, and designating. By taking dominion over the matter and energy of his newly-created world, God shows himself to be the Lord Creator (Genesis 1:6–31).

From Jacob's perspective, the world through which he moves is similarly a world in the process of being created. Because the path is not clear, he must progress "carefully," "stepping gingerly." The metaphor of the fog figures Jacob's experience of the boundless yet uncertain possibility this new land represents for him: "Unlike the English fogs he had known since he could walk, or those way north where he lived now, this one was sun fired, turning the world into thick, hot gold. Penetrating it was like struggling through a dream" (10). Notice the imagery here: the fog is described as "sun fired" and as having the aspect of "thick, hot gold"; it is likened to a dream that one struggles through. As Jacob moves through the mud, the grass, and up onto land, the fog dissipates: "It was only after he reached the live oak trees that the fog wavered and split. He moved faster then, more in control but missing, too, the blinding gold he had come through" (11). Thus does Jacob's movement through space divide water from land, and light from dark. Like the Lord before him, he gains increasing mastery as the world gains definition and clarity.

By linking Jacob to the Judeo-Christian creation story, Morrison subtly suggests that Jacob's desire for mastery is one that can be secured only through the classification and subjugation of others. Furthermore, the creation story is not the only story in Genesis with which Jacob is associated. The Biblical Jacob is, after all, the patriarch who secures dominion over the nations of the earth through less than honorable means. Specifically, he supplants his elder twin, Esau, in two stages, first taking away Esau's birthright and then taking away his blessing (Genesis 25:29–34; 27:5–40). In the first stage, Jacob takes advantage of his elder brother's vulnerability. One day, Esau comes in from the fields faint with hunger and begs his younger brother to give him something to eat. Jacob agrees, but only on the condition that Esau give up his birthright—the right to be recognized and treated as the firstborn son. Famished, Esau agrees to do so in return for a bowl of red pottage. The second time, Jacob engages in outright trickery. With the help of his mother, Rebecca,[10] Jacob fools his elderly father, Isaac, into giving him the blessing that Isaac had intended for Esau. Having twice defrauded his elder twin, once by pressing an unfair advantage in a trade and once through trickery, Jacob sets himself and his descendants up to rule over Esau, Esau's descendants, and all the nations of the earth. This story provides an important context within which to consider Lina's description of the character of Jacob as someone who has a "clever way of getting without giving" (7).

At the end of the chapter, the fog metaphor with which the chapter begins returns, but is notable chiefly for the mention of the fog's absence, as well as for how that absence reflects on Jacob's sense of his own agency. After dinner at a public inn, during which the rum trader Peter Downes regales him with tales about the money to be made in the rum trade, Jacob walks out into the night. The "sky had forgotten completely its morning fire and was tricked out in cool stars on a canvas smooth and dark as Regina's hide" (40). Although Jacob is back in the place where he had encountered the morning fog, this time "nothing was in his way": "no fog, gold or gray, impeded him." Gazing at the reflected starlight in the water, Jacob places his hands in the surf to wash off the "detritus of the day," most notably the blood of the young raccoon he had freed from the trap. The gesture is reminiscent of the actions of Pontius Pilate because the "infant waves [that] died above his wrists" remind us that Jacob is washing off the blood of an innocent (40).[11] After washing his hands, Jacob walks back to the inn. As he does so, he forms a plan that requires him to invest in "a remote labor force" whose embodied experience he decides to ignore:

> And the plan was as sweet as the sugar on which it was based. And there was a profound difference between the intimacy of slave bodies at Jublio and a remote labor force in Barbados. Right? Right, he thought, looking at a sky vulgar with stars. Clear and right. The silver that glittered there was not at all unreachable. And that wide swath of cream pouring through the stars was his for the tasting. (40–41)

Morrison's condemnation of Jacob's decision could not be clearer. The "smooth and dark" horse's hide to which the sky is compared, and against which the "cool stars" glitter, suggests the warm dark skin of the nameless and faceless slaves whose lives and labor will provide the backdrop for the "silver" that Jacob has coolly decided is "not at all unreachable." That his decision is both contemptible and productive of whiteness as a particular and historically-locatable way of being in the world is captured by Morrison's reference to the Milky Way as "that wide swath of cream pouring through the stars." For the reader familiar with Morrison's oeuvre, the cream in this passage evokes the whiteness that Pecola, in a pathetic attempt to be perceived by others as beautiful, tries to imbibe by drinking a massive amount of milk from a Shirley Temple cup in *The Bluest Eye* (19, 23). The whiteness that Morrison condemns in this passage refers not to a particular skin color per se, but rather to the whole system of interactions, institutions, and ideas that create, support, and justify a putative European racial superiority (Morrison, *Playing*; Moya and Markus; Wiegman). From the perspective of hindsight, Morrison knows that this emergent whiteness will confer, in the novel's narrative future, a variety of social and economic advantages to those who can lay claim to it. She also knows that it is available to the light-skinned Anglo-Dutch trader Jacob Vaark (and to Willard, Scully, and Rebekka) in a way that it is not available to the darker-skinned, non-European characters of Lina, Sorrow, and Florens.

Jacob's decision to invest in rum is subsequently mirrored in the calculations made by Scully, who similarly seizes on his own race and gender advantage in accepting the wages Rebekka pays to him and Willard Bond after Jacob dies. Still enslaved at the end of the novel, ignorant of his date of liberation or the amount of his freedom fee, Scully is uncertain what the "dark matter out there, thick, unknowable, aching to be made into a world" will mean for his future prospects. However, he rightly perceives that his future as a white male indentured servant who is *paid* for his labor will separate him from the non-European women he had once considered "a kind of family" (183). And while he feels regret about that separation, his desire for freedom is such that it impels him along a self-interested course. Can we really blame him? After all, no character in the novel, with one notable exception, emerges as blameless. Florens is implicated in her own fate by her actions when she is left alone with the young boy being fostered by Blacksmith. So is Lina, condemned as much by her meek acquiescence to Rebekka's increasingly irrational demands as by her own irrational distrust of Sorrow. Interestingly, the only character that escapes blame is Sorrow. Even Blacksmith could be held to account for ignoring Florens's emotional vulnerability, as well as her relative innocence and lack of maturity, in his condemnation of her (Waegner 98). But it would be a mistake to conclude that Morrison is interested in blaming individual characters—even Jacob. Rather, she writes to reveal the historically derived and institutionalized systems of ideas and practices in which these characters are caught. She is also concerned to show how their human need for love, belonging, and status is perverted by that same system to act as manacles on their bodies and souls.

Recall that the plot of *A Mercy* turns on Florens's misreading of the crucial encounter between her mother and Jacob Vaark. By the time we come to the penultimate chapter of the novel, we understand that Florens has not only misunderstood her mother's motives in offering her to Vaark, but has also misperceived the very details of the exchange itself. But only in the last chapter, which is narrated and focalized by her mother, do we learn the answer to the question that haunts Florens over the course of the novel: "Why did my mother give me away?" Six years old at the time of the encounter, Florens is too young to comprehend why her mother behaves the way she does; she lacks a schema that would enable her to appreciate why her mother might believe that she would be safer leaving with Vaark than staying on the D'Ortega plantation. Having had no experience of sexual assault or exploitation, Florens cannot anticipate what it would be like to be taken into the marital bed of Senhor D'Ortega and his wife to serve as their sexual plaything, as her mother has been. She cannot even imagine that kind of exploitation as a possibility. Moreover, Florens does not understand that her mother perceives Jacob's basic decency, and so calculates that her daughter will be treated more humanely under Jacob's rule than under that of D'Ortega. Nor can Florens realize the fundamental powerlessness of her mother as an enslaved person of African descent in the American colony of Virginia in 1682. Accordingly, Florens can interpret the exchange only through the schema of a mother's love and care—specifically, the withdrawal of it. Although Florens's mother does her best to explain to her daughter why she urged Vaark to take her daughter with him, Florens is incapable of absorbing—even of hearing—what her mother says. Instead, Florens persists in *misreading* the situation through the childlike schema of a mother's love for her children (Jennings 646). The conclusion she comes to is that her mother has preferred her brother to herself. Florens writes: "mothers nursing greedy babies scare me. I know how their eyes go when they choose. How they raise them to look at me hard, *saying something I cannot hear. Saying something important to me, but holding the little boy's hand* (9, emphasis added). The result for Florens of this crucial misreading is a subjectivity built around a sense of profound rejection and abandonment, exacerbated by an irrational jealousy of little boys who claim the attention of the person she loves. Such is the tinderbox into which Blacksmith places the little boy he is fostering when he leaves Florens alone with Malaik for several days while he rides off to tend to Rebekka. The result is not a happy one. The two regard each other with such hostility that Florens ends up hurting Malaik very seriously. We could blame her for not being a good babysitter. But what experience has Florens ever had in caring for a baby? Moreover, according to the schema with which Florens regards him, Malaik is not an innocent; he is not a vulnerable being who both needs and deserves her care. Rather, he is embodiment of everything she most fears—the threat of being "expel" (161–162).

Conclusion

Morrison's retrospective judgment of *The Bluest Eye* is that she centered the narrative on too frail a vehicle. The character of Pecola could not bear the weight brought to bear by the "despising glance" of "racial self-contempt." As a result,

Pecola was doubly victimized—once by the fictional society that deemed her "not beautiful," and again by the book's readers who pitied her rather than asking themselves what role they might have played in her "smashing" ("Afterword" 211). In *A Mercy*, Morrison once again takes up the problem of racial perception and readerly responsibility. But Morrison is a more experienced writer in 2008 than she was in 1972. Her historical time frame has grown longer and her narrative structure has become sturdier—as has her protagonist. Florens may be young, black, female, and enslaved, but she is not a victim.[12] She is disadvantaged by the society in which she lives, but her ability and willingness to "unfold [her] limbs to rise up and bare teeth"—even at great cost to herself and the one she loves—demonstrates a robust resistant emancipatory intentionality (3).

As I have argued throughout this chapter, the narrative structure of the novel is key to the work this novel is doing. Morrison's decision to alternate Florens's with the other characters' perspectives has several important consequences. On the one hand, it gives the narrative a steady, inexorable, forward energy—like a train running on a track. As Figure 7 shows, when the structure is mapped out, it even visually resembles a train track. This is deliberate on Morrison's part; as mentioned earlier, she has described the narrative as moving "like an engine—tchk, tchk, tchk." The effect is to create a retrospective teleology; it enables what Teresa Jimenez has astutely labeled Morrison's "hindsight prophecy." On the other hand, because Morrison distributes the narrative attention among eight different characters, the narrative structure works as a kind of theater in the round. Each character takes a turn at center stage in an arrangement that ensures that all their different "sides," or schemas, will be exposed to view. Jacob, viewed through his own schemas, is a kind, decent, hard-working man who has made his own luck through force of will and native intelligence. According to the schemas Lina employs, he is both a man who has a "clever way of getting without giving" (7) and the likely father of Sorrow's baby. What are we, as readers, to make of the conflicts revealed through the different worlds of sense that are included in the novel? What responsibilities do we as readers have in adjudicating them? By asking us explicitly if we can read, and by giving us different schemas through which to interpret the same event, the novel deliberately invites our participation in the creation of narrative meaning. It alerts us to the fact that we will be expected to evaluate the different characters and situations—that we will be expected to judge them in light of our own schemas, as well as by the schemas and evidence provided by the different characters. For example, it turns out that Jacob is *not* the father of

Sorrow's baby; if we are to believe Sorrow, who is in the best position to know, that honor should be accorded to the Deacon. At the same time, our evaluation of Jacob necessarily incorporates information we receive from perceiving him through his own and Lina's schemas. So, Jacob is both hard-working *and* someone who takes unfair advantage of others to get what he wants.

Other conflicts similarly deserve our judgment. Did Lina kill Sorrow's baby? Did Willard steal the shoat his owner accused him of stealing? Are people of African descent fully human beings with all the inalienable rights and obligations that being fully human implies? In the first case, what is at stake is the sincerity of Lina's appreciation for all living things—specifically her animist orientation to the world. In Scully's case, what is at stake is the scarcity of labor, and the fact that landowners interested in maintaining a workforce frequently extended indentured servants' time illegitimately. And in the last case what is at stake is the justice of enslaving a person for life simply because he or she has African ancestry. This last matter, especially, requires adjudication if any sort of moral righteousness is to be asserted in the context of European Enlightenment claims about the equality of man and the inalienability of the right to life and self-determination. Importantly, the novel does not leave these questions unanswered. Lina does not mourn the death of Sorrow's baby, but neither is there any indication apart from Sorrow's suspicions that Lina had anything to do with the baby's death. The accusation of theft against Willard turns out to be false; his term of service had been illegally extended. And lastly, the humanity of people of African descent is assumed, contested, deliberated upon, and affirmed over the course of the novel as a whole.

By taking us back to before the founding of our country, Morrison provides an alternative history of the United States. She does not give us the triumphalist narrative of good, freedom-loving, and self-reliant patriots defeating evil, slavish, and decadent monarchists (Waegner 91). Instead, she tells a more ambivalent story about individuals and small communities scrabbling for survival and, beyond that, jockeying for position (Jennings 647). She shows us a disorganized, multicultural society that is riven by religious factionalism in a way that makes sense of our founding fathers' decision (a hundred years in the novel's narrative future) to insist upon the separation of church and state. Beyond that, Morrison pushes us to think about what race is, and how and why it developed in the first place. By foregrounding interpretation as a learned practice, Morrison implicitly stages a critique of a biological conception of race and creates the conditions by which her readers might develop racial literacy. Race, as it emerges over the course of the novel, is not a thing that inheres in a person's body or blood. Rather, it is a way of "reading" human others for the purpose of deciding how to interact with them. People do not look out and naturally "see" race; rather we learn from our societies and from each other how to "read" it onto the body of the other.

Finally, by returning us to a time and place "before racism became established," Morrison imaginatively reconstructs a world in which her characters do not always read race onto the body of the others. What might be gained by looking back to a time and place before race? The possibility that we might be able to envision a future beyond it. As with Junot Díaz's story "How to Date," the novel's utopic impulse is found finally not in the plot or the structure of the novel, but rather in the possibility of a transformation of consciousness of the reader that the work of fiction makes possible.

CONCLUSION

Reading Race

The Social Imperative examines a set of literary texts written by contemporary Latina/o and African American authors in order to address current debates about method in literary studies. Over the previous chapters, I have made a case for the social stakes involved in engaging with literature and literary study not by remaining within disciplinary boundaries but by opening out to other disciplines, in particular social psychology. I have done so to emphasize that people do not just "see" race—we also "read" it, actively engaging in interpretive practices that draw upon widely available schemas that attribute particular meanings to different bodies, behaviors, styles, and spaces. Accordingly, the aims I have pursued throughout this book are related to the way schemas in literature—and, in particular, racial and gender schemas—direct attention, condition perception, and shape interpretation.

As a literary critic, I am interested in how schemas work in literature, as well as how they affect the way literature works. As I note in this book's introduction, readers bring to the scene of reading their own sets of schemas, and this affects whether and how they value and enjoy specific works of literature. And as I show throughout the preceding chapters, schemas are embedded into works of literature through a variety of narrative features, including focalization, narrative form, rhetorical devices, and historical and literary allusions. As a part of the social world, literature is a system of social communication through which information, ideas, and norms are transmitted from author to reader, and among different communities of readers. As such, it is not unique. But neither is literature the same as every other system of communication. Literary texts are culturally consecrated; they are highly valued in a way that advertising, for example, is not. Moreover, literary texts work differently than do other forms of social communication. As aesthetic objects that engage readers deeply on the cognitive-affective level over a duration of time, works of literature make us think—but they also makes us feel. They give us language, while also prompting us to form in our minds images that evoke a whole variety of associations. Literary texts have the potential to alter our perceptions and teach us how to interpret unfamiliar phenomena. They shape our cultural imaginaries and build for us schemas through which we interpret the social world.

It matters, then, not only which specific literary texts we literature professors choose to teach, but also how we teach them, and to whom. As teachers, we have the opportunity and the ability to make visible the ideology of individual texts by alerting our students to those features of the text that embody racist and sexist, or anti-racist and anti-sexist, schemas. We can scaffold our students' understanding of a work of literature from an unfamiliar world of sense by articulating its alien logic. We can help students understand how the ideas they believe to be their own have been shaped and supported by the wide variety of cultural products (including literary texts) they come into contact with on a daily basis. But we cannot do any of this without the kind of intensive reading and re-reading that involves a heightened attention to literary language and form in a way that acknowledges the shaping force of culture and society on a text's development and expression. Accordingly, I model in this book a method of close reading that interprets a literary work's themes, structure, plot, and symbolism in terms of the ideas and practices that reflect, promote, and contest the pervasive socio-cultural ideals of the world(s) with which the work engages. My close readings are designed to illuminate features of the texts that remain unaddressed in the scholarly literature. But they also work as sustained explorations of how literary artifacts sometimes reflect, usually comment on, and always help to shape the ideological, institutional, and interpersonal mechanisms through which race/ethnicity, gender, and sexuality are made real.

As a person living in the social world, I am drawn to works of literature that seek to challenge our country's dominant racial schemas. The authors whose writings I focus on in this book are astute cultural critics whose essayistic and fictional works are extended and theoretically sophisticated meditations on and inquiries into race/ethnicity and gender as systems of social distinction. By thematizing the way people read race/ethnicity and gender onto the bodies of others, these authors' writings reveal the social constructedness—the doing—of race/ethnicity and gender. But these authors' writings also go beyond mere investigation and illustration. Toni Morrison, Lorna Dee Cervantes, Helena María Viramontes, Manuel Muñoz, Junot Díaz, and Audre Lorde also employ all the narrative resources available to them to resist the stigmatized meanings their bodies, cultures, and values have been made to bear. And they facilitate, through the use in their texts of metaphors, motifs, and intertextual allusions, and via transformations in narrative form, the development of alternative racial schemas that have a more referentially accurate relationship to the social world than those that circulate broadly in public discourse. Through their writings, these authors work to create racial literacy.

Literature by itself will never change the world or create racial literacy. But it nevertheless remains a highly powerful tool, and an important actor, in the ongoing struggle to imagine, as the Mexican poet and novelist Rosario Castellanos says, another way to be human and free. This is what constitutes the social imperative of literature.

NOTES

Introduction

1. More information about these three programs can be found online: CCSRE <https://ccsre.stanford.edu>; FGSS <http://feminist.stanford.edu>; MTL <http://web.stanford.edu/dept/MTL/cgi-bin/modthought/>.

2. See, e.g., Chute; Aldama, *Brain*; Aldama, *Multicultural*; Hayles, *Mother*; Hayles, *Electronic*.

3. See, e.g., Buell, *Writing*; Buell, *Future*; Heise, *Sense*; Morton, *Ecology*; Morton, *Ecological*.

4. For philosophy and literature see, e.g., Nussbaum, *Love's*; Eldridge, *Oxford Handbook*; Landy, *Philosophy*; Landy, *How to Do*. For law and literature see, e.g., Posner, *Law*; Gutiérrez-Jones, *Critical*; Dolin, *Critical Introduction*.

5. See, e.g., Aldama, *Toward*; Boyd, *Why Lyrics*; Zunshine, *Introduction*; Zunshine, *Getting*; Vermeule, *Why Do*.

6. See, e.g., Moretti, *Distant*; Jockers, *Macroanalysis*; Underwood, *Why Literary*; Algee-Hewitt, "Acts"; and the Stanford Literary Lab pamphlets, available for download at <http://litlab.stanford .edu/?page_id=255>.

7. Social psychology is a social science discipline that is engaged in the experimental study of how people's thoughts, feelings, and behaviors are influenced by the actual, imagined, or implied presence of others—at both the interpersonal and societal levels. Cultural psychology is a related disciplinary subfield that focuses on the mutual constitution of culture and self. Because both social psychology and cultural psychology seek to understand individual behavior in social contexts, they share some concerns and research topics with sociology. The psychologists whose work informs my own use a variety of behavioral and cognitive neuroscientific experimental methods. Experimental social and cultural psychology can be distinguished from clinical psychology (or therapy), which is focused on assessing and treating individuals who are suffering from psychological distress.

8. Levinson counts Charles Altieri, James Soderholm, Ihab Hassan, and Virgil Nemoianu as normative formalists. She names as activist formalists W.J.T. Mitchell and Richard Strier.

9. Booth provides a helpful account of why even the most banal description of a literary text can never be neutral (92–97).

10. My purpose in quoting so many of Best and Marcus's words is to hew closely to "what the text itself is saying" (8).

11. In her trenchant critique of their essay, Rooney faults Best and Marcus for failing to demonstrate the efficacy of the method they propose. Observing that the key elements of Althusser's argument are missing from their critique of his work, she notes that it seems "fair to ask that an argument seeking to persuade us to take 'description' as the test of reading itself offer exemplary descriptions of other texts." She continues: "at a minimum, it ought to demonstrate in its own practice that such a description is possible" (126).

12. Over the next two decades, the demographics of our country will become increasingly non-white. According to Census Bureau estimates, whites will become a minority of the total population sometime between 2042 and 2044 (United States Census Bureau). This fact has elicited a great deal of anxiety from many white Americans, with the result that discussions about race are more visible than ever in the mainstream media.

13. Feminist philosopher María Lugones describes our shared social world as being made up of many alternative domains of intelligibility—or "worlds of sense" (*Pilgrimages* 20–26, 85–93). These worlds of sense each have their own sociality—their own set of values, characteristic ways of interacting, and particular persons who actively inhabit a specific geographical and psychic space.

14. Sociological criticism, and especially quantitative analysis, calls into question the discipline's traditional focus on the singular literary text. Some excellent examples of sociological criticism by contemporary literary critics that have informed my own thinking are Calderón and J. D. Saldívar; Goldstone; González; Guillory, *Cultural*; McGurl; Mignolo, *Darker*; Mignolo, *Local*; Moretti, *Bourgeois*, Moretti, *Graphs*; Moretti, *Signs*; J. D. Saldívar, *Border*; J. D. Saldívar *Dialectics*; J. D. Saldívar, *Trans-Americanity*; R. Saldívar, *Borderlands*; R. Saldívar, *Chicano*; Szalay.

15. I grant that a reader's reading of an individual work might be mediated by a prior exposure to other works that belong to a given genre. Still, a person who is reading usually interacts with only one novel at a time.

16. Because any interpretive approach will reveal some features of the literary work but not others, I embrace methodological pluralism as a disciplinary imperative. Such an embrace is consistent with my understanding, described in detail in a subsequent section of this introduction, of the way schemas direct a reader's attention, condition her perception, and shape the resulting interpretation. This is not to say that I believe all methods are equally illuminating of every text.

17. In developing his theory of characterization, Woloch analyzes the linkages between structure and reference through an analysis of the distribution of character-space in narrative form. It is the "inherently social dimension to narrative form" that he refers to with the neologism "socioformal" (17).

18. For recent explorations of this problem, see, e.g., Aubry; Nussbaum, *Cultivating*; Waxler.

19. Tompkins wrote the introduction and also contributed the final essay.

20. For a helpful introduction to the German literary critic Wolfgang Iser's reception aesthetics, see Iser; Fluck, "Why"; Fluck, "Search."

21. The experimenters selected their examples of literary fiction from among works written by prize-winning (e.g., National Book Award–winning) and canonical authors.

22. Theory of mind (ToM) was introduced in 1978 to describe the abilities of chimpanzees to understand the purposes and behaviors of human actors (Premack and Woodruff). Much of the research done on ToM in the intervening years has focused on children's developmental abilities, and in the impaired ability on the part of autistic individuals to impute mental states to others (see, e.g., Baron-Cohen, Leslie, and Frith). More recently, some literary critics have begun to explore what the theory might contribute to their own understanding of how literature works (see, e.g., Zunshine, *Getting*; Zunshine, *Introduction*; B. Boyd; and Vermeule).

23. The specific tests used were the Reading the Mind in the Eyes Test (Baron-Cohen et al.) and the Yoni task (Shamay-Tsoory and Aharon-Peretz).

24. An earlier study done by researchers at the University of Toronto using a variety of psychological measures came to a very similar conclusion (Mar et al.). But whereas Kidd was concerned specifically with the power of literary fiction, the earlier study made a distinction only between fiction and non-fiction.

25. "Schema" refers to an active organisation of past reactions, or of past experiences, which must always be supposed to be operating in any well-adapted organic response. That is, whenever there is any order or regularity of behaviour, a particular response is possible only because it is related to other similar responses which have been serially organised, yet which operate, not simply as individual members coming one after another, but as a unitary mass. Determination by schemata is the most fundamental of all the ways in which we can be influenced by reactions and experiences which occurred some time in the past. All incoming impulses of a certain kind, or mode, go together to build up an active, organised setting: visual, auditory, various types of cutaneous impulses and the like, at a relatively low level; all the experiences connected by a common interest: in sport, in literature, history, art, science, philosophy and so on, on a higher level. There is not the slightest reason, however, to suppose that each set of incoming impulses, each new group of experiences persists as an isolated member of some passive patchwork. They have to be regarded as constituents of living, momentary settings belonging to the organism, or to whatever parts of the organism are concerned in making a response of a given kind, and not as a number of individual events somehow strung together and stored within the organism. (Bartlett 201)

26. As Markus and Zajonc note: "Perceivers are selective in what they notice, learn, remember, or infer in any situation. These selective tendencies . . . are not random, however. The pervasive errors and biases that result from such selective information processing are very often quite systematic" (142–43).

27. Videos for both the original experiment and its updated version are available at <http://www.theinvisiblegorilla.com/videos.html>.

28. "The self-concept derives not only from the cultural self-schema that is the focus

herein [independent vs. interdependent] but from the complete configuration of self-schemata, including those that are a product of gender, race, religion, social class, and one's particular social and developmental history" (Markus and Kitayama 230, fn. 3).

29. See also Eagleton, *Literary Theory*. He writes: "There is no such thing as a literary work or tradition which is valuable in itself, regardless of what anyone might have said or come to say about it. 'Value' is a transitive term: it means whatever is valued by certain people in specific situations, according to particular criteria and in light of given purposes" (10).

30. For two useful collections that map out a variety of positions on the relationship between ethics and literature, see George; Garber, Hanssen, and Walkowitz.

31. Information about the Future of Minority Studies Research Project is available at <http://www.fmsproject.cornell.edu>.

32. See Alcoff et al., *Identity Politics*; Alcoff, *Visible*; Hames-García, *Fugitive*; Hames-García, *Identity*; Markus and Moya; S. Mohanty; Moya and Hames-García; Moya, *Learning*; Martínez; Siebers, *Disability Theory*; Siebers, *Disability Aesthetics*; Sánchez-Casal and MacDonald; Teuton.

33. See Barad, "Agential"; Barad, "Meeting"; Barad, "Posthumanist."

34. Guinier explains:

In legal terms, the focus on prejudice alone cast a long doctrinal shadow, allowing subsequent courts to limit constitutional relief to remedying acts of *intentional* discrimination by local entities or individuals. Absent evidence that local officials or state actors intentionally manipulated school boundaries *because of racial animus*, *Brown*'s principled conclusion ultimately excused inaction in the face of a gradual return to racially segregated schools that are unquestionably separate *and* unequal. The sociological ramifications—that de facto separation became invisible—were predictable, given the Court's lopsided psychological framing." (96)

35. The concept of possible selves was introduced in 1986 to describe individuals' ideas of what they might become, what they would like to become, and what they are afraid of becoming. An individual's possible future selves are personalized, but they are also social. The possible future selves that one can imagine for oneself are the direct result of previous social comparisons in which the individual's own thoughts, feelings, characteristics, and behaviors have been contrasted to those of others in their social domain. Possible selves thus provide a link between cognition, emotion, and motivation. There is a robust line of research within cultural psychology that explores how possible selves affect motivation and performance in domains as varied as juvenile delinquency and educational achievement (see, e.g., Markus and Nurius; Oyserman and Markus; Oyserman and Fryberg; Oyserman, Bybee, and Terry).

Chapter 1: Racism Is Not Intellectual

1. When I speak of *multicultural literature*, I mean those works of literature that treat race and ethnicity in interesting and complicated ways that also have a referential relationship to empirical reality. Generally, but not always, such works are written by persons who have been constituted as "subaltern" or "minority" or "racialized" subjects

in a society (such as our own) that is economically and socially stratified along the lines of class, gender, sexuality, ability, and race. I am aware that *multicultural* is a contested term, and I use it advisedly in the absence of a better one.

2. This quotation and the block quote below it are taken from "Some Issues about Emotions and Racisms," a paper prepared by Michael Stocker for the proceedings of the "Passions of the Color Line" conference. The planned publication has not appeared in print. Some of the material around the quotes cited in this chapter can be found in Stocker with Hegeman.

3. This and the following quotation are taken from a paper prepared by Mendieta for the same, unpublished, conference proceedings.

4. When I speak of objectivity, I am not appealing to a God's-eye "view from no-where," but rather to a post-positivist conception that acknowledges the unavoidability, and indeed, epistemic necessity of interpretive bias. By itself, the subjectivity of emotion does not disqualify it from contributing to projects that strive for a more objective, less mystified, understanding of our society (see also S. Mohanty; Alcoff, *Real*; Babbitt, "Feminism"; Babbitt, "Identity"; Babbitt, "Stories").

5. I follow Fredrickson's understanding of racism as "not merely an attitude or set of beliefs," but rather something that "expresses itself in the practices, institutions, and structures" in a way that "either directly sustains or proposes to establish a racial order, a permanent group hierarchy that is believed to reflect the laws of nature or the decrees of God" (*Racism* 6). See also Omi and Winant, esp. pp. 69–76.

6. In Book 8, chapter 3 of his *Nicomachean Ethics*, Aristotle distinguishes three kinds of friendship: the friendship of those who love on account of utility, those who love on account of pleasure, and "those who are good and alike in point of virtue." He calls the latter "complete" or "perfect" friendship, from the Greek word *teleia*. This sort of friendship is characterized by friends who wish "good things for their friends, for their friends' sake." It is both stable and virtuous (Bartlett and Collins 168).

7. Friedman continues: "Through seeing what my friend counts as a harm done to her, for example, and seeing how she suffers from it and what she does in response, I can try on, as it were, her interpretive claim and its implications for moral practice. I can attend to what happens as a result of her acquiescence and accommodation or as a result of her resistance and rebellion" (198).

8. Du Bois describes double-consciousness as "a veil," a "second-sight," a "peculiar sensation" born of a "sense of always looking at one's self through the eyes of others, of measuring one's soul by the tape of a world that looks on in amused contempt and pity" (5).

9. I am speaking, of course, from experience. Over my adult life, I have had many friends of various backgrounds who have taught me a great deal about the way race is implicated with other social hierarchies such as class, gender, and sexuality to produce the U.S. racial formation. Perhaps the two friends from whom I initially learned the most about race in this country are two African American women with whom I worked closely (at different times in my life) over the course of several years—one an academic, the other a former schoolteacher and civil servant. These two women are

very different from each other (and from me) in a number of salient ways (sexuality, religious affiliation, age, life trajectory, work experiences, geographical location), but what they have in common (besides the fact that they are both middle-class, college-educated African American women) is that they are incredibly intelligent women who can articulate insightfully what race has meant for the way they and others around them have been gendered, sexualized, and situated within a global economic order. Additionally, they have in common the fact that I care deeply about them. In each case, we have seen and helped each other through some of life's most difficult transitions (death, divorce, job loss, breakups, affairs, moves across the country, parental disappointments, intimate betrayals, murder, and suicide) and celebrated together some of life's most affirming events (marriage, graduations, school acceptances, new romances, new home purchases, parental achievements, job offers, and job promotions). They have each, at different times and in different ways, through their words and through their experiences, helped me discern the subtle racial dynamics that infuse our daily lives and permeate our most intimate interactions. We have learned together through humor and with laughter, in anger, though sorrow, and by way of profound emotional pain. We have pushed each other way past our comfort zones on several notable occasions, and I am the wiser for it.

10. Friedman writes: "I certainly do not preclude the possibility that all of these sources and more, not solely friendship, may contribute to moral transformation" (202).

11. For an excellent book that uses the metaphor of friendship to discuss how readers interact with books they read, see Booth (esp. 169–79). Booth points out that the metaphor of books as friends is an old one, and was especially powerful during the nineteenth century, although it saw a decline at the end of the twentieth.

12. The heteroglossic advantage of the novel (after it fundamentally changed the landscape of literature so that all genres had been "novelized") is that it is longer (more voices can enter the text simply by virtue of the fact that there is more space for them to exist in) and that its form is looser (thus allowing for a wider variety of types of voices to be incorporated into the same work).

13. As discussed in the introduction, conceiving of a long, complex work of literature as a heteroglossic orchestrated unity that sounds differently to different people can help us to think more complexly about the question of literary value. Those of us who are trained in the academy are duly educated into some works of literature—but not others. Some canonical works of literature may not so much have trans- or cross-cultural value as that their new readers are taught to become good readers of them. In other words, apprentice readers—as part of their entry fee into the academy—develop through their education the schemas appropriate to a full appreciation of the canonized texts.

14. Morrison sees this sort of contextual dialogism as a desirable aspect of the novel-reader relation. In an interview with Nellie McKay, she explains: "[t]he open-ended quality that is sometimes a problematic in the novel form reminds me of the uses to which stories are put in the black community. The stories are constantly being retold, constantly being imagined within a framework" (Morrison, "Interview" 427).

15. If I am to believe my many students who tell me so (and I have no reason not

to), good multicultural literature really does have the capacity to powerfully implicate its readers and make them examine their own relation to the economic and social structures that reinforce racial and cultural hierarchies.

16. For instance, she begins the poem with a reference to her own imaginative universe, a land in which there are "no distinctions. . . . no boundaries . . . no hunger, no / complicated famine or greed." She asserts, "I am not a revolutionary. / I don't even like political poems" (Cervantes 35).

Chapter 2: Not One and the Same Thing

1. Morrison reminds us that when you pull something out by the roots, it will not grow back. She further notes that while both nightshade and blackberry are connotative of blackness, they are otherwise opposed. One is familiar, the other exotic; one is harmless, the other dangerous. And finally, whereas one produces a nourishing berry, the other delivers toxic poisons ("Unspeakable" 25).

2. Having been persuaded that her original opening was not welcoming to the non-black reader, Morrison labored to craft an alternative opening that would work as a "threshold" between "the reader" and the "black-topic text" she intended the novel to be ("Unspeakable" 24–27).

3. A paradox is sometimes defined as "a statement or a condition which seems on its face to be logically contradictory or absurd, yet turns out to be interpretable in a way that made good sense" (Abrams 201). Within literary criticism, the term is sometimes used to describe a linguistic or structural device that serves to contrast the conventional view of a situation with a more inclusive view or that allows for the coexistence of opposites (Brooks). Both of these meanings are applicable to the paradoxes in *Sula*, as is another sense that, according to the *Oxford English Dictionary*, is obsolete: "A statement or tenet contrary to received opinion or belief, *esp.* one that is difficult to believe."

4. Critics have made much of Sula's missing self, interpreting it in various ways. Grant reads Sula as "enigma" or "mystery," and the novel as a whole has "a prime postmodernist text" that complicates, if not entirely thwarts, the reader's interpretive enterprise (94). Lee reads it as symptomatic of the novel's larger concern with the elusiveness of meaning as conveyed by language. For Lee, *Sula* thematizes "the notion of signification's duplicity" (582). McDowell sees it as indicative of the novel's figuration of character, not as essence, but as process (81).

5. One might be tempted to explain this narrative delay by arguing that waiting to introduce Sula facilitates the setting of the historical and cultural context of the novel and allows for a richer understanding of the effect she will have on the community. The problem with this interpretation is that the novel continues for twenty-five years and two full chapters after Sula's death.

6. This has occasioned some critics to see Nel/Sula as a dual protagonist. For example, Hoffarth-Zelloe reads Sula and Nel as "separate aspects of one being." More precisely, she read them as two aspects of the author's (Morrison's) "fragmented personality," resulting from being both an artist and a responsible member of her community (114–15). Grant also reads Nel and Sula as "co-protagonists" (91).

7. It is not clear to whom Nel is speaking in the section that she narrates. At one point she appears to be speaking to Jude, at other points she is talking to an anonymous third person—to us, the reader.

8. *Sula* has been in print for over forty years now, and over that time it has generated many different, often very illuminating, readings. What critics have written about the novel has changed over time. Its earliest critics discuss it as a text that illuminates the black female experience (e.g., Smith, "Beautiful"; Bell). Some critics—most of whom were writing in the 1980s and 1990s, during the heyday of poststructuralism—interpret its paradoxes as symptoms of the novel's indeterminacy of meaning (e.g., McDowell; Bergenholtz; Grant; Lee). Rather than reading *Sula* as indeterminate, Hunt reads the novel as parable, a form that grapples with ethical or moral issues but is open-ended and subversive because inexplicit. Hunt's interpretation is alive to the Biblical resonances and historical contexts of Morrison's writings; she does a good job of situating the novel in relation to the African American experience of war. Gillespie and Kubitschek take a different approach. They read *Sula* in the context of Nancy Chodorow's theory of the reproduction of mothering and Carol Gilligan's theory of women's moral and psychological development. As am I, they are concerned to track the relationship between the self and her community, attending to how race, class, and gender constrain and enable the development of human selves. Writing at the turn of the millennium, Phillip Novak interprets the novel in terms of "an ongoing wake, a ceaseless celebration of African American culture born of an acute sensitivity to the culture's continuing fragility" (191–92). Jackson provides a compelling reading of the novel as subversively reconstructing a lynching narrative. Although different from each other, these and other essays collectively make up a rich body of knowledge about this remarkable novel.

9. As Lee notes in her reading of the novel: "Variability of meaning, whether articulated or silent, derives from a relativity of perspective" (574).

10. I am certainly not unique in reading the novel as an ethical exploration on Morrison's part (see, e.g., Gillespie and Kubitschek; Nissen; Wu). Nissen sees the novel as attempting to answer the broad question "How should one live?" by entering the debate "as to whether individual experience or general ethical principles are the sounder basis for personal ethics" (265). Combining a narratological with an ethical approach, he ends by deciding that the character of Eva is the most ethically meritorious in the novel. Nissen's positive valuation of Eva is prefigured by Bell. Gillespie and Kubitschek, by contrast, judge Eva to be lacking in the empathy that is a crucial element for completing the process of female development (35–37).

11. This is a central tenet of McDowell's interpretation of the novel. I agree that Sula is a subject-in-process, but I do not see the novel's primary purpose as questioning "assumptions about the self in Afro-American literature" (McDowell 60). For a critique of McDowell's poststructuralist emphasis, see Awkward.

12. For McDowell, the birthmark signifies different aspects of Sula's "figurative 'selves,' her multiple identity" (61). Hunt reads each image allegorically as referencing Christian iconography: the flower of the Virgin Mary, the serpent in the garden, and the seals on the foreheads of the servants in the Book of Revelation (454).

13. Gillespie and Kubitschek note that Nel is aware of the boundaries between them in a way that Sula is not (41).

14. On racial injury, see Gutíerrez-Jones.

15. This is the primary reason why I cannot read *Sula* as a lesbian novel, if by that we mean a novel that assumes the existence of a sexual relationship between Nel and Sula. For a reading that does, see Smith, "Toward."

16. In this, Nel has a very Kantian view of marriage. In the entry on "Marriage and Domestic Partnership" in *The Stanford Encyclopedia of Philosophy*, Brake describes Kant's attitude toward marriage this way:

> The marriage right, a "right to a person akin to a right to a thing," gives spouses "lifelong possession of each other's sexual attributes," a transaction supposed to render sex compatible with respect for humanity: "while one person is acquired by the other *as if it were a thing*, the one who is acquired acquires the other in turn; for in this way each reclaims itself and restores its personality." (n. pag.)

17. Lugones's concept of "faithful witness" has been usefully developed by Martínez (see esp. 112–36).

18. Hunt reads the deweys as a "disturbing fulfillment of the mystery of the Trinity (God, Christ, and the Holy Spirit)" (445).

19. This is not to say that racial and gendered conflict is not present in the novel; it is, although I have chosen in this essay not to focus on it in favor of a focus on the relationship between the novel's two protagonists. *Sula* is a rich and complex novel that can bear multiple interpretations. Nevertheless, I stand by my contention that the novel is not primarily about racism or sexism.

Chapter 3: Another Way to Be

1. For a longer discussion of schemas, see the introduction to this book.

2. Critiques of historical contextualization that take aim at New Historicism and the "hermeneutics of suspicion" often make this sort of claim (see, e.g., Felski; Sedgwick, esp. 138–43; Best and Marcus).

3. As a practical matter, similarly situated readers who share overlapping sets of schemas often produce nearly convergent readings.

4. Context-eschewing "surface readings," even when "close," will be likely to produce less intense reader-text relationships, and so shallower interpretations. And just as I would not turn to a particular person's acquaintance if I hoped to gain a profound knowledge and appreciation of that person, neither am I inclined to turn to a literary critic who has failed to examine the explicit and implicit contexts from which a work has emerged. Attending to context is vitally important for how we literary critics do our work; it is one fundamental way we contribute to the production of knowledge about the system of communication we call literature.

5. The gender of the story's narrator is established in the first sentence of the second paragraph, when she says, "Not that I was her favorite granddaughter or anything special."

6. For the history of people of Mexican descent in this country, see, e.g., Camarillo; Montejano; Gutiérrez; Foley; Ruíz, *Cannery*; Ruíz, *Out*; Sánchez.

7. It is no accident that the first literary prize awarded by Chicanos for Chicano literature was called the Premio Quinto Sol. El Quinto Sol, or the Fifth Sun, is a reference to the present age in the Aztec cosmology (Calderón).

8. "U.S. Third World feminism" was an analogous term employed by some women of color in the 1980s and 1990s. It was used primarily to signal an experiential connection with non-white or "Third World" women living in countries other than the U.S., particularly in what is now called the Global South.

9. See also Collins; S. Mohanty; Moya, *Learning*; Moya and Hames-García; Alexander and Mohanty; Alcoff et al.

10. The past perfect verb tense refers to an action completed before something else that happened in the past.

11. A schema does not have to be explicit in the mind of the author to organize her approach to the matters that concern her.

12. For more on the experience of being gay and Latino, see Hames-García and Martínez.

13. As one of Limón's informants so charmingly puts it: "*¡Es puro pedo de viejas!*" (168).

Chapter 4: Dismantling the Master's House

1. Sáez's suggestion that there are multiple Yuniors who appear across Díaz's oeuvre is provocative, but finally unconvincing (529–33). There is too much continuity in the character, and Díaz himself speaks about Yunior as a recurring character (Díaz, "Search").

2. The critiques of identity politics are almost too manifold to mention, since criticizing identity politics has become a shibboleth for many humanities scholars anxious to distance themselves from naïve forms of essentialism. For a useful review (and rebuttal) of this tendency, see Moya and Hames-García; Hames-García, *Identity*; Alcoff, *Visible Identities*; Alcoff, "Who's Afraid?"; Alcoff and Mohanty. Of course some scholars, especially women and queers of color, continue to draw on Lorde's insights (see, e.g., Hames-García, *Fugitive*; Hames-García, *Identity*; Martínez; J. Muñoz; Holland, *Raising*; Holland, *Erotic*; Ferguson).

3. Race is thus an "assemblage" in the sense outlined by Latour in his introduction to Actor-Network-Theory in *Reassembling the Social*—although it is by no means a recent one. Rather, race is an evolving assemblage that requires constant making and remaking to maintain its ongoing efficacy.

4. Political scientist Alexander P. Lamis and a newspaper reporter conducted the interview on July 8, 1981, but in the first edition of Lamis's *The Two-Party South*, Atwater was identified only as a "Republican official in Ronald Reagan's White House" (26). Lamis named him as the interviewee in *Southern Politics in the 1990s*, published after Atwater's death.

5. Such attacks did not go unanswered. For powerful defenses of the use of identity, see Alcoff, *Visible*; Alcoff et al.; Hames-García, *Fugitive*; Hames-García, *Identity*; S. Mohanty; Moya, *Learning*; Moya and Hames-García; Teuton.

6. For example, Senate Majority Leader Harry Reid found himself the target of

conservative race-baiting in January 2010 when advance publicity for a book about the Obama presidential campaign revealed that he had, several years earlier, made a fairly innocuous observation about President Obama's relative acceptability to white voters. For more about that incident, see Moya, "Harry." For an account of a 2008 incident involving former vice presidential candidate Geraldine Ferraro, see Li (5–6).

7. On March 27, 2010, Sherrod, who is African American, gave a moving speech to the Georgia chapter of the NAACP, in which she described her difficult but successful effort to overcome her fear of and resentment toward white people. For a link to a video of the speech see Sherrod. For news accounts of the incident, see Shahid; Nicholas and Hennessey. For an in-depth media analysis of the incident, see Jencks et al.

8. My knowledge of women of color theory has been acquired through years of reading and teaching a large volume of the writings—fictional, essayistic, and scholarly—of women of color. Scholars interested in consulting some key sources might begin with Alexander and Mohanty; Anzaldúa, *Borderlands*; Baca Zinn and Dill; Bambara, *The Black Woman*; Chow; hooks; Hurtado; Lorde, *Sister*; C. Mohanty, Russo, and Torres; Moraga; Moraga and Anzaldúa; Moya, *Learning*; Ramos; Smith, "Toward"; Smith, *Home*; Smith, "Beautiful"; Wong, Woo, and Yamada. For a helpful account of the historical development of and relationships among Chicana, black, and white feminisms, see Roth.

9. Perspiration, spilled breast milk, and menstrual blood figure prominently in the writings of women of color. Representative fictional examples include Milkman's extended nursing in Morrison's *Song of Solomon*, Sethe's stolen milk in Morrison's *Beloved*, the sweat that trickles down between Estrella's breasts in Viramontes's *Under the Feet of Jesus*, and the menstrual blood that so bedevils Velma in Bambara's *The Salt Eaters*.

10. The self as figured by women of color thus anticipates as well the interdependent self described in the studies about different cultural models of the self done by Markus and Kitayama. Although their early work focused on the different types of selves associated with middle-class Japanese college students (interdependent) compared to middle-class European American college students (independent), subsequent work in cultural psychology demonstrates that factors of class and race affect the extent to which an American is likely to be an independent as opposed to an interdependent self (Markus and Conner).

11. In 1968, sociologist Erving Goffman helpfully catalogued the features associated with American normativity when he wrote: "in an important sense there is only one complete unblushing male in America: a young, married, white, urban, northern, heterosexual Protestant father of college education, fully employed, of good complexion, weight and height and a recent record in sports" (128). Compare this to the list of features Lorde associates with herself in her essay "Age, Race, Class, and Sex: Women Redefining Difference," and it becomes clear why she understands herself to be a paradigmatic outsider: "As a forty-nine-year-old Black lesbian feminist socialist mother of two, including one boy, and a member of an inter-racial couple, I usually find myself a part of some group defined as other, deviant, inferior, or just plain wrong" (114).

12. An abbreviated version of the essay was published in *Essence* 14.6 (October 1983).

This and all essays by Lorde referred to in this chapter are collected in her book *Sister Outsider*.

13. Compare Anzaldúa's observation that internalized oppression negatively affects Chicanas' relationships with each other: "To be close to another Chicana is like looking in the mirror. We are afraid of what we'll see there. *Pena*. Shame. Low estimation of self" (*Borderlands* 58).

14. As Moraga notes, the hardest part of remembering what it "feels like to be a victim" in a way that would preclude our victimization of others is that "it may mean giving up whatever privileges we have managed to squeeze out of this society by virtue of our gender, race, class, or sexuality" (*Loving* 53).

15. "Alma," "Miss Lora," and "The Cheater's Guide to Love." Yunior, who narrates all four stories, is presumably talking to himself in each. A fourth story in *This Is How You Lose Her*, "Flaca," is also written using second-person narration with Yunior as the narrator, but in that story Yunior is talking not to himself, but to a former girlfriend with that nickname.

16. Steele defines an *identity contingency* as the specific set of responses that a person with a given identity has to cope with in a specific setting (*Whistling*).

17. It is worth noting that the word *don't* appears seventeen times in this approximately 1600-word story, eleven of which represent a direct order from Yunior to himself toward the end of the story when he is becoming increasingly agitated about the possibility of his failure to get the love he so desperately desires.

18. Díaz emphasizes how important it is for people of color to confront their own participation in the perpetuation of the ideas and practices that support a system of white supremacy:

> How can you change something if you won't even acknowledge its existence, or if you downplay its significance? . . . The silence around white supremacy is like the silence around Sauron in *The Lord of the Rings*, or the Voldemort name that must never be uttered in the Harry Potter novels. And yet here's the rub: if a critique of white supremacy doesn't first flow through you . . . you have, in fact, almost guaranteed its survival and reproduction. There's that old saying: the devil's greatest trick is that he convinced people that he doesn't exist. Well, white supremacy's greatest trick is that it has convinced people that, if it exists at all, it exists always in other people, never in us. (Díaz, "Search")

19. While not unrelated, Dominicans' attitude regarding the relationship between hair texture and race differs somewhat from African Americans' understanding of the same in the relative priority Dominicans put on hair texture (as opposed to skin color) as the primary marker of race.

20. Candelario lists a series of regionally anomalous events that further account for Dominicans' distinctive racial formation and relation to whiteness: the relatively short duration and limited importance of plantation slavery; the massive depopulations caused by white emigration; the impoverishment of the remaining white and creole colonials during the seventeenth century; and the heavy reliance on blacks and mulattos in the armed forces and religious infrastructure (3). What seems clear is that people in the Dominican Republic with visible African ancestry—who might have faced resistance

had they been living in a society with more people with European ancestry in positions of power—had the economic, political, and social power to construct themselves as "white" (224). See also Moya Pons (206–07).

Chapter 5: The Misprision of Mercy

1. In a radio interview with NPR's Michele Norris on October 27, 2008, Morrison cites as an influence on her thinking a book by Don Jordan and Michael Walsh. *White Cargo* recounts the experience of poor whites in Britain, some of whom were orphan children, who were kidnapped, impressed, or otherwise pushed into servitude in seventeenth- and eighteenth-century America (Morrison, "Morrison Finds").

2. See Handlin and Handlin; Morgan, *American*; Morgan, "Slavery"; Breen and Innes; Fredrickson, *Arrogance*; Fredrickson, "Toward."

3. See also Degler; Vaughn, "Blacks"; Jordan.

4. For an informative and easy to read timeline of slavery, see the Educational Broadcasting Corporation's web resource, "Slavery and the Making of America—Time and Place."

5. In her review of the novel in the *Guardian*, the novelist Hilary Mantel notices that Morrison "is not inquiring about any simple kind of literacy. She means, can you read the nature of the world? Do you understand omens?" On the whole, however, Mantel's reading of the book lacks understanding. She never enters into the life of any character other than Jacob (she judges the other characters as "insubstantial"), and she cannot perceive the logic of the narrative structure (she describes it as a "wisp"). This allows her to imagine that the book "emphasises . . . a sort of grim equality based on suffering," and is nothing more than a belated precursor to *Beloved*.

6. Elinor Teele registers this in her perceptive review of the novel published in the *California Literary Review*. She writes: "When Morrison takes us into a world, we do not visit it; we inhabit it."

7. Not named as such in the novel, Bacon's Rebellion is referred to as "that 'people's war'" (11). It was an armed rebellion led by Nathaniel Bacon against the governor of the colony of Virginia, William Berkeley, in 1675–76. In his declaration of rebellion, Bacon claimed that Berkeley had advanced the fortunes of a small circle of his favorites while failing to protect the interests of the settlers against unjust taxes and Indian attacks. About a thousand Virginians of all classes, including formerly indentured European and African servants, rose up together to drive Berkeley out of Virginia and burn down the capital of Virginia, Jamestown. The rebellion failed in its purpose to remove all Indians from Virginia and eventually petered out after Nathaniel Bacon died from dysentery. But the alliance of poor whites and poor blacks was disturbing to the English King and to land-owning whites, and led to a series of new laws that helped to institutionalize the association between blackness and unpaid servitude (Morgan, *American* 250–70). For a text of the declaration, see Bacon.

8. Lugones defines *modernist agency* as "a mirage of individual autonomous action" in which the social, political, and economic institutions that back up the successful agent are effectively obscured (211).

9. *Tiktaalik roseae* is a 375-million-year-old fossil fish that was discovered in the Canadian Artic in 2004. It shares anatomical features with both primitive fish and the first four-legged animals, called tetrapods. It is interesting to scientists as a transitional fossil between fish and land animals (see University of Chicago; Wilford).

10. Morrison reinforces Vaark's association with this Bible story by naming his wife Rebekka.

11. See Matthew 27: 24–26. Pontius Pilate is the Roman prefect who sought to avoid personal responsibility for Jesus's impending crucifixion by washing his hands with water in front of the frenzied crowd, as a gesture symbolizing his abdication of blame for the blood that would be shed.

12. This is not to say that *A Mercy* cannot or will not be misread. It already has been. David Gates's review of the novel in the *New York Times Sunday Book Review* provides a good example. He reads the novel as a pastoral, presumably because it is set on a farm amidst nature. This causes him to judge the novel a failure: "for these characters, living in the midst of it, nature doesn't signify." And while Gates recognizes that the characters have "conflicting motivations," he misses the importance of the narrative structure and the anomalous distribution of character-space. Finally, because he does not attend to race as an object of inquiry, he derives from the novel a banal moral—"exploitation is evil"—and judges it a tragedy. John Updike's review in the *New Yorker* is similarly blinkered. Updike can read the words of the novel, but he completely misses the sense. Updike emphasizes the fact that the women in the novel are "unmastered" by the three white men who fail to provide them with lasting guidance or relief. The only process in the novel he judges to be "intelligible" and available to all the characters is "procreation." Without an adequate schema with which to read the novel, Updike finally judges it "a vision, both turgid and static, of a new world turning old, and poisoned from the start."

WORKS CITED

Abrams, M. H. *A Glossary of Literary Terms*. 7th ed. Orlando: Harcourt, 1999. Print.

Ahern, Maureen, ed. *A Rosario Castellanos Reader: An Anthology of Her Poetry, Short Fiction, Essays and Drama*. Trans. Maureen Ahern. Austin: University of Texas Press, 1988. Print.

Alaimo, Stacy. "Trans-Corporeal Feminisms and the Ethical Space of Nature." *Material Feminisms*. Ed. Stacy Alaimo and Susan J. Hekman. Bloomington: Indiana University Press, 2008. 237–64. Print.

Alcoff, Linda Martín. "Anti-Latino Racism." *Decolonizing Epistemologies: Latina/o Theology and Philosophy*. Ed. Ada Isasi-Díaz and Eduardo Mendieta. New York: Fordham University Press, 2012. 107–26. Print.

———. *Real Knowing*. Ithaca: Cornell University Press, 1996. Print.

———. *Visible Identities: Race, Gender, and the Self*. New York: Oxford University Press, 2006. Print.

———. "Who's Afraid of Identity Politics?" Moya and Hames-García. 312–44. Print.

Alcoff, Linda Martín, Michael Hames-García, Satya P. Mohanty, and Paula M. L. Moya, eds. *Identity Politics Reconsidered*. New York: Palgrave Macmillan, 2006. Print. The Future of Minority Studies.

Alcoff, Linda Martín, and Satya P. Mohanty. "Reconsidering Identity Politics: An Introduction." Alcoff et al. 1–9. Print.

Aldama, Frederick Luis. *Multicultural Comics: From Zap to Blue Beetle*. Austin: University of Texas Press, 2010. Print. Cognitive Approaches to Literature and Culture Series.

———. *Toward a Cognitive Theory of Narrative Acts*. Austin: University of Texas Press, 2010. Print. Cognitive Approaches to Literature and Culture Series.

———. *Your Brain on Latino Comics: From Gus Arriola to Los Bros Hernandez*. Austin: University of Texas Press, 2009. Print.

Alexander, M. Jacqui, and Chandra Talpade Mohanty, eds. *Feminist Genealogies, Colonial Legacies, Democratic Futures*. New York: Routledge, 1997. Print.

Algee-Hewitt, Mark. "Acts of Aesthetics: Publishing as Recursive Agency in the Long Eighteenth Century." *Romanticism and Victorianism on the Net* 58 (2010) Web. 23 Aug. 2015. <http://www.erudit.org/revue/ravon/2010/v/n57-58/1006517ar.html>.

Althusser, Louis. "Ideology and Ideological State Apparatuses (Notes towards an Investigation)." *Lenin and Philosophy and Other Essays*. New York: Monthly Review Press, 1971. 127–86. Print.

Anzaldúa, Gloria. *Borderlands/La Frontera: The New Mestiza*. San Francisco: Spinsters/ Aunt Lute Books, 1987. Print.

———, ed. *Making Face, Making Soul—Haciendo Caras: Creative and Critical Perspectives by Women of Color*. San Francisco: Aunt Lute Books, 1990. Print.

Attridge, Derek. "Context, Idioculture, Invention." *New Literary History* 42.4 (2011): 681–99. Print.

Aubry, Timothy. *Reading as Therapy: What Contemporary Fiction Does for Middle-Class Americans*. Iowa City: University of Iowa Press, 2011. Print.

Austen, Jane. *Pride and Prejudice*. Ed. Richard Bain. New York: Cambridge University Press, 1996. Print. Cambridge Literature.

Awkward, Michael. "Response [to Deborah McDowell]." *Afro-American Literary Study in the 1990s*. Ed. Houston A. Baker Jr. and Patricia Redmond. Chicago: University of Chicago Press, 1989. 73–77. Print.

Babbitt, Susan. "Feminism and Objective Interests: The Role of Transformation Experiences in Rational Deliberation." *Feminist Epistemologies*. Ed. Linda Alcoff and Elizabeth Potter. New York: Routledge, 1993. 245–64. Print.

———. "Identity, Knowledge, and Toni Morrison's *Beloved*: Questions about Understanding Racism." *Hypatia* 9.3 (1994): 1–18. Print.

———. "Stories from the South: A Question of Logic." *Hypatia* 20.3 (2005): 1–21. Print.

Baca Zinn, Maxine, and Bonnie Thornton Dill, eds. *Women of Color in U.S. Society*. Philadelphia: Temple University Press, 1994. Print.

Bacon, Nathaniel. "Bacon's Rebellion: The Declaration (1676)." *History Matters*. Web. 11 June 2014. <http://historymatters.gmu.edu/d/5800>.

Bakhtin, Mikhail M. *The Dialogic Imagination: Four Essays by M. M. Bakhtin*. Trans. Caryl Emerson and Michael Holquist. Ed. Michael Holquist. Austin: University of Texas Press, 1981. Print.

Bambara, Toni Cade. *The Black Woman: An Anthology*. New York: New American Library, 1970. Print.

———. *The Salt Eaters*. New York: Vintage, 1981. Print.

Barad, Karen. "Agential Realism: Feminist Interventions in Understanding Scientific Practices." *The Science Studies Reader*. Ed. Mario Biagioli. New York: Routledge, 1998. 1–11. Print.

———. "Meeting the Universe Halfway: Realism and Social Construction without Contradiction." *Feminism, Science, and the Philosophy of Science*. Ed. Lynn Hankinson Nelson and Jack Nelson. Dordrecht: Kluwer, 1996. 161–94. Print.

———. "Posthumanist Performativity: Toward an Understanding of How Matter Comes to Matter." *Signs: Journal of Women in Culture and Society* 28.3 (2003): 801–31. Rpt. in *Material Feminisms*. Ed. Stacy Alaimo and Susan J. Hekman. Bloomington: Indiana University Press, 2008. 120–54. Print.

Baron-Cohen, Simon, Alan M. Leslie, and Uta Frith. "Does the Autistic Child Have a 'Theory of Mind'?" *Cognition* 21.1 (1985): 37–46. Web. 12 April 2014.

Baron-Cohen, Simon, Sally Wheelwright, Jacqueline Hill, Yogini Raste, and Ian Plumb. "The 'Reading the Mind in the Eyes Test' Revised Version: A Study with Normal Adults, and Adults with Asberger Syndrome, or High-Functioning Austism." *Child Psychology and Psychiatry* 42.2 (2001): 241–51. Print.

Bartlett, Frederic C. *Remembering: A Study in Experimental and Social Psychology.* Cambridge: Cambridge University Press, 1932. Print.

Bartlett, Robert C., and Susan D. Collins, eds. *Aristotle's Nicomachean Ethics.* Trans. Robert C. Bartlett and Susan D. Collins. Chicago: University of Chicago Press, 2011. Print.

Bell, Roseann P. "Review of *Sula.*" *Obsidian* 2 (Winter 1976): 93–95. Rpt. in McKay, *Critical Essays.* 24–27. Print.

Bergenholtz, Rita A. "Toni Morrison's *Sula*: A Satire on Binary Thinking." *African American Review* 30.1 (1996): 89–98. Print.

Best, Stephen, and Sharon Marcus. "Surface Reading: An Introduction." *Representations* 108.1 (2009): 1–21. Print.

Bonilla-Silva, Eduardo. *Racism without Racists: Color-Blind Racism and the Persistence of Racial Inequality in the United States.* Lanham: Rowman & Littlefield, 2003. Print.

Booth, Wayne C. *The Company We Keep: An Ethics of Fiction.* Berkeley: University of California Press, 1988. Print.

Bourdieu, Pierre. *The Field of Cultural Production: Essays on Art and Literature.* Ed. Randal Johnson. New York: Columbia University Press, 1993. Print.

Boyd, Brian. *Why Lyrics Last: Evolution, Cognition, and Shakespeare's Sonnets.* Cambridge: Harvard University Press, 2012. Print.

Boyd, James. "Nixon's Southern Strategy: 'It's All in the Charts.'" *New York Times Magazine* 17 May 1970: 25, 105–11. Print.

Brake, Elizabeth. "Marriage and Domestic Partnership." *The Stanford Encyclopedia of Philosophy,* Ed. Edward N. Zalta. Fall 2012 ed. Web 20 Aug 2015. <http://plato.stanford.edu/archives/fall2012/entries/marriage/>.

Bransford, John D., and Marcia K. Johnson. "Contextual Prerequisites for Understanding: Some Investigations of Comprehension and Recall." *Journal of Verbal Learning and Verbal Behavior* 11 (1972): 717–26. Print.

Breen, T. H., and Stephen Innes. *"Myne Owne Ground": Race and Freedom on Virginia's Eastern Shore, 1640–1676.* New York: Oxford University Press, 1980. Print.

Brooks, Cleanth. *The Well Wrought Urn: Studies in the Structure of Poetry.* San Diego: Harcourt, 1975. Print.

Brotherston, Gordon. Conversation with author. Stanford, CA, 17 Jan. 2006.

Browne, William Hand, ed. *Archives of Maryland. Proceedings and Acts of the General Assembly of Maryland, January 1637/8–September 1664. Published by Authority of the State, Under the Direction of the Maryland Historical Society.* Maryland Historical Society, 1883. Print.

Bruner, Jerome S. *Beyond the Information Given: Studies in the Psychology of Knowing.* New York: Norton, 1973. Print.

Buell, Lawrence. *The Future of Environmental Criticism: Environmental Crisis and Literary Imagination*. Malden: Blackwell. 2005. Print. Blackwell Manifestos.

———. *Writing for an Endangered World: Literature, Culture, and Environment in the U.S. and Beyond*. Cambridge: Belknap Press of Harvard University Press, 2001. Print.

Calderón, Hector. *Narratives of Greater Mexico: Essays on Chicano Literary History, Genre, and Borders*. Austin: University of Texas Press, 2005. Print.

Calderón, Héctor, and José David Saldívar, eds. *Criticism in the Borderlands: Studies in Chicano Literature, Culture, and Ideology*. Durham: Duke University Press, 1991. Print. Post-Contemporary Interventions.

Camarillo, Albert. *Chicanos in a Changing Society: From Mexican Pueblos to American Barrios in Santa Barbara and Southern California, 1848–1930*. Cambridge: Harvard University Press, [1979] 1996. Print.

Campbell, James, and James Oakes. "The Invention of Race: Rereading *White over Black*." *Reviews in American History* 21.1 (1993): 172–83. Print.

Candelario, Ginetta E. B. *Black behind the Ears: Dominican Racial Identity from Museums to Beauty Shops*. Durham: Duke University Press, 2007. Print.

———. "Hair Race-ing: Dominican Beauty Culture and Identity Production." *Meridians* 1.1 (2000): 128–56. Print.

Castellanos, Rosario. "Meditation on the Brink." Ahern. 111. Print.

Cervantes, Lorna Dee. "Poem for the Young White Man Who Asked Me How I, an Intelligent, Well-Read Person Could Believe in the War Between Races." *Emplumada*. Pittsburgh: University of Pittsburgh, 1981. 35–37. Print.

Chabris, Christopher F., and Daniel J. Simons. *The Invisible Gorilla: And Other Ways Our Intuitions Deceive Us*. New York: Crown, 2010. Print.

Chentsova-Dutton, Yulia E., and Jeanne L. Tsai. "Self-Focused Attention and Emotional Reactivity: The Role of Culture." *Journal of Personality and Social Psychology* 98.3 (2010): 507–19. Print.

Chow, Esther Ngan-Ling. "The Development of Feminist Consciousness among Asian American Women." *Gender and Society* 1.3 (1987): 284–99. Print.

Chute, Hillary L. *Graphic Women: Life Narrative and Contemporary Comics*. New York: Columbia University Press, 2010. Print.

Cohen, Patricia. "Next Big Thing in English: Knowing They Know That You Know." *New York Times* 31 Mar 2010: sec. C1. Print.

Collins, Patricia Hill. *Black Feminist Thought: Knowledge, Consciousness, and the Politics of Empowerment*. New York: Routledge, 1991. Print.

Culler, Jonathan. "Literary Competence." *Reader-Response Criticism: From Formalism to Post-Structuralism*. Ed. Jane P. Tompkins. Baltimore: Johns Hopkins University Press, 1980. 101–17. Print.

Damasio, Antonio R. *Descartes' Error: Emotion, Reason, and the Human Brain*. New York: Putnam, 1994. Print.

Davis, Angela Y. "Afro Images: Politics, Fashion, and Nostalgia." *Critical Inquiry* 21.1 (1994): 37–45. Print.

Degler, Carl N. *Neither Black nor White: Slavery and Race Relations in Brazil and the United States*. Madison: University of Wisconsin Press, [1971] 1986. Print.

de Sahagún, Fray Bernardino. *Florentine Codex: A General History of the Things of New Spain. Book 3: The Origin of the Gods*. Trans. Arthur J. Anderson, and Charles E. Dibble. Salt Lake City: University of Utah Press, [1540–1585] 1982. Print.

Desmond, Matthew, and Mustafa Emirbayer. *Racial Domination, Racial Progress: The Sociology of Race in America*. New York: McGraw-Hill, 2010. Print.

Díaz, Junot. *The Brief Wondrous Life of Oscar Wao*. New York: Riverhead Books, 2007. Print.

———. "Dark America." Anne and Loren Kieve Distinguished Lecture. Stanford University. 18 May 2012. M4A file.

———. *Drown*. New York: Riverhead Books, 1996. Print.

———. "How to Date a Browngirl, Blackgirl, Whitegirl, or Halfie." *Drown*. 143–49. Print.

———. "The Search for Decolonial Love." Parts I & II. Interview by Paula M. L. Moya. *Boston Review* (June 2012): 26–27. Web. 14 Aug. 2012. Rpt. in *Salon*. <http://www.salon.com/2012/07/02/the_search_for_decolonial_love/>.

———. *This Is How You Lose Her*. New York: Riverhead Books, 2012. Print.

Dickinson, Emily. *The Complete Poems of Emily Dickinson*. Ed. Thomas Herbert Johnson. Boston: Little, Brown, 1960. Print.

Dolin, Kieran. *A Critical Introduction to Law and Literature*. New York: Cambridge University Press, 2007. Print.

Dorris, Michael. *The Broken Cord*. New York: Harper Perennial, 1990. Print.

Du Bois, W.E.B. *The Souls of Black Folk*. Ed. Donald B. Gibson and Monica E. Elbert. New York: Penguin Classics, 1989. Print.

Dussel, Enrique D. *The Underside of Modernity: Apel, Ricoeur, Rorty, Taylor, and the Philosophy of Liberation*. Trans. and ed. Eduardo Mendieta. Atlantic Highlands: Humanities Press, 1996. Print.

Eagleton, Terry. *After Theory*. New York: Allen Lane, 2003. Print.

———. *Literary Theory: An Introduction*. Minneapolis: University of Minnesota Press, 1983. Print.

Educational Broadcasting Corporation. "Slavery and the Making of America: Time and Place." 2004. Web. 24 June 2014. <http://www.pbs.org/wnet/slavery/timeline/>.

Eldridge, Richard. *The Oxford Handbook of Philosophy and Literature*. New York: Oxford University Press, 2009. Print.

Elliott, Jane, and Derek Attridge. *Theory after "Theory."* New York: Routledge, 2011. Print.

Fanon, Frantz. *Black Skin, White Masks*. Trans. Richard Philcox. New York: Grove Press, [1952] 2008. Print.

Felski, Rita. "'Context Stinks!'" *New Literary History* 42.4 (2011): 573–91. Print.

Ferguson, Roderick A. *Aberrations in Black: Toward a Queer of Color Critique*. Minneapolis: University of Minnesota Press, 2004. Print.

Fish, Stanley E. "Interpreting the *Variorum*." *Reader-Response Criticism: From Formalism to Post-Structuralism*. Ed. Jane P. Tompkins. Baltimore: Johns Hopkins University Press, 1980. 164–84. Print.

Fluck, Winfried. "The Search for Distance: Negation and Negativity in Wolfgang Iser's Literary Theory." *New Literary History* 31.1 (2000): 175–210. Print.

———. "Why We Need Fiction: Reception Aesthetics, Literary Anthropology, *Funktionsgeschichte.*" *Romance with America? Essays on Culture, Literature, and American Studies.* Ed. Laura Bieger and Johannes Voelz. Heidelberg: Universitätsverlag Winter, 2009. 365–384. Print.

Foley, Neil. *The White Scourge: Mexicans, Blacks, and Poor Whites in Texas Cotton Culture.* Berkeley: University of California Press, 1997. Print.

Fredrickson, George M. *The Arrogance of Race: Historical Perspectives on Slavery, Racism, and Social Inequality.* Middletown: Wesleyan University Press, 1988. Print.

———. *Racism: A Short History.* Princeton: Princeton University Press, 2002. Print.

———. "Toward a Social Interpretation of the Development of American Racism." *Key Issues in the Afro-American Experience.* Ed. Nathan I. Huggins, Martin Kilson, and Daniel M. Fox. Vol. 1. New York: Harcourt, 1971. 240–54. Print.

Freud, Sigmund. "On the Universal Tendency to Debasement in the Sphere of Love (Contributions to the Psychology of Love II)." *The Freud Reader.* Ed. Peter Gay. New York: Norton, [1912] 1989. 394–400. Print.

Friedman, Marilyn. *What Are Friends For? Feminist Perspectives on Personal Relationships and Moral Theory.* Ithaca: Cornell University Press, 1993. Print.

Frye, Marilyn. *The Politics of Reality: Essays in Feminist Theory.* Trumansburg: Crossing Press, 1983. Print.

Garber, Marjorie B., Beatrice Hanssen, and Rebecca L. Walkowitz. *The Turn to Ethics.* New York: Routledge, 2000. Print.

García, Alma M., ed. *Chicana Feminist Thought: The Basic Historical Writings.* New York: Routledge, 1997. Print.

Gates, David. "Original Sins." *New York Times Sunday Book Review* 28 Nov. 2008. Web. 20 Jul. 2010.

George, Stephen K., ed. *Ethics, Literature, and Theory: An Introductory Reader.* 2nd ed. Lanham: Rowman & Littlefield, 2005. Print.

Gillespie, Diane, and Missy Dehn Kubitschek. "Who Cares? Women-Centered Psychology in *Sula.*" *Black American Literature Forum* 24.1 (1990): 20–48. Print.

Gilligan, Carol. *In a Different Voice: Psychological Theory and Women's Development.* Cambridge: Harvard University Press, 1982. Print.

Goffman, Erving. *Stigma: Notes on the Management of Spoiled Identity.* Englewood Cliffs: Prentice Hall, 1963. Print.

Goldstone, Andrew. *Fictions of Autonomy: Modernism from Wilde to de Man.* New York: Oxford University Press, 2013.

González, Marcial. *Chicano Novels and the Politics of Form: Race, Class, and Reification.* Ann Arbor: University of Michigan Press, 2009. Print.

Grant, Robert. "Absence into Presence: The Thematics of Memory and 'Missing' Subjects in Toni Morrison's *Sula.*" McKay. 91–103. Print.

Guillory, John. "Close Reading: Prologue and Epilogue." *ADE Bulletin* 149.8 (2010): 8–14. Print.

———. *Cultural Capital: The Problem of Literary Canon Formation*. Chicago: University of Chicago Press, 1993.

Guinier, Lani. "From Racial Liberalism to Racial Literacy: *Brown v. Board of Education* and the Interest-Divergence Dilemma." *Journal of American History* 91.1 (2004): 92–118. Print.

Gutiérrez, David. *Walls and Mirrors: Mexican Americans, Mexican Immigrants, and the Politics of Ethnicity*. Berkeley: University of California Press, 1995. Print.

Gutiérrez-Jones, Carl Scott. *Critical Race Narratives: A Study of Race, Rhetoric, and Injury*. New York: New York University Press, 2001. Print. Critical America.

Hadden, Sally E. "The Fragmented Laws of Slavery in the Colonial and Revolutionary Eras." *The Cambridge History of Law in America*. Ed. Michael Grossberg and Christopher L. Tomlins. New York: Cambridge University Press, 2008. 253–87. Print.

Hames-García, Michael R. *Fugitive Thought: Prison Movements, Race, and the Meaning of Justice*. Minneapolis: University of Minnesota Press, 2004. Print.

———. *Identity Complex: Making the Case for Multiplicity*. Minneapolis: University of Minnesota Press, 2011. Print.

Hames- García, Michael Roy, and Ernesto Javier Martínez. *Gay Latino Studies: A Critical Reader*. Durham: Duke University Press, 2011. Print.

Handlin, Oscar, and Mary F. Handlin. "Origins of the Southern Labor System." *William and Mary Quarterly* 7.2 (1950): 199–222. Print.

Harjo, Joy. "I Give You Back." *She Had Some Horses*. New York: Thunder's Mouth Press, 1983. Print.

Hayles, Katherine. *Electronic Literature: New Horizons for the Literary*. Notre Dame: University of Notre Dame Press, 2008. Print. University of Notre Dame Ward-Phillips Lectures in English Language and Literature.

———. *My Mother Was a Computer: Digital Subjects and Literary Texts*. Chicago: University of Chicago Press, 2005. Print.

Hegel, Georg Wilhelm Friedrich. *The Phenomenology of Spirit*. Trans. A. V. Miller. Oxford: Oxford University Press, 1977. Print.

Heidegger, Martin. *Basic Writings*. Ed. David Farrell. New York: Harper, 1977. Print.

Heise, Ursula K. *Sense of Place and Sense of Planet: The Environmental Imagination of the Global*. New York: Oxford University Press, 2008. Print.

Hening, William Waller, ed. *The Statutes at Large: Being a Collection of All the Laws of Virginia, from the First Session of the Legislature, in the Year 1619: Published Pursuant to an Act of the General Assembly of Virginia, Passed on the Fifth Day of February One Thousand Eight Hundred and Eight*. Vol. 2. Richmond: Samuel Pleasants Junior, Printer to the Commonwealth, 1810. Google Books. Web. 24 June 2014.

Herrera-Sobek, María. "The Devil in the Discotheque: A Semiotic Analysis of a Contemporary Legend." *Monsters with Iron Teeth: Perspectives on Contemporary Legend*. Ed. Gillian Bennett and Paul Smith. Sheffield: Sheffield Academic Press, 1988. 147–58. Print.

Hills, Rust. *Writing in General and the Short Story in Particular*. Rev. ed. Boston: Houghton Mifflin, 2000. Print.

Hoffarth-Zelloe, Monika. "Resolving the Paradox? An Interlinear Reading of Toni Morrison's *Sula*." *Journal of Narrative Technique* 22.2 (1992): 114–27. Print.

Holland, Sharon Patricia. *The Erotic Life of Racism*. Durham: Duke University Press, 2012. Print.

———. *Raising the Dead: Readings of Death and (Black) Subjectivity*. Durham: Duke University Press, 2000. Print.

hooks, bell. *Feminist Theory: From Margin to Center*. Boston: South End Press, 1984. Print.

Hunt, Patricia. "War and Peace: Transfigured Categories and the Politics of *Sula*." *African American Review* 27.3 (1993): 443–59. Print.

Hurtado, Aida. "Relating to Privilege: Seduction and Rejection in the Subordination of White Women and Women of Color." *Signs: Journal of Women in Culture and Society* 14.4 (1989): 833–55. Print.

Instituto Nacional de Antropología e Historia. "Sala 4: Huitzilopochtli." Museo del Templo Mayor. Web. 5 July 2008.

Iser, Wolfgang. "The Reading Process: A Phenomenological Approach." *Reader-Response Criticism: From Formalism to Post-Structuralism*. Ed. Jane P. Tompkins. Baltimore: Johns Hopkins University Press, 1980. 50–69. Print.

Jackson, Chuck. "A 'Headless Display': *Sula*, Soldiers, and Lynching." *Modern Fiction Studies* 52.2 (2006): 374–92. Print.

Jameson, Fredric. *The Political Unconscious: Narrative as a Socially Symbolic Act*. Ithaca: Cornell University Press, 1981. Print.

Jay, Martin. "Historical Explanation and the Event: Reflections on the Limits of Contextualization." *New Literary History* 42.4. (2011): 557–71. Print.

Jencks, Fae, et al. *Timeline of Breitbart's Sherrod Smear*. MediaMatters for America, 2010. Web. 24 June 2014.

Jennings, La Vinia Delois. "Toni Morrison Plots the Formation of Racial Slavery in Seventeenth-Century America." *Callaloo* 32.2 (2009): 645–703. Print.

Jimenez, Teresa. "They Hatch Alone: The Alienation of the Colonial American Subject in Toni Morrison's *A Mercy*." Undergraduate Honors Thesis. University of California, Berkeley. May 2012.

Jockers, Matthew Lee. *Macroanalysis: Digital Methods and Literary History*. Urbana: University of Illinois Press, 2013. Print. Topics in the Digital Humanities.

Johnson, Thomas. "Negro Leaders See Bias in Call of Nixon for 'Law and Order.'" *New York Times* 13 Aug 1968: 27. Print.

Jordan, Don, and Michael Walsh. *White Cargo: The Forgotten History of Britain's White Slaves in America*. New York: New York University Press, 2008. Print.

Jordan, Winthrop D. *White over Black: American Attitudes toward the Negro*. Chapel Hill: University of North Carolina Press, 1968. Print.

Joyce, James. *A Portrait of the Artist as a Young Man*. New York: Viking, 1964. Print.

Kelley, Robin D. G. "Nap Time: Historicizing the Afro." *Fashion Theory* 1.4 (1997): 339–52. Print.

Kidd, David Comer, and Emanuele Castano. "Reading Literary Fiction Improves Theory of Mind." *Science* 18 Oct. 2013: 377–80. Print.

Lamis, Alexander P. *Southern Politics in the 1990s.* Baton Rouge: Louisiana State University Press, 1999. Print.

———. *The Two-Party South.* New York: Oxford University Press, 1984. Print.

Landy, Joshua. *How to Do Things with Fictions.* New York: Oxford University Press, 2012.
Print.

———. *Philosophy as Fiction: Self, Deception, and Knowledge in Proust.* New York: Oxford University Press, 2004. Print.

Latour, Bruno. *Reassembling the Social: An Introduction to Actor-Network-Theory.* New
York: Oxford University Press, 2005. Print.

———. *We Have Never Been Modern.* Cambridge: Harvard University Press, 1993. Print.

Lee, Rachel. "Missing Peace in Toni Morrison's *Sula* and *Beloved.*" *African American
Review* 28.4 (1994): 571–83. Print.

Levenson, Michael. "Novelty, Modernity, Adjacency." *New Literary History* 42.4 (2011):
663–80. Print.

Levinson, Marjorie. "What Is New Formalism?" *PMLA* 122.2 (2007): 558–69. Print.

Levins Morales, Aurora, and Rosario Morales. *Getting Home Alive.* Ithaca: Firebrand
Books, 1986. Print.

Li, Stephanie. *Signifying without Specifying: Racial Discourse in the Age of Obama.* New
Brunswick: Rutgers University Press, 2012. Print.

Limón, José. *Dancing with the Devil: Society and Cultural Poetics in Mexican-American
South Texas.* Madison: University of Wisconsin Press, 1994. Print.

Lorde, Audre. "Age, Race, Class, and Sex: Women Redefining Difference." *Sister Outsider.* 114–23. Print.

———. "Eye to Eye: Black Women, Hatred, and Anger." *Sister Outsider.* 145–75. Print.

———. "Man Child: A Black Lesbian Feminist's Response." *Sister Outsider.* 72–80. Print.

———. "The Master's Tools Will Never Dismantle the Master's House." *Sister Outsider.*
110–13. Print.

———. *Sister Outsider.* Freedom: The Crossing Press, 1984. Print.

———. "The Uses of Anger: Women Responding to Racism." *Sister Outsider.* 124–33.
Print.

Love, Heather. "Close but Not Deep: Literary Ethics and the Descriptive Turn." *New
Literary History* 41 (2010): 371–91. Print.

Lugones, María. *Pilgrimages/Peregrinajes: Theorizing Coalition against Multiple Oppressions.* Lanham: Rowman & Littlefield, 2003. Print.

Mantel, Hilary. *Bring Up the Bodies: A Novel.* New York: Henry Holt, 2012. Print.

———. "How Sorrow Became Complete." *Guardian* 8 Nov. 2008. Web. 20 Jun. 2010.

———. *Wolf Hall: A Novel.* New York: Henry Holt, 2009. Print.

Mar, Raymond A., et al. "Bookworms versus Nerds: Exposure to Fiction versus Non-
Fiction, Divergent Associations with Social Ability, and the Simulation of Fictional
Social Worlds." *Journal of Research in Personality* 40 (2006): 694–712. Print.

Markus, Hazel Rose, and Alana Conner. *Clash! 8 Cultural Conflicts That Make Us Who We Are*. New York: Hudson Street Press, 2013. Print.

Markus, Hazel Rose, and Shinobu Kitayama, "Culture and the Self: Implications for Cognition, Emotion, Motivation." *Psychological Review* 98.2 (1991): 224–53. Print.

Markus, Hazel Rose, Shinobu Kitayama, and Rachel J. Heiman. "Culture and 'Basic' Psychological Principles." *Social Psychology: Handbook of Basic Principles*. Ed. Edward Tory Higgins and Arie W. Kruglanski. New York: Guilford Press, 1996. 857–913. Print.

Markus, Hazel Rose, and Paula M. L. Moya, eds. *Doing Race: 21 Essays for the 21st Century*. New York: Norton, 2010. Print.

Markus, Hazel Rose, and Paula Nurius. "Possible Selves." *American Psychologist* 41.9 (1986): 954–69. Print.

Markus, Hazel Rose, and Robert B. Zajonc. "The Cognitive Perspective in Social Psychology." *Handbook of Social Psychology* 1 (1985): 137–230. Print.

Martínez, Ernesto Javier. *On Making Sense: Queer Race Narratives of Intelligibility*. Stanford: Stanford University Press, 2013. Print. Stanford Studies in Comparative Race and Ethnicity.

Marx, Karl. *Capital*. Vol. 1. Trans. Ben Fowkes. New York: Penguin, 1977. Print.

McDowell, Deborah E. "Boundaries: Or Distant Relations and Close Kin." *Afro-American Literary Study in the 1990s*. Ed. Houston A. Baker Jr. and Patricia Redmond. Chicago: University of Chicago Press, 1989. 51–70. Print.

McGurl, Mark. *The Program Era: Postwar Fiction and the Rise of Creative Writing*. Cambridge: Harvard University Press, 2009.

McKay, Nellie Y. *Critical Essays on Toni Morrison*. Boston: G. K. Hall, 1988. Print. Critical Essays on American Literature.

McQuillan, Martin. *Post-Theory: New Directions in Criticism*. Edinburgh: Edinburgh University Press, 1999. Print.

Mendieta, Eduardo. "Technologies of the Racist Self." Unpublished manuscript. 2001. Print.

Mercer, Kobena. "Black Hair/Style Politics." *Welcome to the Jungle: New Positions in Black Cultural Studies*. New York: Routledge, 1994. 97–130. Print.

Michaels, Walter Benn. "The Interpreter's Self: Peirce on the Cartesian Subject." *Reader-Response Criticism: From Formalism to Post-Structuralism*. Ed. Jane P. Tompkins. Baltimore: Johns Hopkins University Press, 1980. 185–200. Print.

Mignolo, Walter. *The Darker Side of the Renaissance: Literacy, Territoriality, and Colonization*. Ann Arbor: University of Michigan Press, 1995. Print.

———. *Local Histories/Global Designs: Coloniality, Subaltern Knowledges, and Border Thinking*. Princeton: Princeton University Press, 2000. Print.

Mohanty, Chandra Talpade, Ann Russo, and Lourdes Torres, eds. *Third World Women and the Politics of Feminism*. Bloomington: Indiana University Press, 1991. Print.

Mohanty, Satya. *Literary Theory and the Claims of History: Postmodernism, Objectivity, Multicultural Politics*. Ithaca: Cornell University Press, 1997. Print.

Montejano, David. *Anglos and Mexicans in the Making of Texas, 1836–1986*. Austin: University of Texas Press, 1987. Print.

Moraga, Cherríe. *Loving in the War Years: lo que nunca pasó por sus labios*. Boston: South End Press, 1983. Print.

Moraga, Cherríe, and Gloria Anzaldúa, eds. 1981. *This Bridge Called My Back: Writings by Radical Women of Color*. 2nd ed. New York: Kitchen Table/Women of Color Press, 1983. Print.

Moretti, Franco. *The Bourgeois: Between History and Literature*. Brooklyn: Verso, 2013. Print.

——. *Distant Reading*. New York: Verso, 2013. Print.

——. *Graphs, Maps, Trees: Abstract Models for a Literary History*. New York: Verso, 2005. Print.

——. *Signs Taken for Wonders: On the Sociology of Literary Forms*. New York: Verso, [1983] 2005. Print. Radical Thinkers.

Morgan, Edmund S. *American Slavery, American Freedom: The Ordeal of Colonial Virginia*. New York: Norton, 1975. Print.

——. "Slavery and Freedom: The American Paradox." *Journal of American History* 59.1 (1972): 5–29. Print.

Morrison, Toni. "Afterword." *The Bluest Eye*. New York: Plume, 1993. 209–16. Print.

——. *Beloved: A Novel*. New York: Knopf, 1987. Print.

——. *The Bluest Eye*. New York: Pocket Books, 1972. Print.

——. "An Interview with Toni Morrison." By Bessie Jones. *The World of Toni Morrison: Explorations in Literary Criticism*. Ed. Bessie Jones and Audrey Vinson. Dubuque: Kendall/Hunt, 1985. 127–51. Print.

——. "An Interview with Toni Morrison." By Nellie Y. McKay. *Contemporary Literature* 24.4 (1983): 413–29. Print.

——. *A Mercy*. New York: Vintage, 2008. Print.

——. *Playing in the Dark: Whiteness and the Literary Imagination*. Cambridge: Harvard University Press, 1992. Print.

——, ed. *Race-ing Justice, En-gendering Power: Essays on Anita Hill, Clarence Thomas, and the Construction of Social Reality*. New York: Pantheon Books, 1992. Print.

——. *Song of Solomon*. New York: Knopf, 1977. Print.

——. *Sula*. 1973. New York: Plume. 1982. Print.

——. "Toni Morrison Discusses 'A Mercy.'" Video interview by Lynn Neary. NPR 27 Oct. 2008. Web video. 17 Jul. 2010. <http://www.npr.org/templates/story/story.php?storyId=95961382>.

——. "Toni Morrison Discusses Her Inspiration for *A Mercy*." 2008. Web video. 17 Jun. 2010. <http://www.amazon.com/gp/mpd/permalink/m3KGCJoMBF16TZ>.

——. "Toni Morrison Finds 'A Mercy' in Servitude." Interview by Michele Norris. *All Things Considered*. NPR, 27 Oct. 2008. Radio. Web. 17 Jul. 2010.

——. "Unspeakable Things Unspoken: The Afro-American Presence in American Literature." *Michigan Quarterly Review* 28.1 (1989): 1–34. Print.

Morton, Timothy. *The Ecological Thought*. Cambridge: Harvard University Press, 2010. Print.

———. *Ecology without Nature: Rethinking Environmental Aesthetics*. Cambridge: Harvard University Press, 2009. Print.

Moya, Paula M. L. "Harry Reid's Remarks about Race, Or Much Ado about Nothing." *Arcade*: a digital salon, 2010. Web. 24 June 2014.

———. "Introduction: Reclaiming Identity." Moya and Hames-García. 1–26. Print.

———. *Learning from Experience: Minority Identities, Multicultural Struggles*. Berkeley: University of California Press, 2002. Print.

———. "A Symphony of Anger: Notes toward a Transformation of Feminist Politics." *Phoebe*: an interdisciplinary journal of feminist scholarship, theory and aesthetics, 8.1,2 (1996): 1–13. Print.

Moya, Paula M. L., and Michael R. Hames-García, eds. *Reclaiming Identity: Realist Theory and the Predicament of Postmodernism*. Berkeley: University of California Press, 2000. Print.

Moya, Paula M. L., and Hazel Markus. "Doing Race: An Introduction." Markus and Moya. 1–102. Print.

Moya Pons, Frank. *The Dominican Republic: A National History*. New Rochelle: Hispaniola Books, 1995. Print.

Muñoz, Carlos. *Youth, Identity, Power: The Chicano Movement*. Rev. and expanded ed. New York: Verso, 2007. Print.

Muñoz, José Esteban. *Disidentifications: Queers of Color and the Performance of Politics*. Minneapolis: University of Minnesota Press, 1999. Print.

Muñoz, Manuel. "The Third Myth." *Zigzagger*. 20–30. Print.

———. "The Unimportant Lila Parr." *Zigzagger*. 36–46. Print.

———. *Zigzagger*. Evanston: Northwestern University Press, 2003. Print.

———. "Zigzagger." *Zigzagger*. 5–19. Print.

New York (Colony) et al. *The Colonial Laws of New York from the Year 1664 to the Revolution, Including the Charters to the Duke of York, the Commission and Instructions to Colonial Governors, the Dukes Laws, the Laws of the Donagan and Leisler Assemblies, the Charters of Albany and New York and the Acts of the Colonial Legislatures from 1691 to 1775 Inclusive*. Albany: J. B. Lyon, state printer, 1896. Print.

Nicholas, Peter, and Kathleen Hennessey. "Shirley Sherrod Dismissal a Rash Decision." *Los Angeles Times* 7 Oct 2010. Print.

Nissen, Alex. "Form Matters: Toni Morrison's *Sula* and the Ethics of Fiction." *Contemporary Literature* 40.2 (1999): 263–85. Print.

Novak, Phillip. "'Circles and Circles of Sorrow': In the Wake of Morrison's *Sula*." *PMLA* 114.2 (1999): 184–93. Print.

Nussbaum, Martha. *Cultivating Humanity: A Classical Defense of Reform in Liberal Education*. Cambridge: Harvard University Press, 1997. Print.

———. *Love's Knowledge: Essays on Philosophy and Literature*. New York: Oxford University Press, 1990. Print.

Olds, Sharon. *Satan Says*. Pittsburgh: University of Pittsburgh Press, 1980. Print.

Omi, Michael, and Howard Winant. *Racial Formation in the United States: From the 1960s to the 1990s*. 2nd ed. New York: Routledge, 1994. Print.

Oyserman, Daphna, Deborah Bybee, and Kathy Terry. "Possible Selves and Academic Outcomes: How and When Possible Selves Impel Action." *Journal of Personality and Social Psychology* 91.1 (2006): 188–204. Print.

Oyserman, Daphna, and Stephanie Fryberg. "The Possible Selves of Diverse Adolescents: Content and Function across Gender, Race and National Origin." *Possible Selves: Theory, Research, and Application*. Huntington: Nova, 2006. Print.

Oyserman, Daphna, and Hazel R. Markus. "Possible Selves and Delinquency." *Journal of Personality and Social Psychology* 59.1 (1990): 112–25. Print.

"Patriarchy." Draft revision. *The Oxford English Dictionary*, Mar. 2000. Web.

Pérez Firmat, Gustavo. *Bilingual Blues*. Tempe: Bilingual Press/Editorial Bilingüe, 1995. Print.

Plascencia, Salvador. *The People of Paper*. Orlando: Harcourt, 2006. Print.

Posner, Richard A. *Law and Literature*. 3rd ed. Cambridge: Harvard University Press, 2009. Print.

Premack, David, and Guy Woodruff. "Does the Chimpanzee Have a Theory of Mind?" *Behavioral and Brain Sciences* 1.4 (1978): 515–26. Print.

Quijano, Anibal. "Coloniality of Power, Eurocentrism, and Latin America." *Nepantla: Views from South* 1.3 (2000): 533–80. Print.

Ramos, Juanita, ed. *Compañeras: Latina Lesbians*. 1987. New York: Routledge, 1994. Print.

Rashomon. Dir. Akira Kurosawa. Prod. Minoru Jingo and Masaichi Nagata. Perf. Toshirô Mifune, Machiko Kyô, and Masayuki Mori. Daiei Motion Picture Company, 1950. Film.

Rasmussen, Birgit Brander. *Queequeg's Coffin: Indigenous Literacies and Early American Literature*. Durham: Duke University Press, 2012. Print.

Richards, I. A. *Practical Criticism: A Study of Literary Judgment*. London: K. Paul, Trench, Trubner, 1929. Print.

———. *Principles of Literary Criticism*. New York: Harcourt, 1924. Print.

Rooney, Ellen. "Live Free or Describe: The Reading Effect and the Persistence of Form." *Differences: A Journal of Feminist Cultural Studies* 21.3 (2010): 112–39. Print.

Roth, Benita. *Separate Roads to Feminism: Black, Chicana, and White Feminist Movements in America's Second Wave*. New York: Cambridge University Press, 2004. Print.

Ruíz, Vicki. *Cannery Women, Cannery Lives: Mexican Women, Unionization, and the California Food Processing Industry, 1930–1950*. Albuquerque: University of New Mexico Press, 1987. Print.

———. *From Out of the Shadows: Mexican Women in Twentieth-Century America*. New York: Oxford University Press, 1998. Print.

Sáez, Elena Machado. "Dictating Desire, Dictating Diaspora: Junot Díaz's *The Brief Wondrous Life of Oscar Wao* as Foundational Romance." *Contemporary Literature* 53.2 (2011): 522–55. Print.

Saldívar, José David. *Border Matters: Remapping American Cultural Studies.* Berkeley: University of California Press, 1997. Print.

———. *The Dialectics of Our America: Genealogy, Cultural Critique, and Literary History.* Durham: Duke University Press, 1991. Print. Post-Contemporary Interventions.

———. *Trans-Americanity: Subaltern Modernities, Global Coloniality, and the Cultures of Greater Mexico.* Durham: Duke University Press, 2012. Print. New Americanists.

Saldívar, Ramón. *The Borderlands of Culture: Américo Paredes and the Transnational Imaginary.* Durham: Duke University Press, 2006. Print. New Americanists.

———. *Chicano Narrative: The Dialectics of Difference.* Madison: University of Wisconsin Press, 1990. Print.

———. "Historical Fantasy, Speculative Realism, and Postrace Aesthetics in Contemporary American Fiction." *American Literary History* 23.3 (2011): 574–99. Print.

Saldívar-Hull, Sonia. Conversation with author. Austin, 22 Mar. 2008.

Sánchez, George J. *Becoming Mexican American: Ethnicity, Culture, and Identity in Chicano Los Angeles, 1900–1945.* New York: Oxford University Press, 1993. Print.

Sánchez-Casal, Susan, and Amie A. Macdonald. *Identity in Education.* New York: Palgrave Macmillan, 2009. Print. The Future of Minority Studies.

Sedgwick, Eve Kosofsky. *Touching Feeling: Affect, Pedagogy, Performativity.* Durham: Duke University Press, 2003. Print.

Shahid, Aliyah. "Shirley Sherrod, Ex-USDA Worker: White House Forced Me to Resign over Fabricated Racial Controversy." *New York Daily News* 20 July 2010. Web. 14 Aug 2012.

Shamay-Tsoory, Simone G., and Judith Aharon-Peretz. "Dissociable Prefrontal Networks for Cognitive and Affective Theory of Mind: A Lesion Study." *Neuropsychologia* 45 (2007): 3054–67. Print.

Sherrod, Shirley. "Address at the Georgia NAACP 20th Annual Freedom Fund Banquet." 27 Mar. 2010. Web. 24 June 2014. <http://www.naacp.org/news/entry/video_sherrod>.

Siebers, Tobin. *Disability Aesthetics.* Ann Arbor: University of Michigan Press, 2010. Print.

———. *Disability Theory.* Ann Arbor: University of Michigan Press, 2008. Print.

Silko, Leslie. *Ceremony.* New York: Viking, 1977. Print.

Smith, Barbara. "Beautiful, Needed, Mysterious." *Freedomways,* no 14 (1st quarter 1974): 69–72. Rpt. in McKay, *Critical Essays.* 21–24. Print.

———, ed. *Home Girls: A Black Feminist Anthology.* New York: Kitchen Table/Women of Color Press, 1983. Print.

———. "Toward a Black Feminist Criticism." *Conditions: Two* 1 (1977): 25-44. Print.

Source Code. Dir. Duncan Jones. Perf. Jake Gyllenhaal, Michelle Monaghan, and Vera Farmiga. Vendome Pictures. 2011. Film.

Stanford Literary Lab. Pamphlets. Apr. 2014. Web. 24 June 2014. <http://litlab.stanford.edu>.

Steele, Claude M. *Whistling Vivaldi: And Other Clues to How Stereotypes Affect Us.* New York: Norton, 2010. Print.

Steele, Claude M., Stephen J. Spencer, and Joshua Aronson. "Contending with Group

Image: The Psychology of Stereotype and Social Identity Threat." *Advances in Experimental Social Psychology 34 (2002): 379–440. Print.*

Stocker, Michael. "Some Issues about Emotions and Racisms." Unpublished manuscript. 2001. 1–29.

Stocker, Michael, with Elizabeth Hegeman. *Valuing Emotions.* Cambridge: Cambridge University Press, 1996. Print. Cambridge Studies in Philosophy.

Szalay, Michael. *Hip Figures: A Literary History of the Democratic Party.* Stanford: Stanford University Press, 2012. Print.

Tanenhaus, Sam, and Sean P. Farrell. "A Conversation with Toni Morrison." *New York Times Sunday Book Review* 30 Nov. 2008. Print.

Tavris, Carol, and Elliot Aronson. *Mistakes Were Made (But Not by Me): Why We Justify Foolish Beliefs, Bad Decisions, and Hurtful Acts.* Orlando: Harcourt, 2007. Print.

Teele, Elinor. "Untold History, Unheard Voices." *California Literary Review* 16 Dec. 2008. n. pag. Web. 20 Jul. 2010.

Teuton, Sean Kicummah. *Red Land, Red Power: Grounding Knowledge in the American Indian Novel.* Durham: Duke University Press, 2008. Print.

Thomas, Laurence. "Moral Deference." *Theorizing Multiculturalism: A Guide to Current Debate.* Ed. Cynthia Willett. Malden: Blackwell, 1998. 359–81. Print.

Tompkins, Jane P. "An Introduction to Reader-Response Criticism." *Reader-Response Criticism: From Formalism to Post-Structuralism.* Ed. Jane P. Tompkins. Baltimore: Johns Hopkins University Press, 1980. ix–xxvi. Print.

———. "The Reader in History: The Changing Shape of Literary Response: *Reader-Response Criticism: From Formalism to Post-Structuralism.* Ed. Jane P. Tompkins. Baltimore: Johns Hopkins University Press, 1980. 201–32. Print.

Tsai, Jeanne L. "Ideal Affect: Cultural Causes and Behavioral Consequences." *Perspectives on Psychological Science* 2.3 (2007): 242–59. Print.

Tucker, Herbert F. "Introduction." *New Literary History* 42.4, (2011): vii–xii. Print.

Twine, France Winddance. *A White Side of Black Britain: Interracial Intimacy and Racial Literacy.* Durham: Duke University Press, 2010. Print.

Underwood, Ted. *Why Literary Periods Mattered: Historical Contrast and the Prestige of English Studies.* Stanford: Stanford University Press, 2013. Print.

United States Census Bureau. "U.S. Census Bureau Projections Show a Slower Growing, Older, More Diverse Nation a Half Century from Now." 12 Dec. 2012. Web. 31 Jan. 2015. <http://www.census.gov/newsroom/releases/archives/population/cb12-243.html>.

University of Chicago. *Tiktaalik Roseae.* 2006–2009. Web. 31 Jan. 2015. <http://tiktaalik.uchicago.edu/index.html>.

Updike, John. "Dreamy Wilderness: Unmastered Women in Colonial Virginia." *New Yorker* 03 Nov. 2008. n. pag. Web. 20 Jul. 2010.

Vaughn, Alden T. "Blacks in Virginia: A Note on the First Decade." *William and Mary Quarterly* 3rd ser. 29 (1972): 469–78. Print.

———. "The Origins Debate: Slavery and Racism in Seventeenth-Century Virginia." *Virginia Magazine of History and Biography* 97.3 (1989): 311–54. Print.

Vermeule, Blakey. *Why Do We Care about Literary Characters?* Baltimore: Johns Hopkins University Press, 2010. Print.

Viramontes, Helena María. Conversation with author. Stanford, CA, 4 Feb. 2002.

——. "The Moths." *The Moths and Other Stories.* 21–28. Print.

——. *The Moths and Other Stories.* Houston: Arte Publico Press, 1985. Print.

——. *Their Dogs Came with Them.* New York: Atria Books, 2007. Print.

——. *Under the Feet of Jesus.* New York: Dutton, 1995. Print.

Waegner, Cathy Covell. "Ruthless Epic Footsteps: Shoes, Migrants, and the Settlement of the Americas in Toni Morrison's *A Mercy.*" *Post-National Enquiries.* Ed. Jopi Nyman. Newcastle upon Tyne: Cambridge Scholars, 2009. 91–112. Print.

Waxler, Robert P. *The Risk of Reading: How Literature Helps Us to Understand Ourselves and the World.* New York: Bloomsbury Academic, 2014. Print.

Whitehead, Colson. "The Year of Living Postracially." *New York Times* 4 Nov 2009: sec. A, 31. Print.

Whitmore, William Henry, ed. *The Colonial Laws of Massachusetts: Reprinted from the Edition of 1660, with the Supplements to 1672: Containing also, the Body of Liberties of 1641.* Boston. 1889. Print.

Wiegman, Robyn. "Whiteness Studies and the Paradox of Particularity." *Boundary 2* 26.3 (1999): 115–50. Print.

Wilford, John N. "Fossil Called Missing Link from Sea to Land Animals." *New York Times* 6 Apr. 2006. Web.

Wilkerson, William S. "Is There Something You Need to Tell Me? Coming Out and the Ambiguity of Experience." Moya and Hames-García. 251–78. Print.

Williams, Raymond. "Ideas of Nature." *Culture and Materialism: Selected Essays.* New York: Verso, 2005. 67–85. Print. Radical Thinkers.

——. *Marxism and Literature.* Oxford: Oxford University Press, 1977. Print.

Wimsatt, W. K., Jr., and Monroe Beardsley. "The Affective Fallacy." *The Verbal Icon: Studies in the Meaning of Poetry.* Ed. William K. Wimsatt. Lexington: University of Kentucky Press, 1954. Print.

Woloch, Alex. *The One vs. the Many: Minor Characters and the Space of the Protagonist in the Novel.* Princeton: Princeton University Press, 2003. Print.

Wong, Nellie. "When I Was Growing Up." Moraga and Anzaldúa. 7–8. Print.

Wong, Nellie, Merle Woo, and Mitsuye Yamada. *3 Asian American Writers Speak Out on Feminism.* San Francisco: SF Radical Women, 1979. Print.

Wong, Ying, and Jeanne L. Tsai. "Cultural Models of Shame and Guilt." *The Self-Conscious Emotions: Theory and Research.* Ed. Jessica L. Tracy, Richard W. Robins, and June Price Tangney. New York: Guilford Press, 2007. 210–23. Print.

Woo, Merle. "Letter to Ma." Moraga and Anzaldúa. 140–47. Print.

Wu, Yung-Hsing. "Doing Things with Ethics: *Beloved, Sula,* and the Reading of Judgment." *Modern Fiction Studies* 49.4 (2003): 780–805. Print.

Yamada, Mitsuye. "Invisibility Is an Unnatural Disaster: Reflections of an Asian American Woman." *Bridge: An Asian American Perspective* 7.1 (1979): 11–13. Rpt. in Moraga and Anzaldúa. 35–40. Print.

Zunshine, Lisa. *Getting inside Your Head: What Cognitive Science Can Tell Us about Popular Culture*. Baltimore: Johns Hopkins University Press, 2012. Print.

———. *Introduction to Cognitive Cultural Studies*. Baltimore: Johns Hopkins University Press, 2010. Print.

INDEX

Printed in the USA
CPSIA information can be obtained
at www.ICGtesting.com
LVHW041113191223
766862LV00004B/492